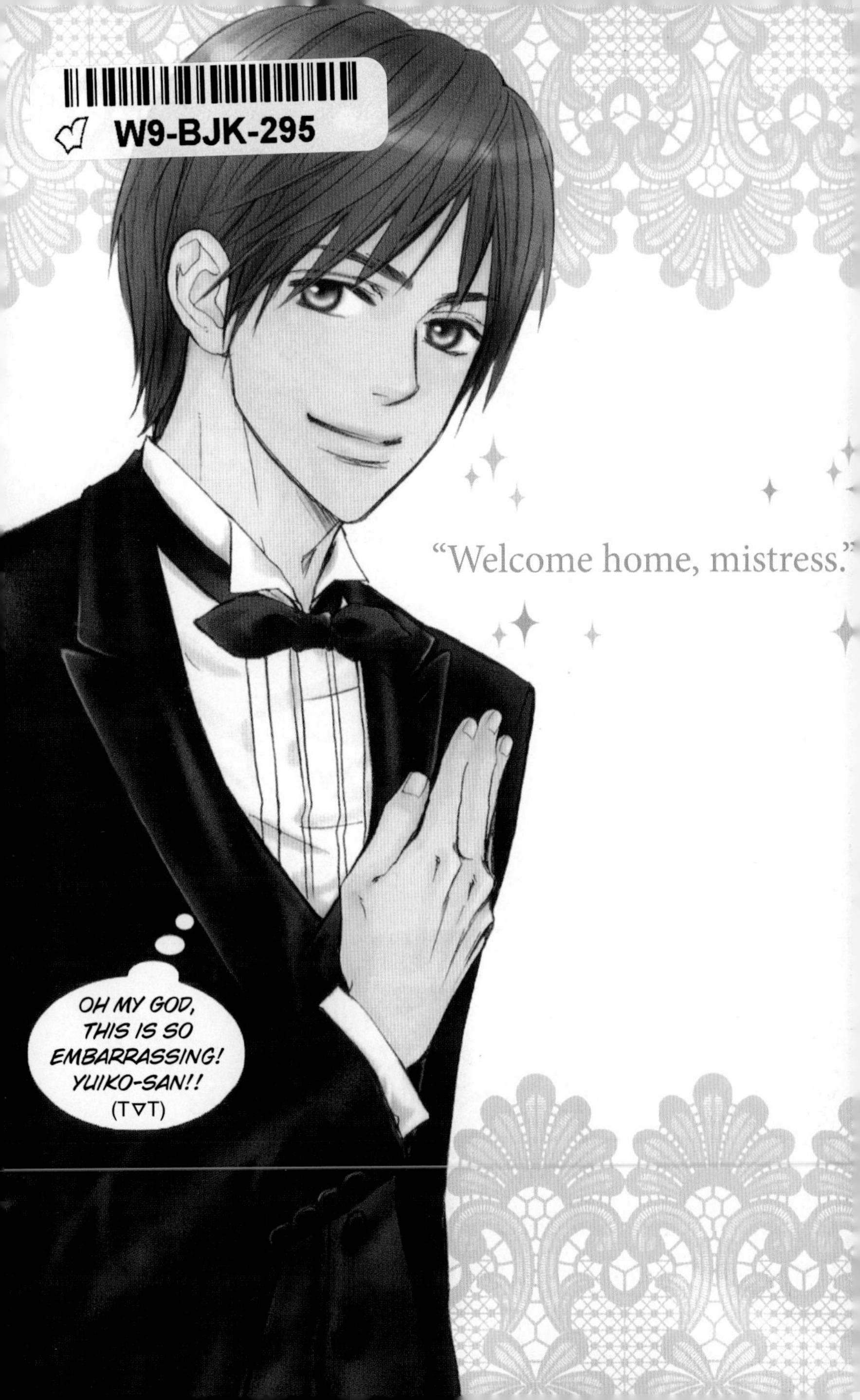
"Welcome home, mistress."
OH MY GOD, THIS IS SO EMBARRASSING! YUIKO-SAN!! (T▽T)

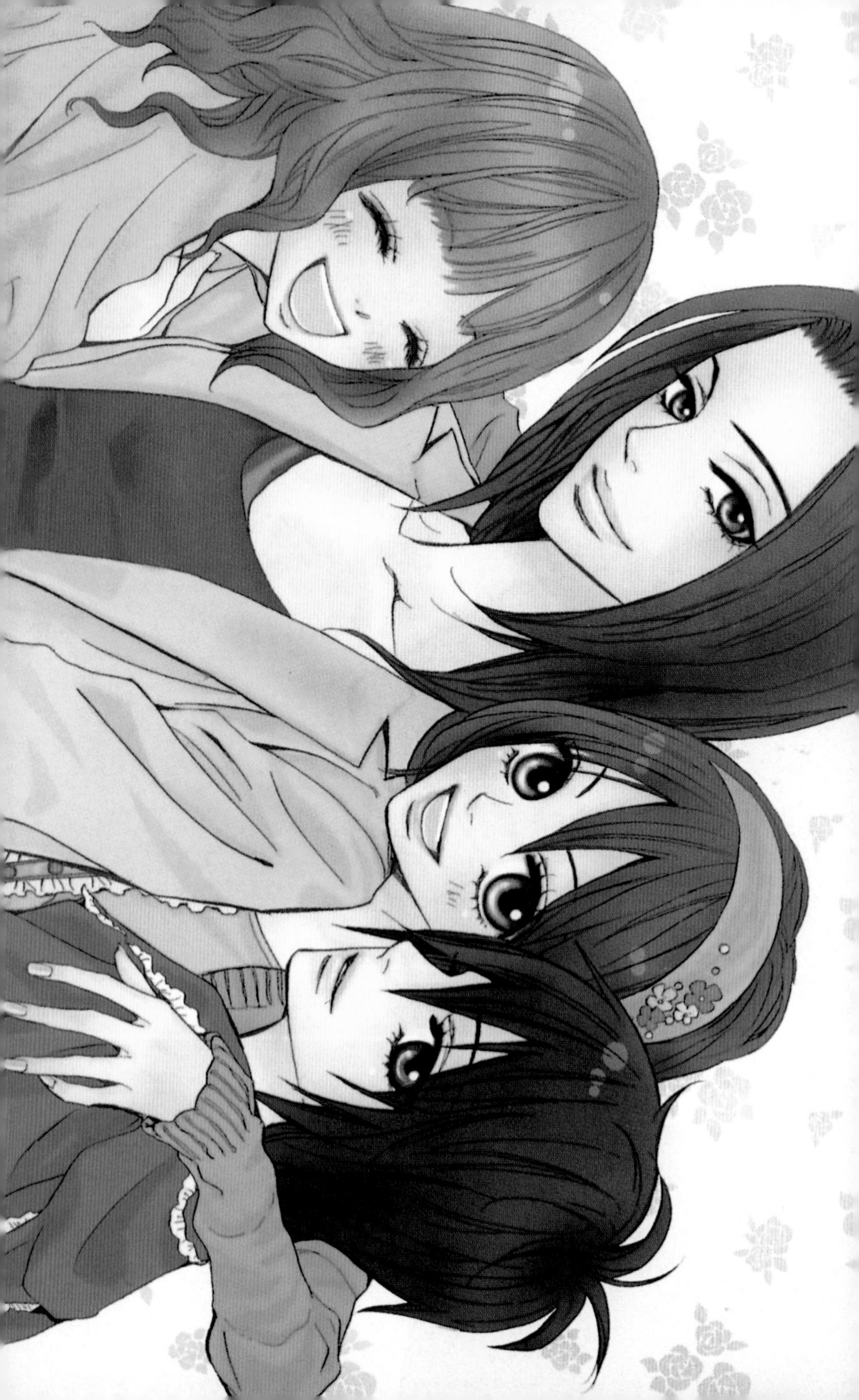

My Girlfriend's a GEEK

4

RIZE SHINBA
STORY: PENTABU

My Girlfriend's a GEEK

AT A GLANCE

THE STORY SO FAR

College student Taiga Mutou is in a loving relationship with his new, older girlfriend Yuiko-san… who happens to be a *fujoshi*! Between his new nickname of "Sebas" and being dragged to various *otaku* events, Taiga's getting his chain jerked around by Yuiko on a daily basis. Then there's the introduction of an oddly classy rival for Yuiko's affections. Will Taiga's love life ever find peace and tranquility again!?

SACCHIN

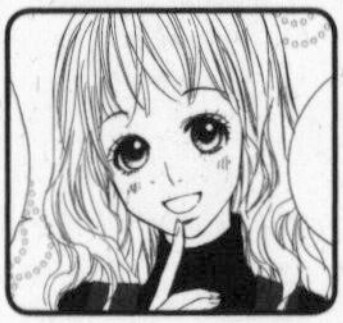

Yuiko-san's friend and partner. She's crazy enough about voice actors to recognize that Taiga's voice is similar to Akira Kubokoji's.

MASA-NEE

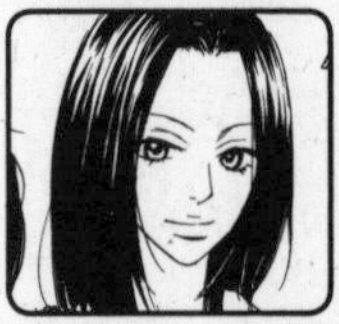

She's got the details on every anime on TV! She visits every single event on the weekends! A legendary *fujoshi* and *dojin* novel writer.

FUJOSHI FRIENDS

TAIGA MUTOU

A normal college student. He wears glasses, but only during class. Totally whipped by Yuiko-san. His current life goal is to be a "*moe seme*"!

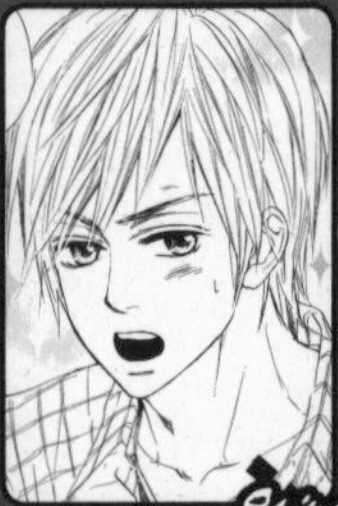

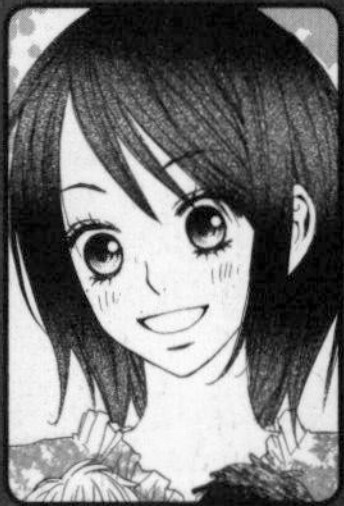

YUIKO AMEYA

By day, a nice, pretty OL. But by night, she turns into a hard-core *fujoshi*! She loves cosplay, particularly when she can knock Taiga out with a cat-eared nurse outfit.♥

…I WON'T BE OUTDONE BY HIM!

FRIENDS

ON THE PROWL

…UGH.

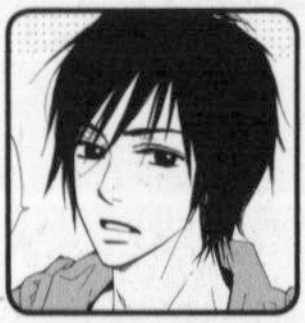

KOUJI SETO

A good friend and former high school classmate of Taiga's. Whenever she sees the two of them together, Yuiko starts making up B.L. stories.

NAOTO KASHIWABARA

A stylish "Milanese" gentleman. The ladies are crazy for him, but he doesn't trip any of Yuiko's *moe* sensors. He considers Taiga a rival in love.

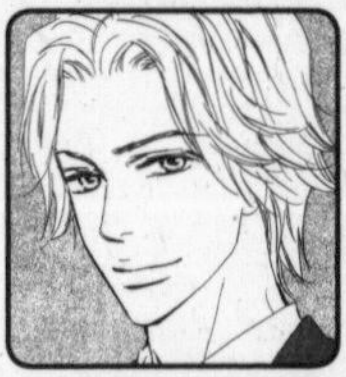

SIBLINGS

SENPAI!

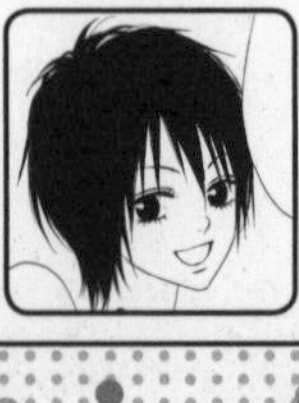

AKARI SETO

Kouji's sister. Her *moe*-style voice is labeled "Genocidal Lolita" by her brother.

HIT ON HER♥

TRANS-FORM! ☆

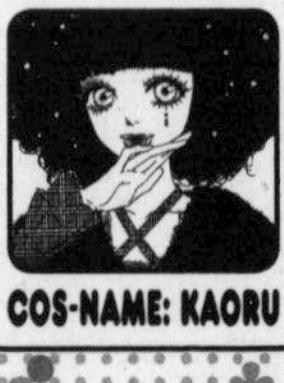

COS-NAME: KAORU

FUJOSHI NEWS

SHOUNEN MANGA

SEPATTE TAKURO

A SHOOTING STAR IN THE WORLD OF SHOUNEN MANGA CURRENTLY BEING SERIALIZED IN *WEEKLY SHOUNEN STEP*. GLOOMY AND WITHDRAWN MIDDLE SCHOOLER TAKURO SEBA IS POSSESSED BY THE MYSTERIOUS SEPA SPIRIT. WITH HIS CAPTAIN AND TEAMMATES OF THE MAREI MIDDLE SCHOOL SEPAK TAKRAW TEAM, HE SETS HIS SIGHTS ON THE NATIONAL TOURNAMENT. IT'S A PERFECTLY NORMAL AND TRADITIONAL SHOUNEN MANGA, BUT FOR SOME REASON, TAIGA IS BEING FORCED TO WRITE A CAPTAIN x TAKURO B.L. NOVEL.

GAME FOR GIRLS

DREAMING NOUVELLE MARIE

AN INSTALLMENT OF THE ETERNAL SWEET ROMANCE SERIES ("ESROMA" AMONG FANS), A WILDLY POPULAR LINE OF GAMES FOR GIRLS. THE HEROINE, MARIE HANABISHI, IS A POTENTIAL BRIDE FOR A LIST OF HANDSOME PRINCES FROM ANOTHER WORLD. YUIKO-SAN'S FAVORITE IS PRINCE MAXIMILLIAN. BUT HER TOP COUPLING IS ANSELM (THE SMART ONE WITH GLASSES) x HEROLD (THE DARK AND HANDSOME ONE).

THESE ARE BOTH ORIGINAL TO THE MANGA VERSION OF "MY GIRLFRIEND'S A GEEK"! YOU WON'T FIND THEM ANYWHERE ELSE! ♡

HERE'S THE ORIGINAL ★
MY GIRLFRIEND'S A GEEK
WRITTEN BY PENTABU

A love diary about a *fujoshi* and a normal man? The infamous blog has made the transition to paperback! Pentabu lovingly dishes out withering smackdowns to every nerdy *fujoshi* comment his girlfriend makes. Feel the sympathy course through your veins as you witness his daily struggles!

If you haven't checked out the inspiration for this manga, what are you waiting for? ♥

Volumes 1 and 2 available now!

Now enjoy Volume 4!

My Girlfriend's a **GEEK**

"This manga is a work of fiction based upon *My Girlfriend's a Geek*, Volumes 1 and 2, by Pentabu."

CONTENTS

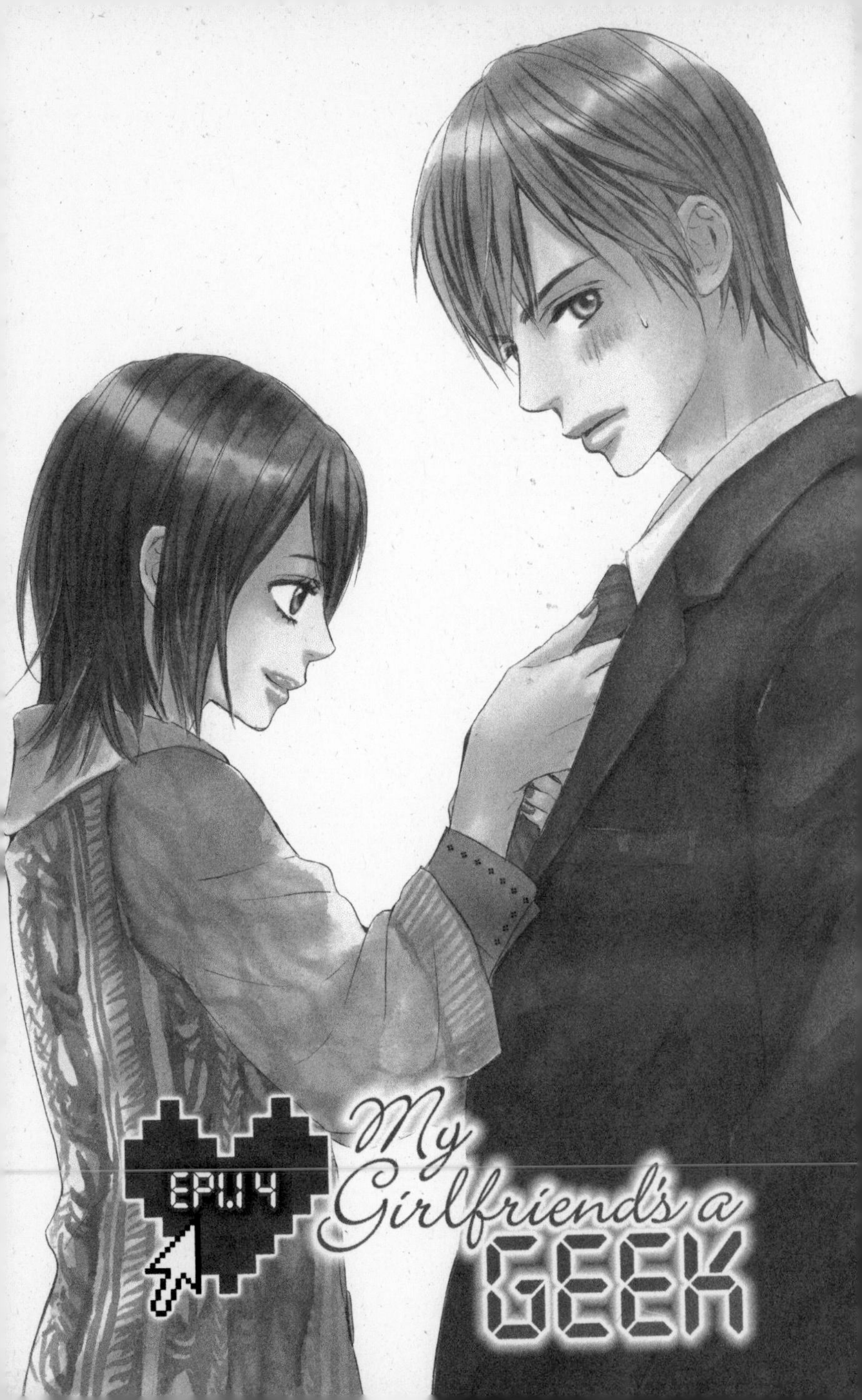
EP1.1 4
My Girlfriend's a GEEK

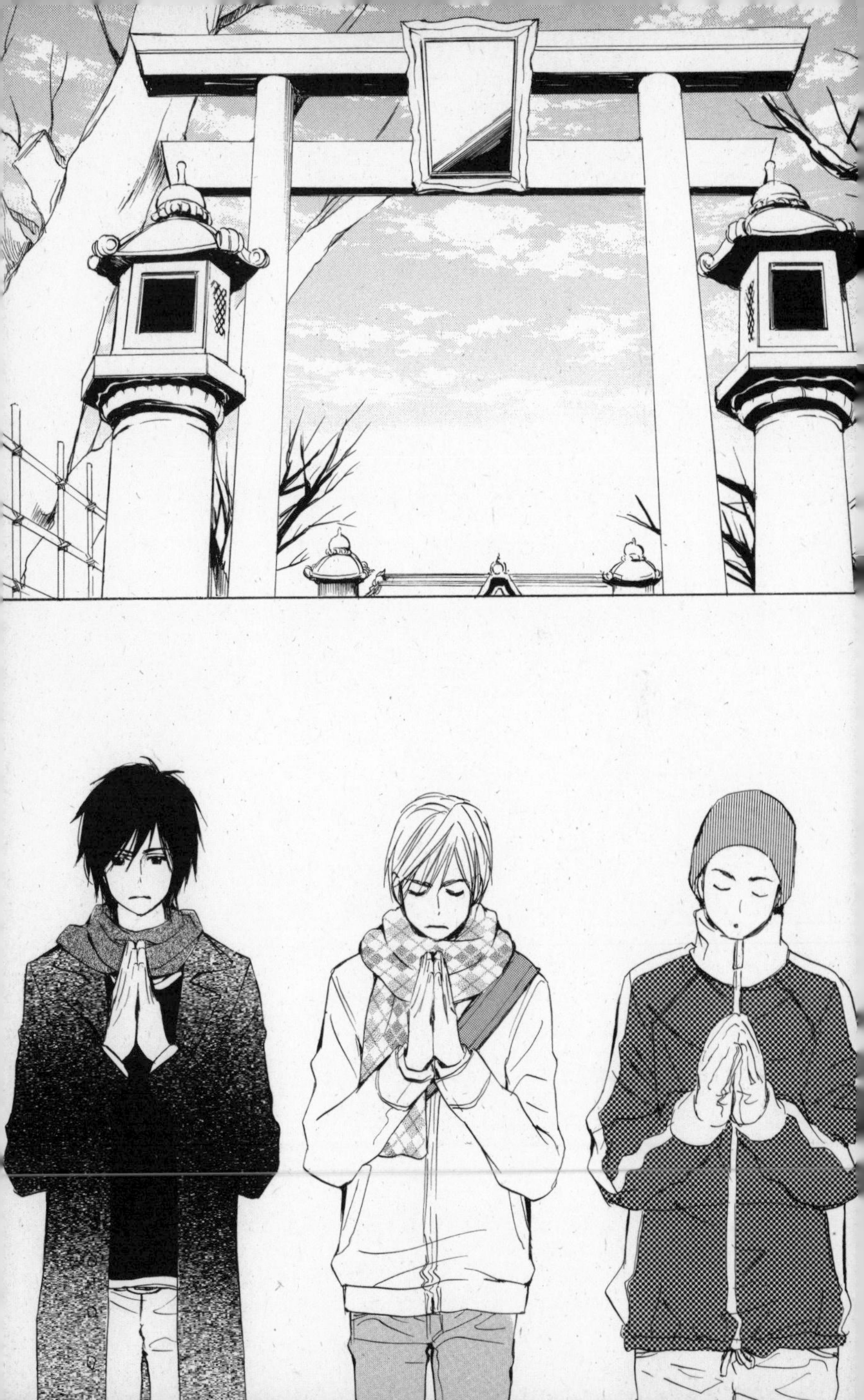

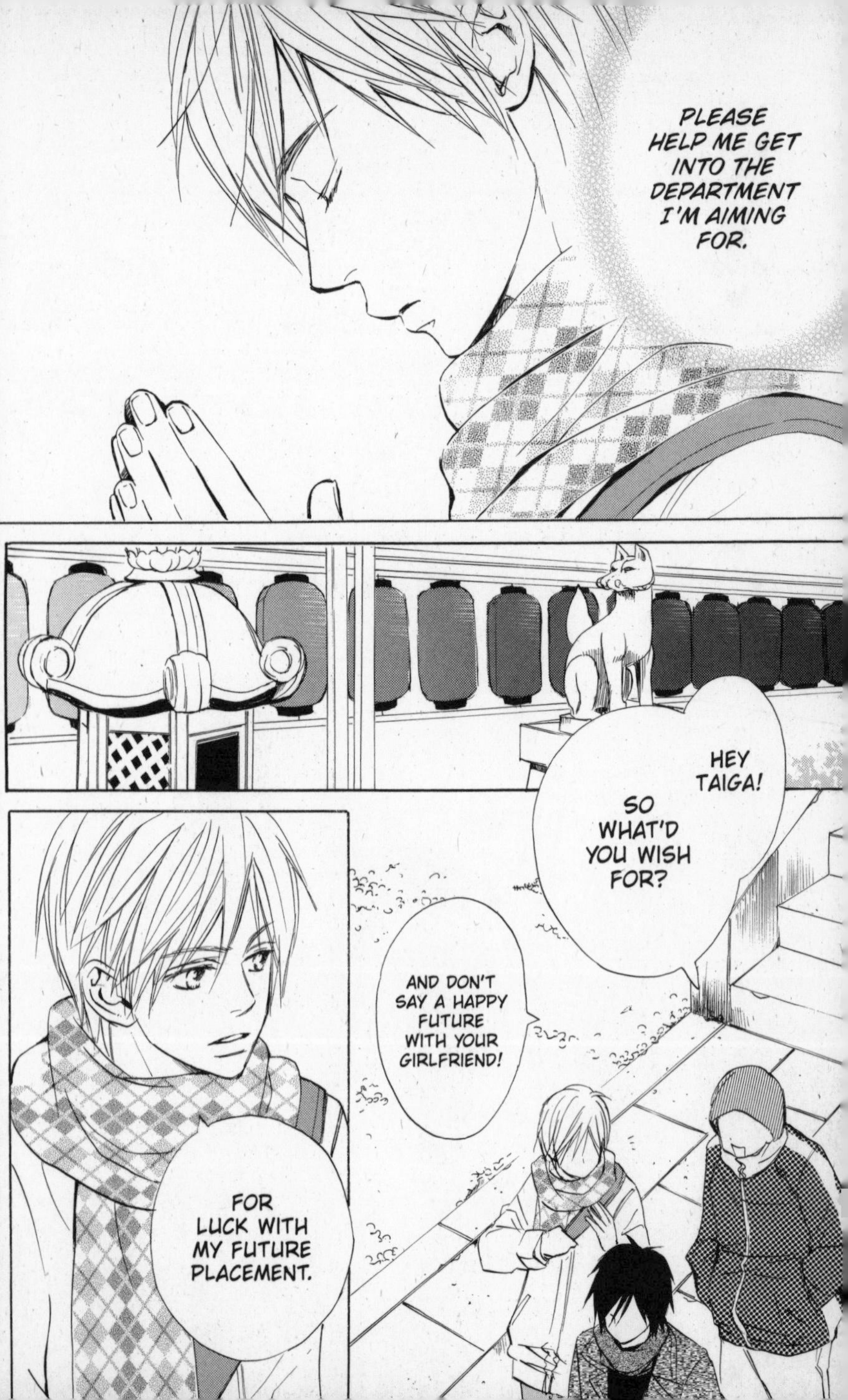
PLEASE HELP ME GET INTO THE DEPARTMENT I'M AIMING FOR.
HEY TAIGA!
SO WHAT'D YOU WISH FOR?
AND DON'T SAY A HAPPY FUTURE WITH YOUR GIRLFRIEND!
FOR LUCK WITH MY FUTURE PLACEMENT.

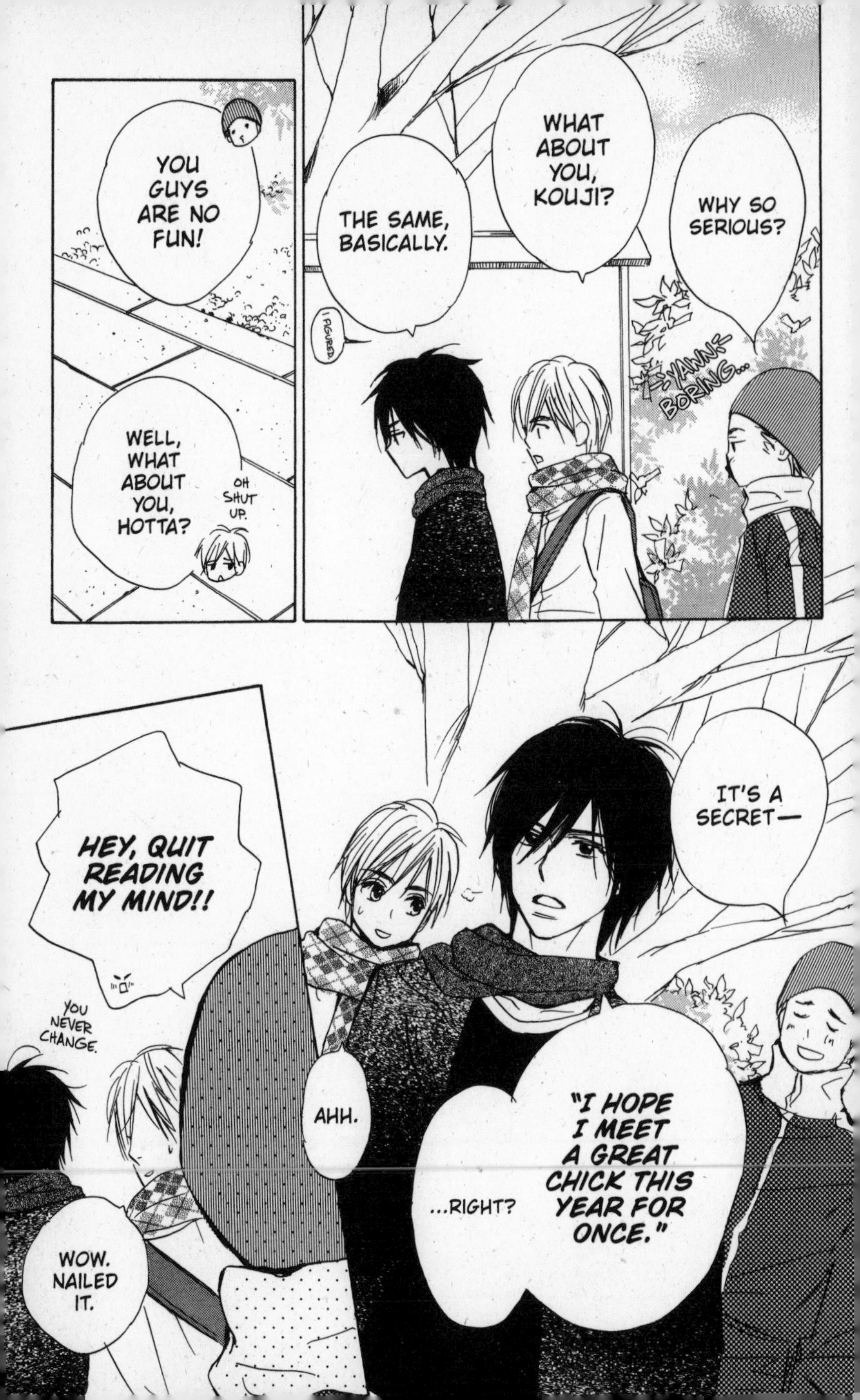
WHY SO SERIOUS?
WHAT ABOUT YOU, KOUJI?
THE SAME, BASICALLY.
I FIGURED.
YAWN BORING...
YOU GUYS ARE NO FUN!
WELL, WHAT ABOUT YOU, HOTTA?
OH SHUT UP.
IT'S A SECRET—
"I HOPE I MEET A GREAT CHICK THIS YEAR FOR ONCE."
...RIGHT?
AHH.
HEY, QUIT READING MY MIND!!
YOU NEVER CHANGE.
WOW. NAILED IT.

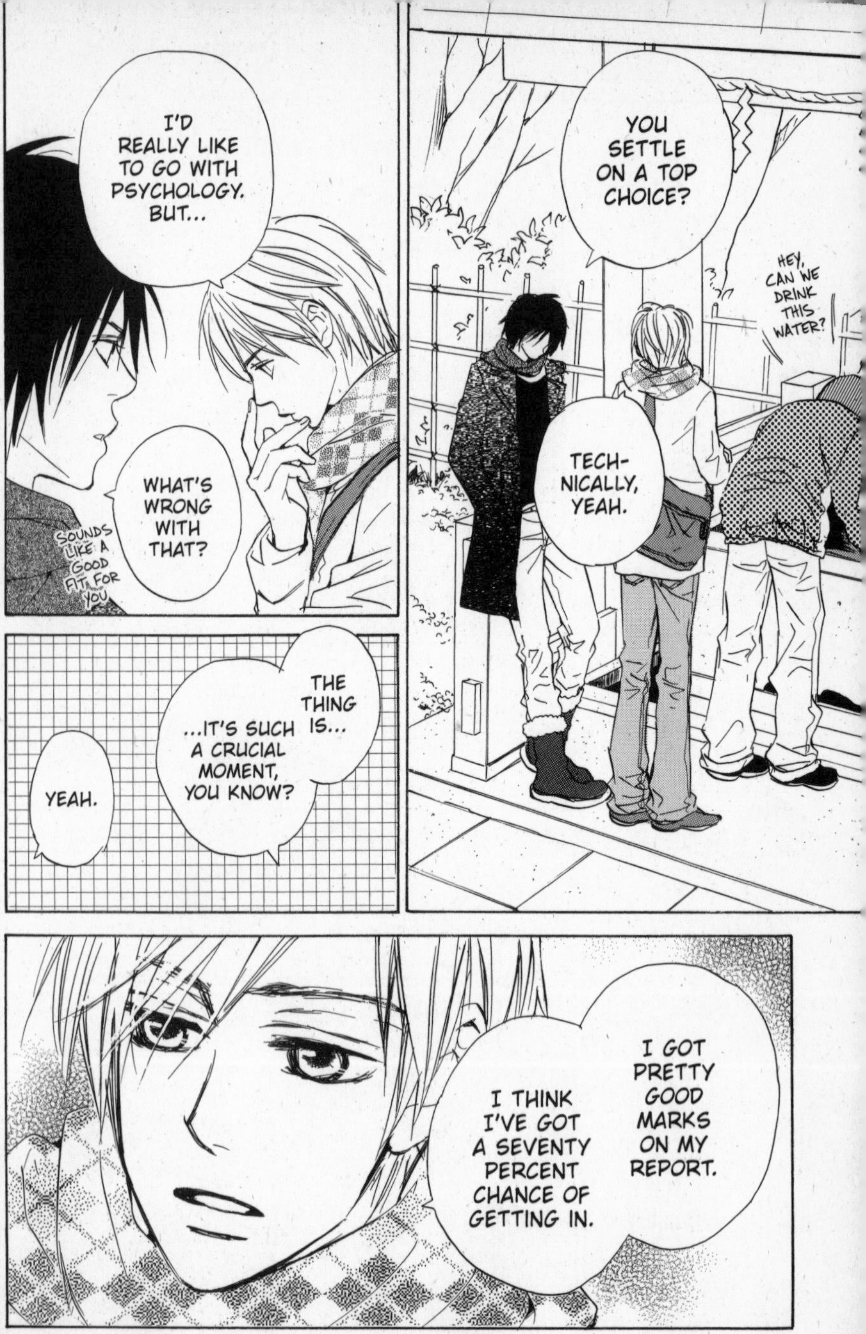
YOU SETTLE ON A TOP CHOICE?
HEY, CAN WE DRINK THIS WATER?
TECH-NICALLY, YEAH.
I'D REALLY LIKE TO GO WITH PSYCHOLOGY. BUT...
WHAT'S WRONG WITH THAT?
SOUNDS LIKE A GOOD FIT FOR YOU
THE THING IS...
...IT'S SUCH A CRUCIAL MOMENT, YOU KNOW?
YEAH.
I GOT PRETTY GOOD MARKS ON MY REPORT.
I THINK I'VE GOT A SEVENTY PERCENT CHANCE OF GETTING IN.

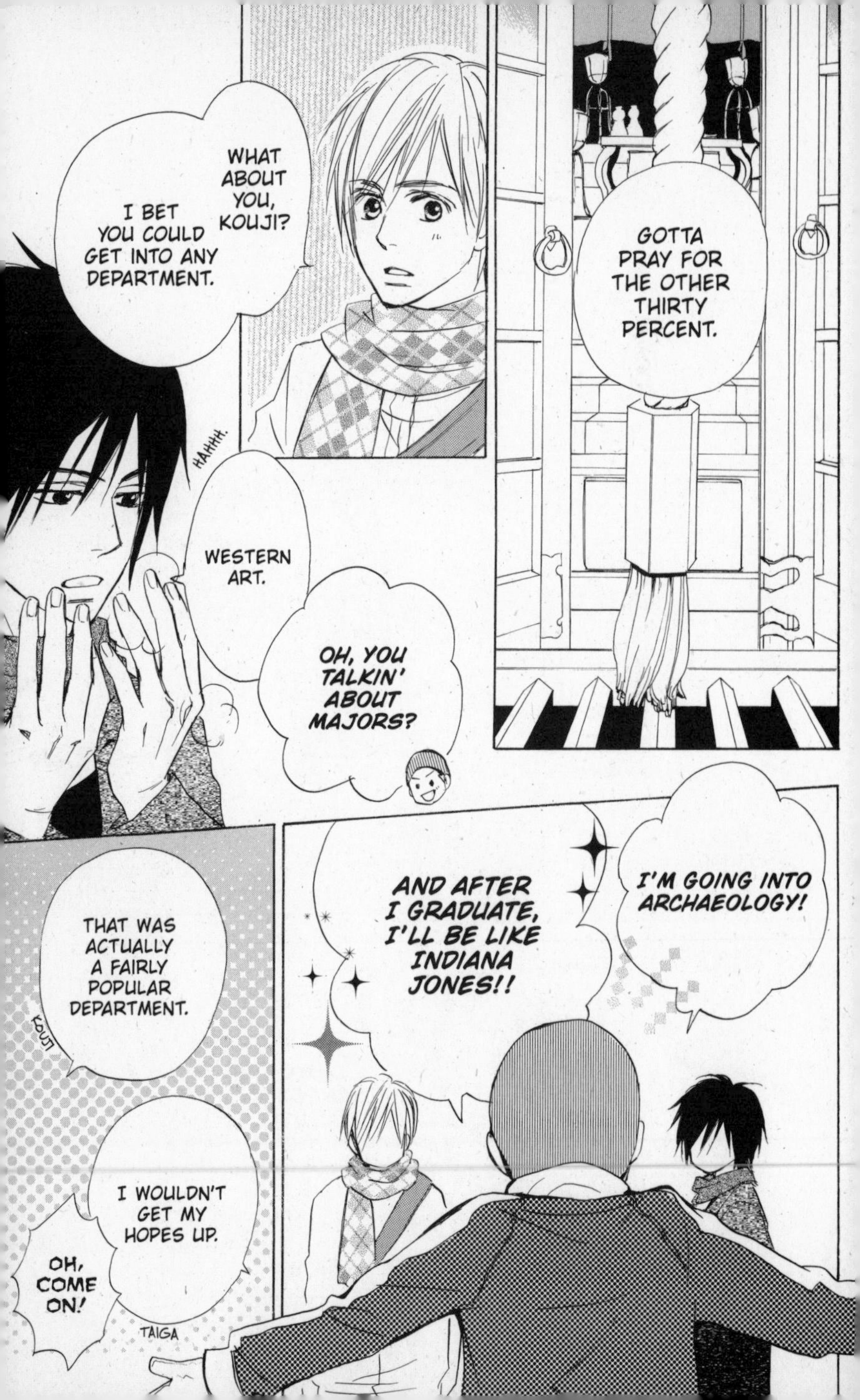
GOTTA PRAY FOR THE OTHER THIRTY PERCENT.
WHAT ABOUT YOU, KOUJI?
I BET YOU COULD GET INTO ANY DEPARTMENT.
HAHHH.
WESTERN ART.
OH, YOU TALKIN' ABOUT MAJORS?
I'M GOING INTO ARCHAEOLOGY!
AND AFTER I GRADUATE, I'LL BE LIKE INDIANA JONES!!
THAT WAS ACTUALLY A FAIRLY POPULAR DEPARTMENT.
KOUJI
I WOULDN'T GET MY HOPES UP.
TAIGA
OH, COME ON!

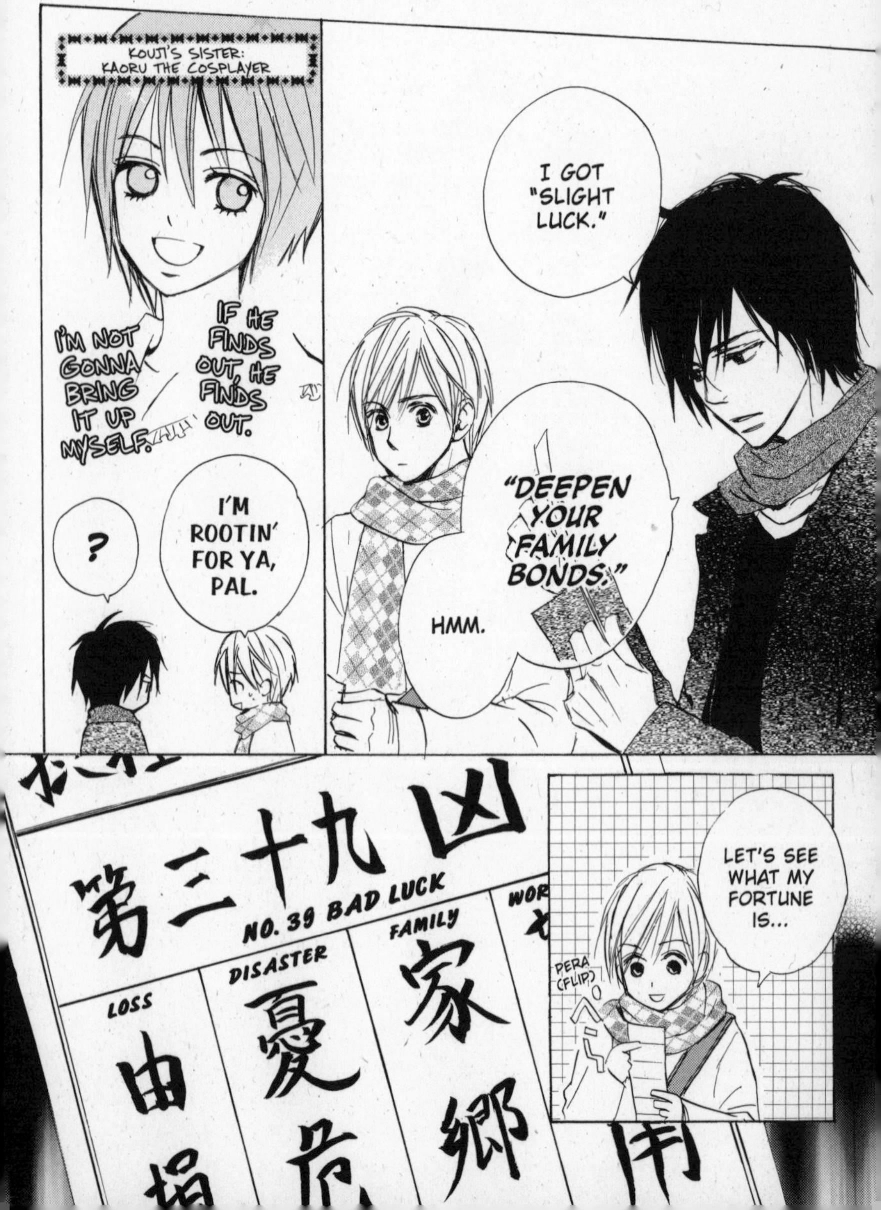
I GOT "SLIGHT LUCK."
"DEEPEN YOUR FAMILY BONDS."
HMM.
KOUJI'S SISTER: KAORU THE COSPLAYER
IF HE FINDS OUT, HE FINDS OUT.
I'M NOT GONNA BRING IT UP MYSELF.
I'M ROOTIN' FOR YA, PAL.
?
LET'S SEE WHAT MY FORTUNE IS...
PERA (FLIP)
第三十九凶
NO. 39 BAD LUCK
FAMILY
DISASTER
LOSS

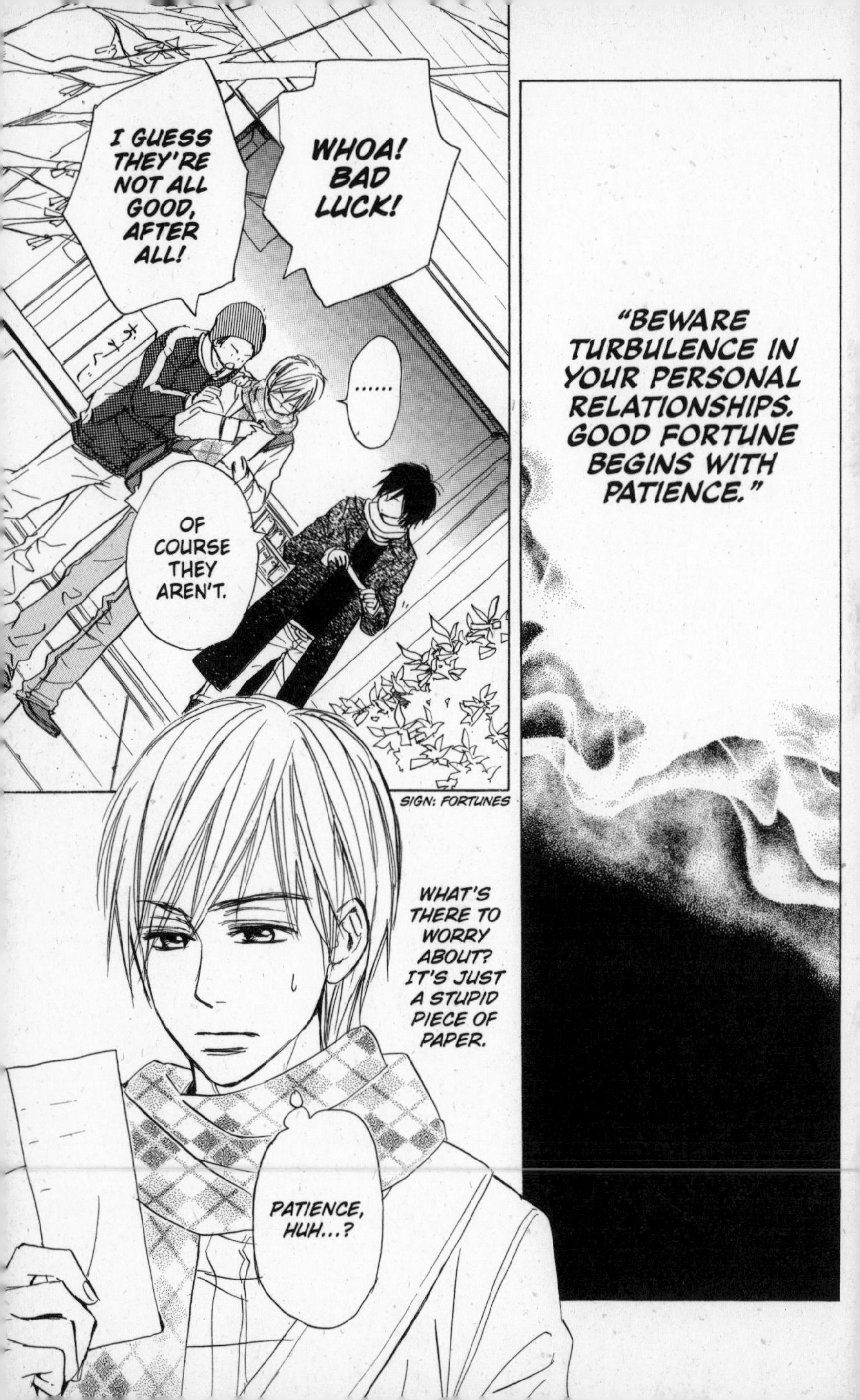
"BEWARE TURBULENCE IN YOUR PERSONAL RELATIONSHIPS. GOOD FORTUNE BEGINS WITH PATIENCE."
WHOA! BAD LUCK!
I GUESS THEY'RE NOT ALL GOOD, AFTER ALL!
......
OF COURSE THEY AREN'T.
SIGN: FORTUNES
WHAT'S THERE TO WORRY ABOUT? IT'S JUST A STUPID PIECE OF PAPER.
PATIENCE, HUH...?

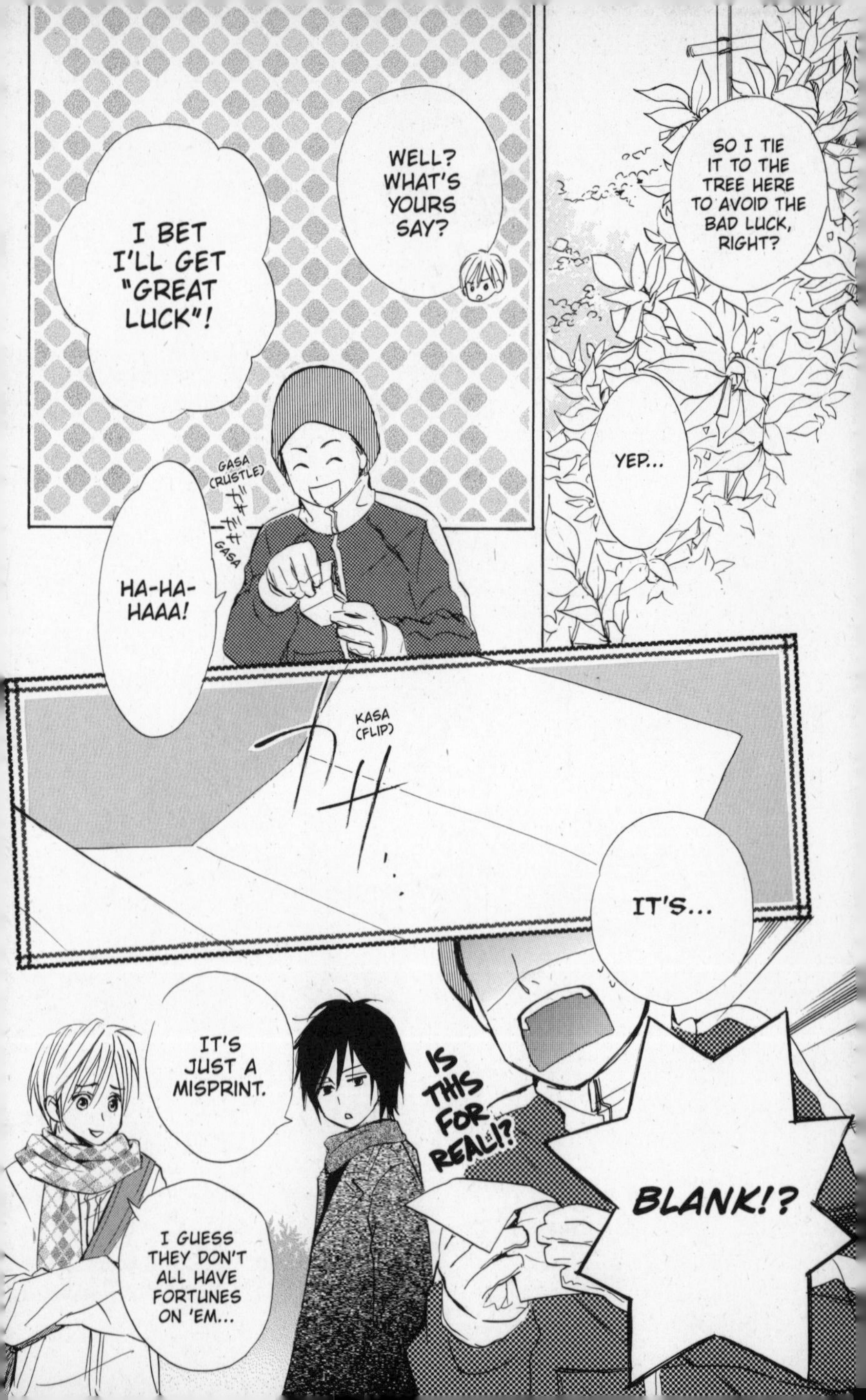
SO I TIE IT TO THE TREE HERE TO AVOID THE BAD LUCK, RIGHT?
YEP...
WELL? WHAT'S YOURS SAY?
I BET I'LL GET "GREAT LUCK"!
GASA (RUSTLE)
GASA
HA-HA-HAAA!
KASA (FLIP)
IT'S...
BLANK!?
IS THIS FOR REAL!?
IT'S JUST A MISPRINT.
I GUESS THEY DON'T ALL HAVE FORTUNES ON 'EM...

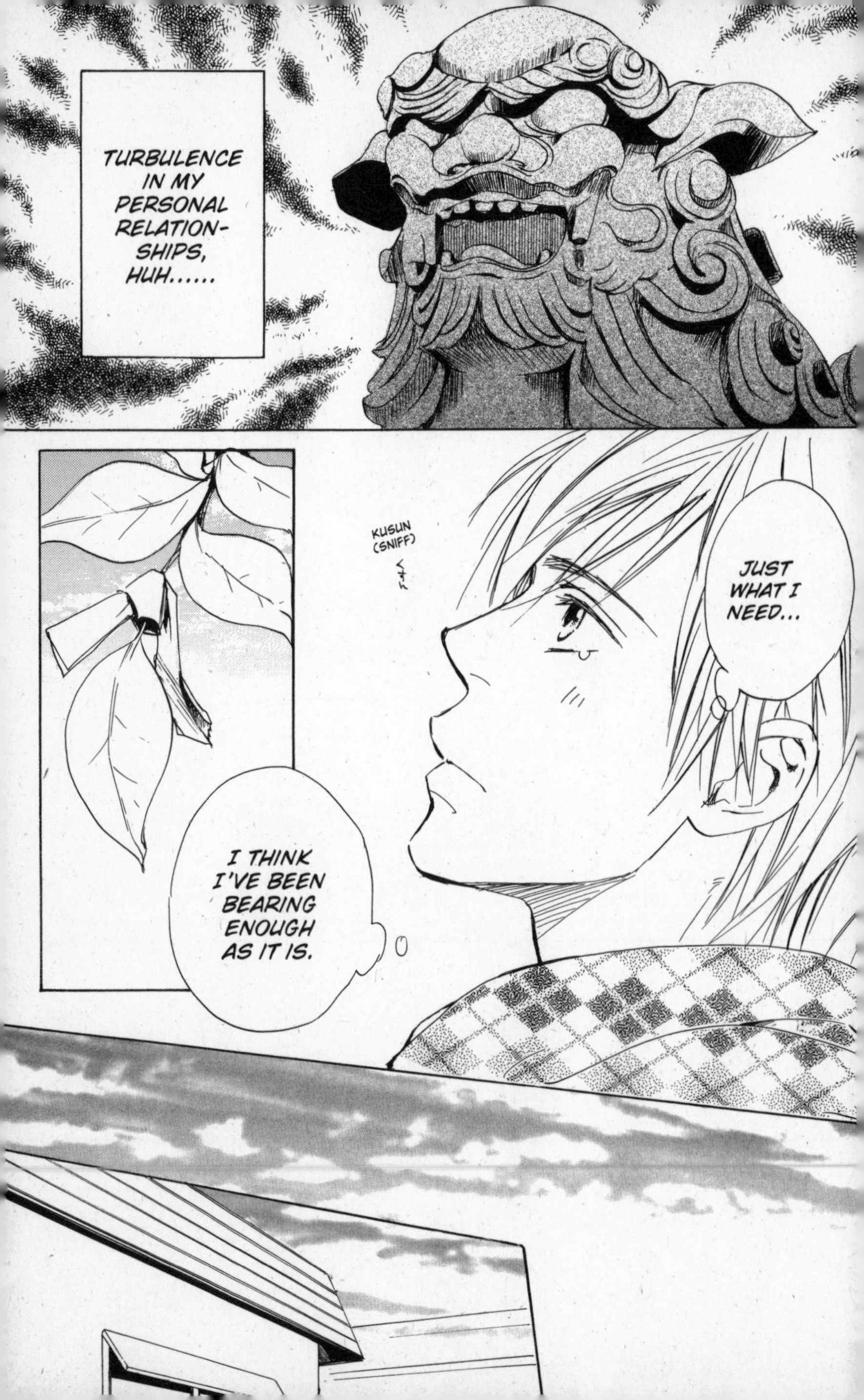
TURBULENCE IN MY PERSONAL RELATION-SHIPS, HUH......
KUSUN (SNIFF)
JUST WHAT I NEED...
I THINK I'VE BEEN BEARING ENOUGH AS IT IS.

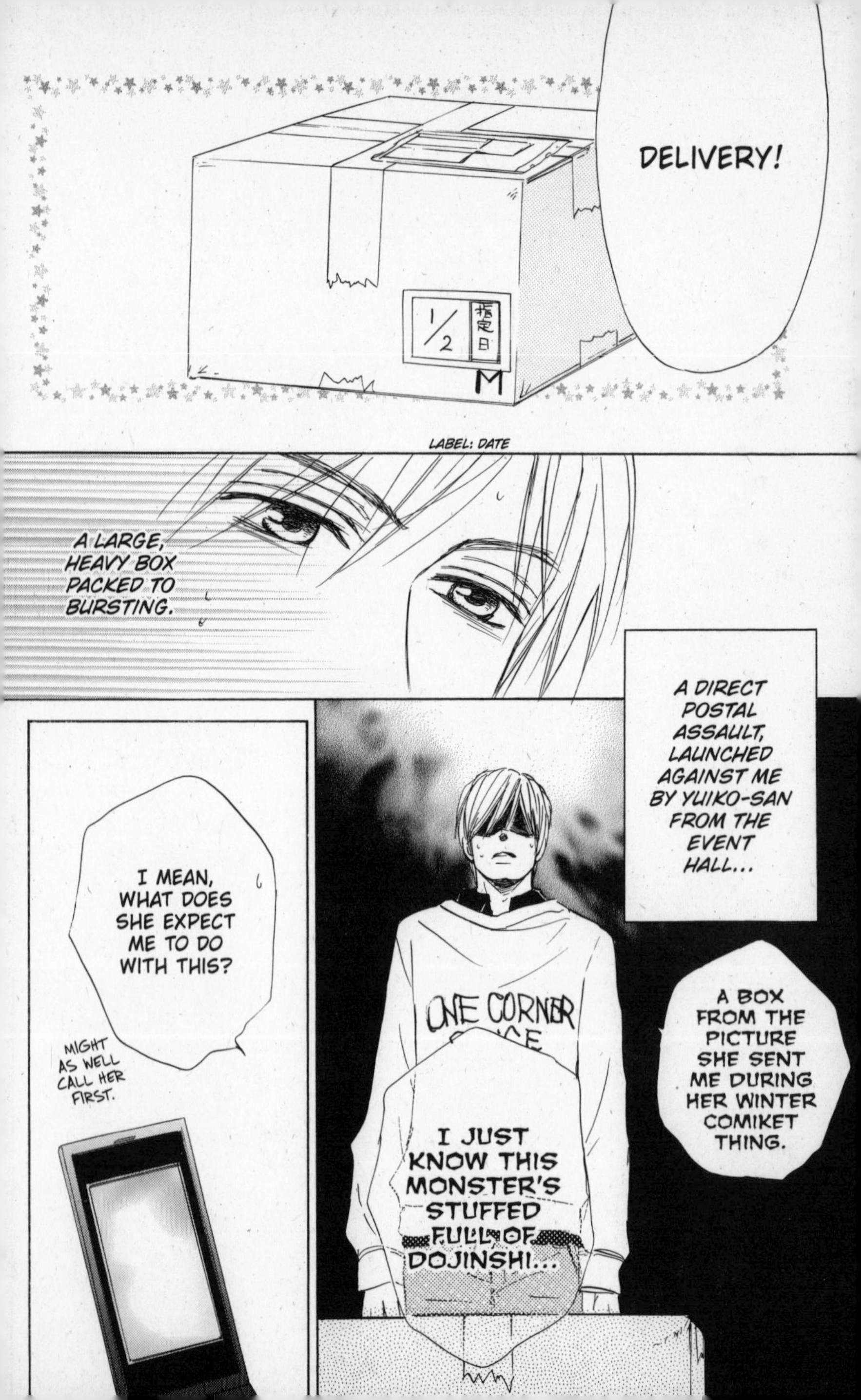

DELIVERY!
1/2
指定日
M
LABEL: DATE
A LARGE, HEAVY BOX PACKED TO BURSTING.
A DIRECT POSTAL ASSAULT, LAUNCHED AGAINST ME BY YUIKO-SAN FROM THE EVENT HALL...
A BOX FROM THE PICTURE SHE SENT ME DURING HER WINTER COMIKET THING.
ONE CORNER
I JUST KNOW THIS MONSTER'S STUFFED FULL OF DOJINSHI...
I MEAN, WHAT DOES SHE EXPECT ME TO DO WITH THIS?
MIGHT AS WELL CALL HER FIRST.

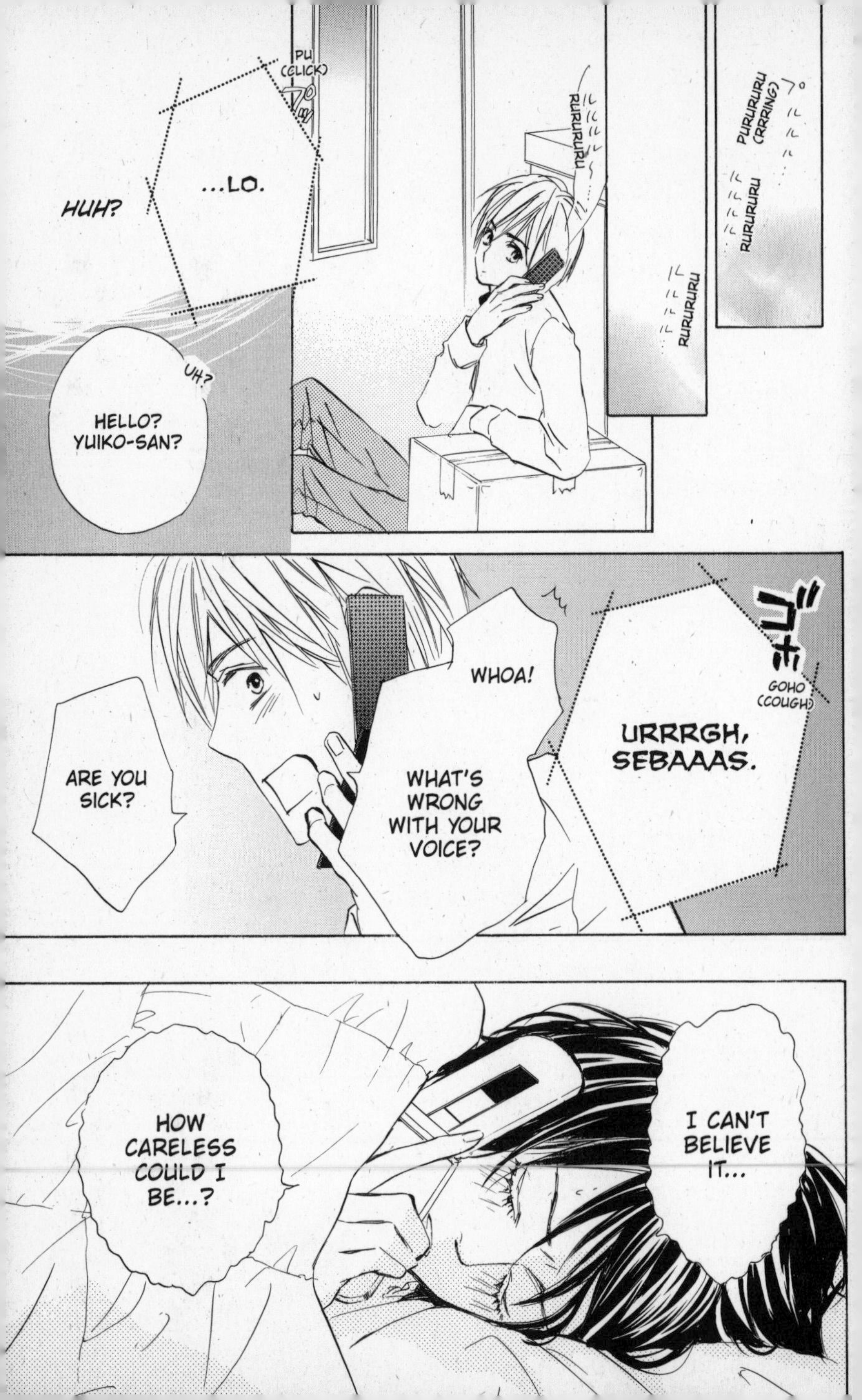
PURURURU (RRRING)
RURURURU
RURURURU
RURURURU
PU (CLICK)
...LO.
HUH?
UH?
HELLO? YUIKO-SAN?
GOHO (COUGH)
URRRGH, SEBAAAS.
WHOA!
WHAT'S WRONG WITH YOUR VOICE?
ARE YOU SICK?
I CAN'T BELIEVE IT...
HOW CARELESS COULD I BE...?

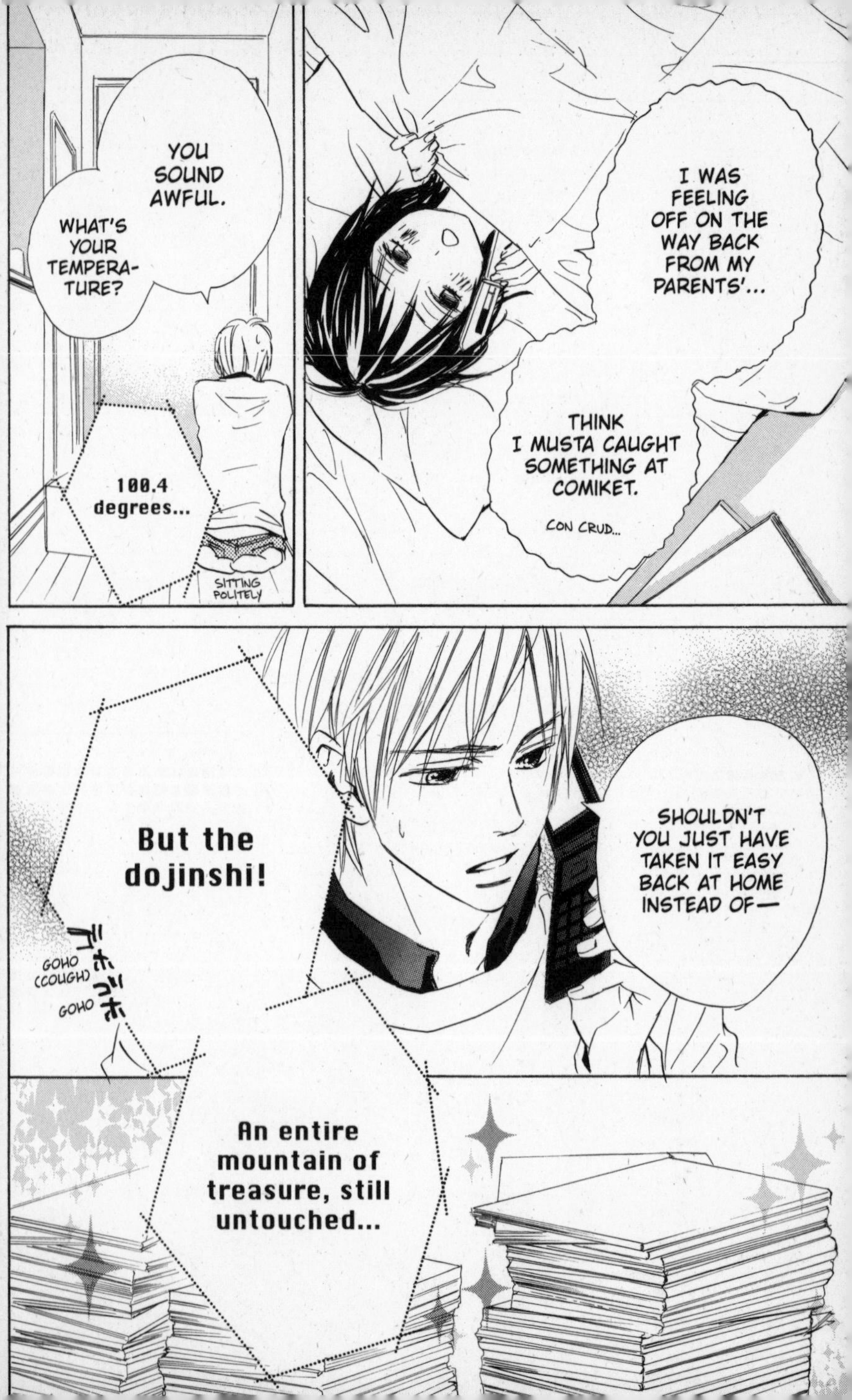
I WAS FEELING OFF ON THE WAY BACK FROM MY PARENTS'...
THINK I MUSTA CAUGHT SOMETHING AT COMIKET.
CON CRUD...
YOU SOUND AWFUL.
WHAT'S YOUR TEMPERA-TURE?
100.4 degrees...
SITTING POLITELY
SHOULDN'T YOU JUST HAVE TAKEN IT EASY BACK AT HOME INSTEAD OF—
But the dojinshi!
ゴホゴホ
GOHO (COUGH) GOHO
An entire mountain of treasure, still untouched...

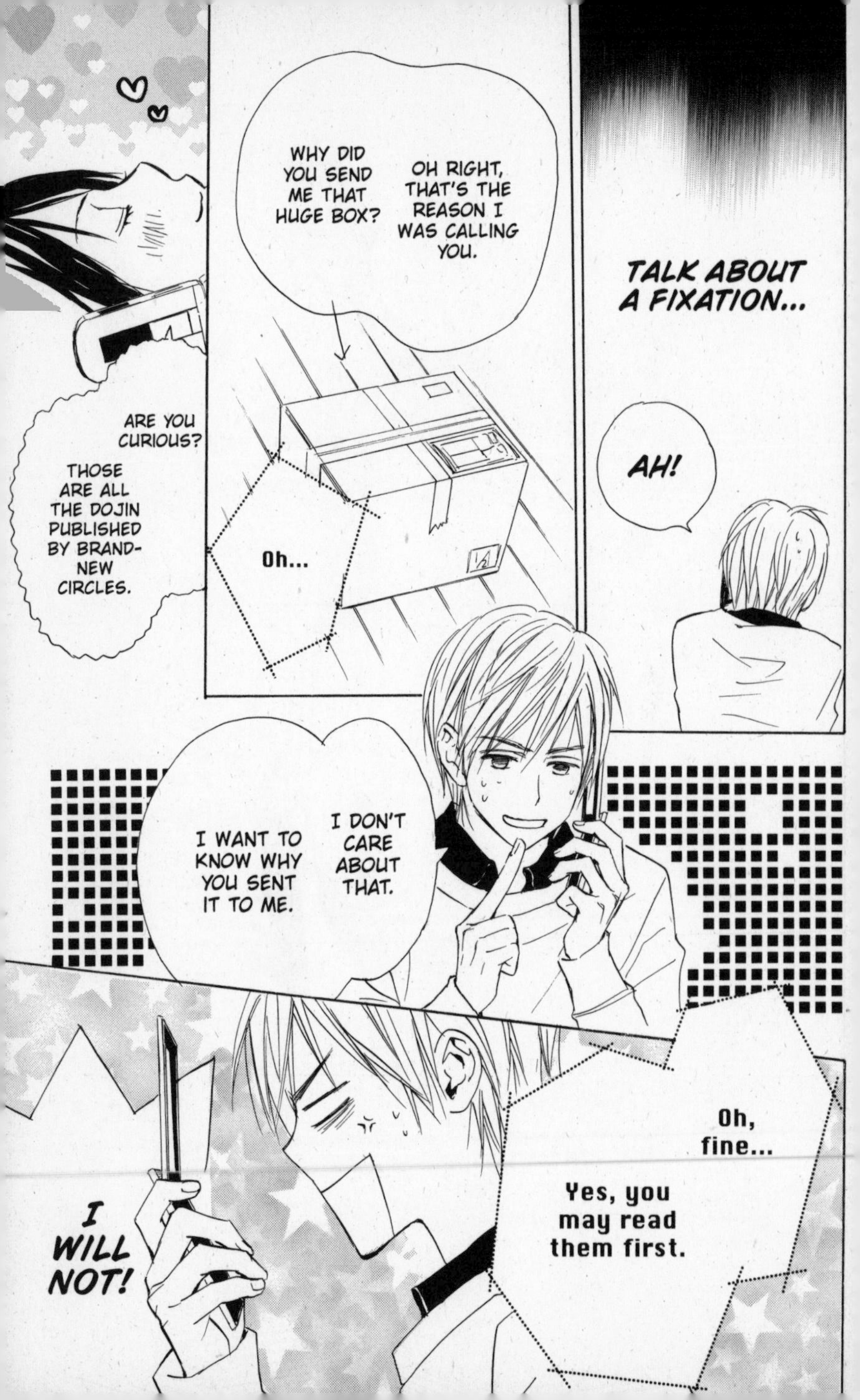
TALK ABOUT A FIXATION...
AH!
OH RIGHT, THAT'S THE REASON I WAS CALLING YOU.
WHY DID YOU SEND ME THAT HUGE BOX?
Oh...
ARE YOU CURIOUS?
THOSE ARE ALL THE DOJIN PUBLISHED BY BRAND-NEW CIRCLES.
I DON'T CARE ABOUT THAT.
I WANT TO KNOW WHY YOU SENT IT TO ME.
Oh, fine...
Yes, you may read them first.
I WILL NOT!

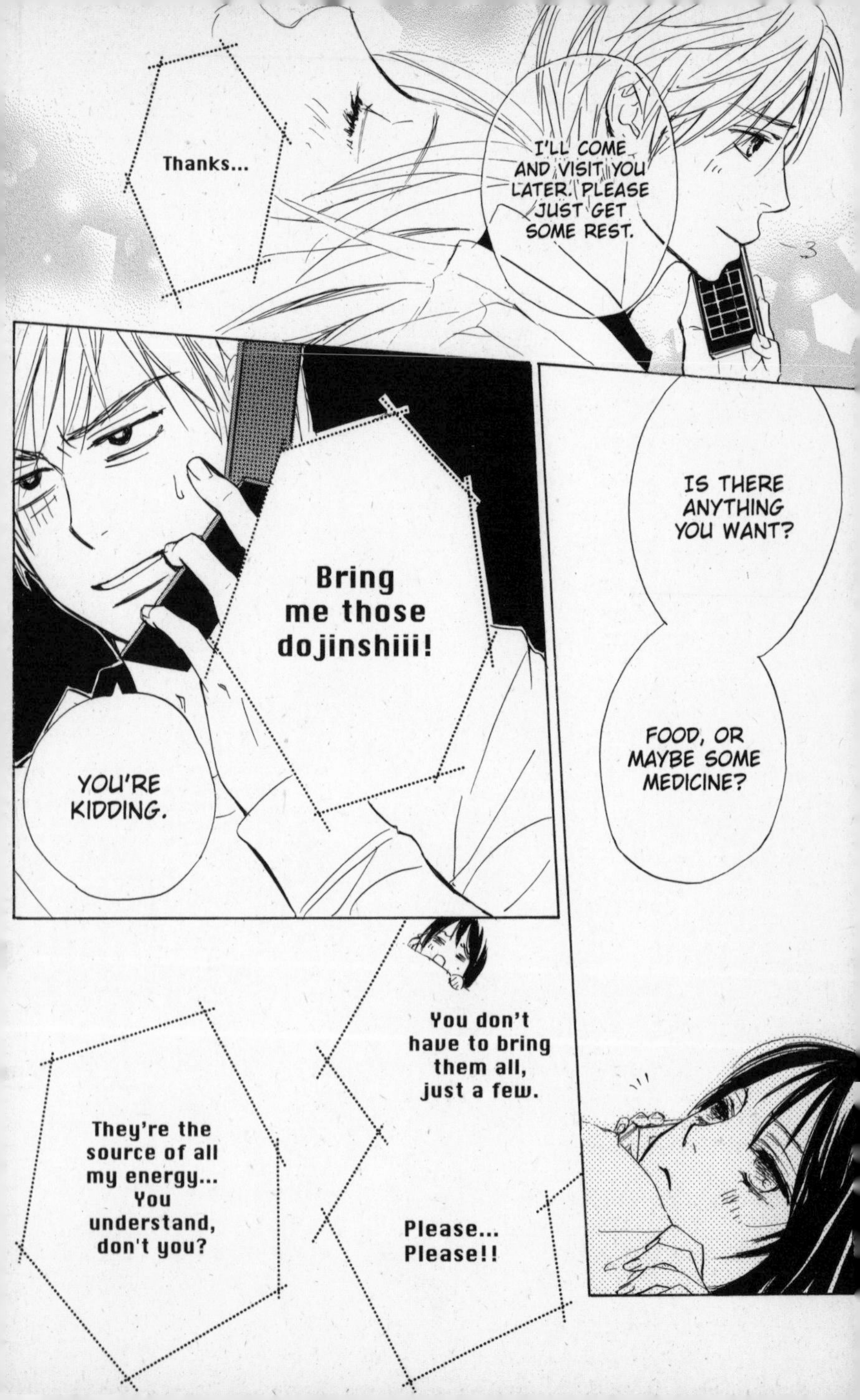
I'LL COME AND VISIT YOU LATER. PLEASE JUST GET SOME REST.
Thanks...
IS THERE ANYTHING YOU WANT?
FOOD, OR MAYBE SOME MEDICINE?
Bring me those dojinshiii!
YOU'RE KIDDING.
You don't have to bring them all, just a few.
They're the source of all my energy... You understand, don't you?
Please... Please!!

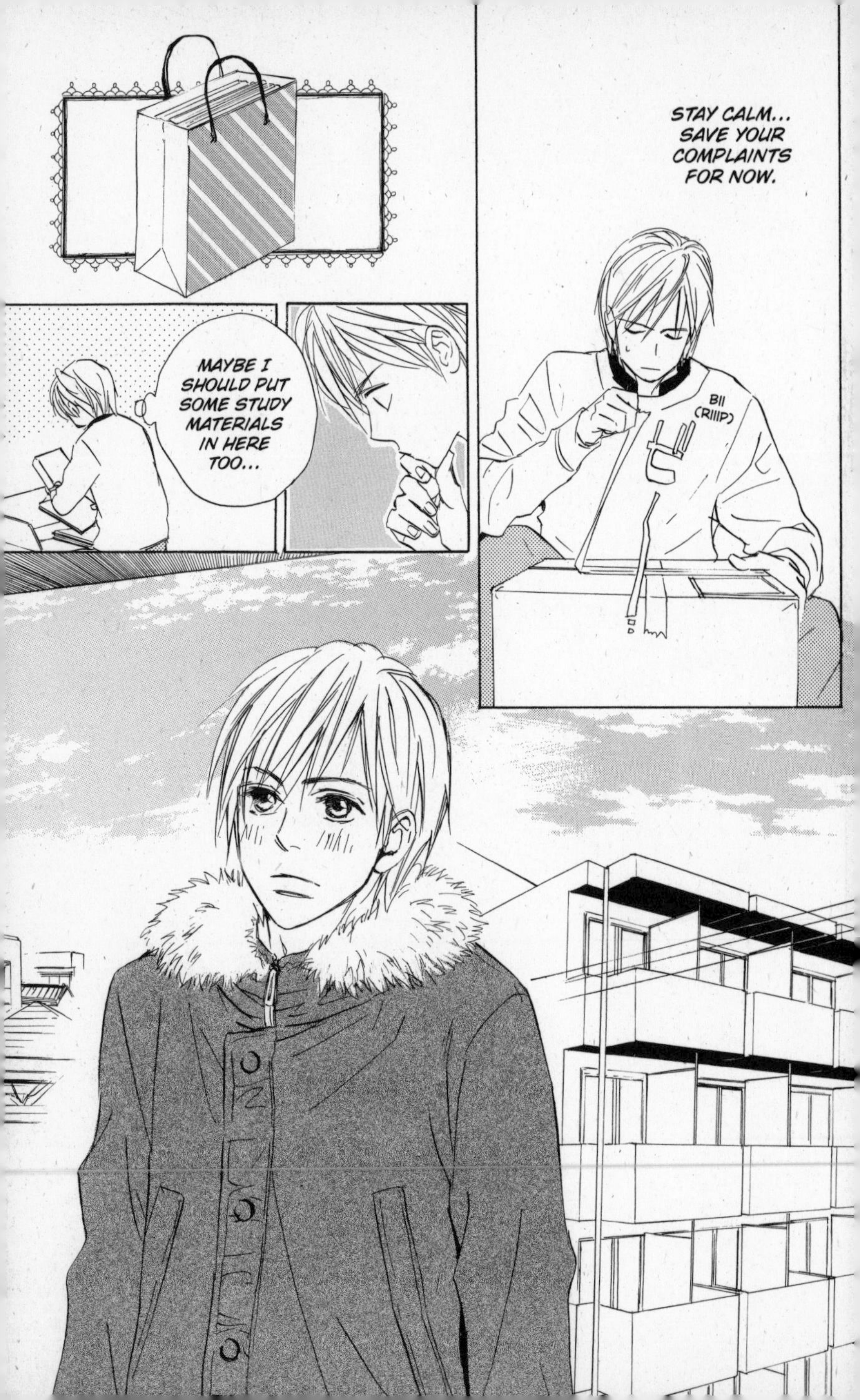
STAY CALM... SAVE YOUR COMPLAINTS FOR NOW.
BII (RIIIP)
MAYBE I SHOULD PUT SOME STUDY MATERIALS IN HERE TOO...

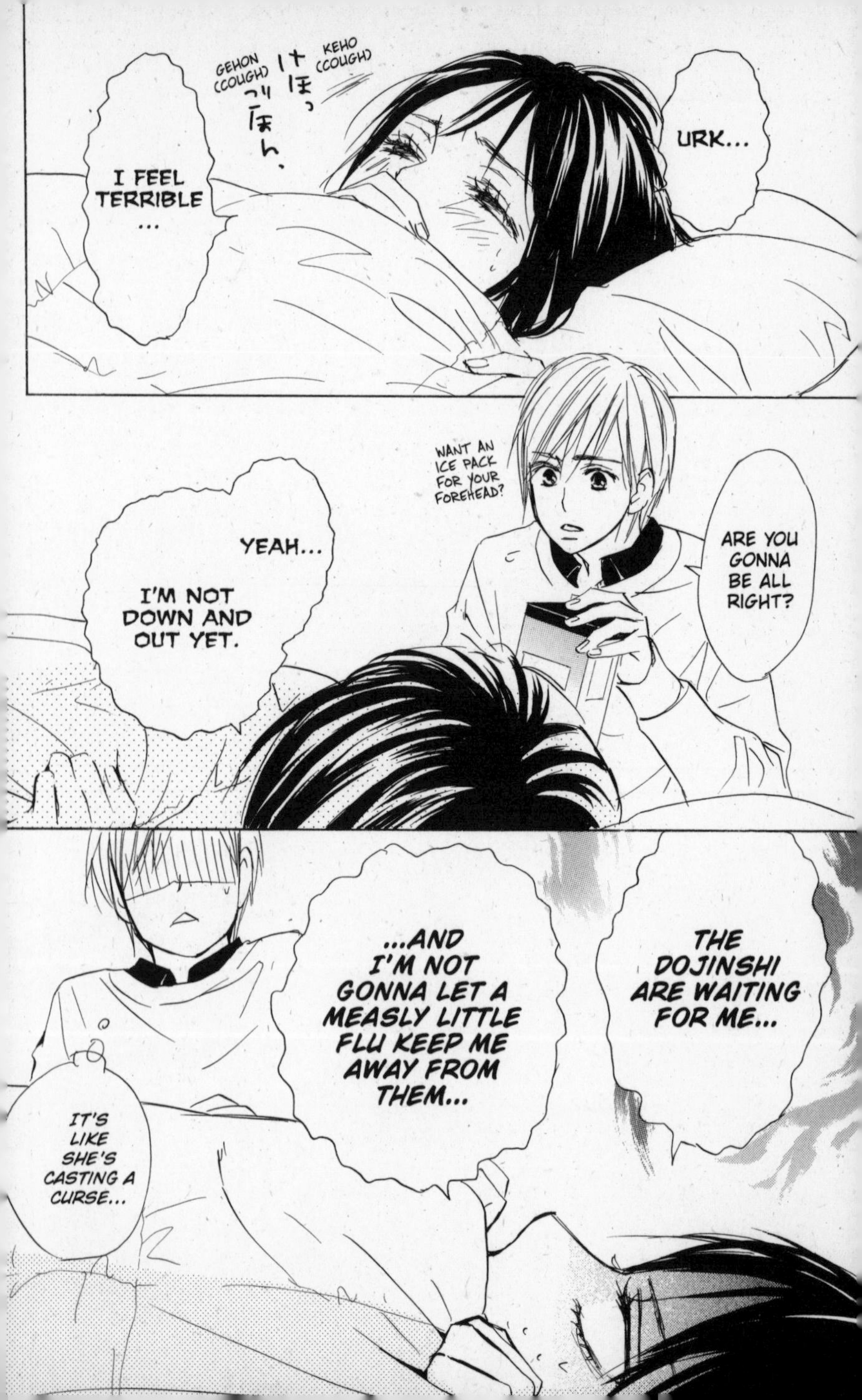
URK...
KEHO (COUGH)
けほっ
GEHON (COUGH)
ごほん.
I FEEL TERRIBLE ...
ARE YOU GONNA BE ALL RIGHT?
WANT AN ICE PACK FOR YOUR FOREHEAD?
YEAH... I'M NOT DOWN AND OUT YET.
THE DOJINSHI ARE WAITING FOR ME...
...AND I'M NOT GONNA LET A MEASLY LITTLE FLU KEEP ME AWAY FROM THEM...
IT'S LIKE SHE'S CASTING A CURSE...

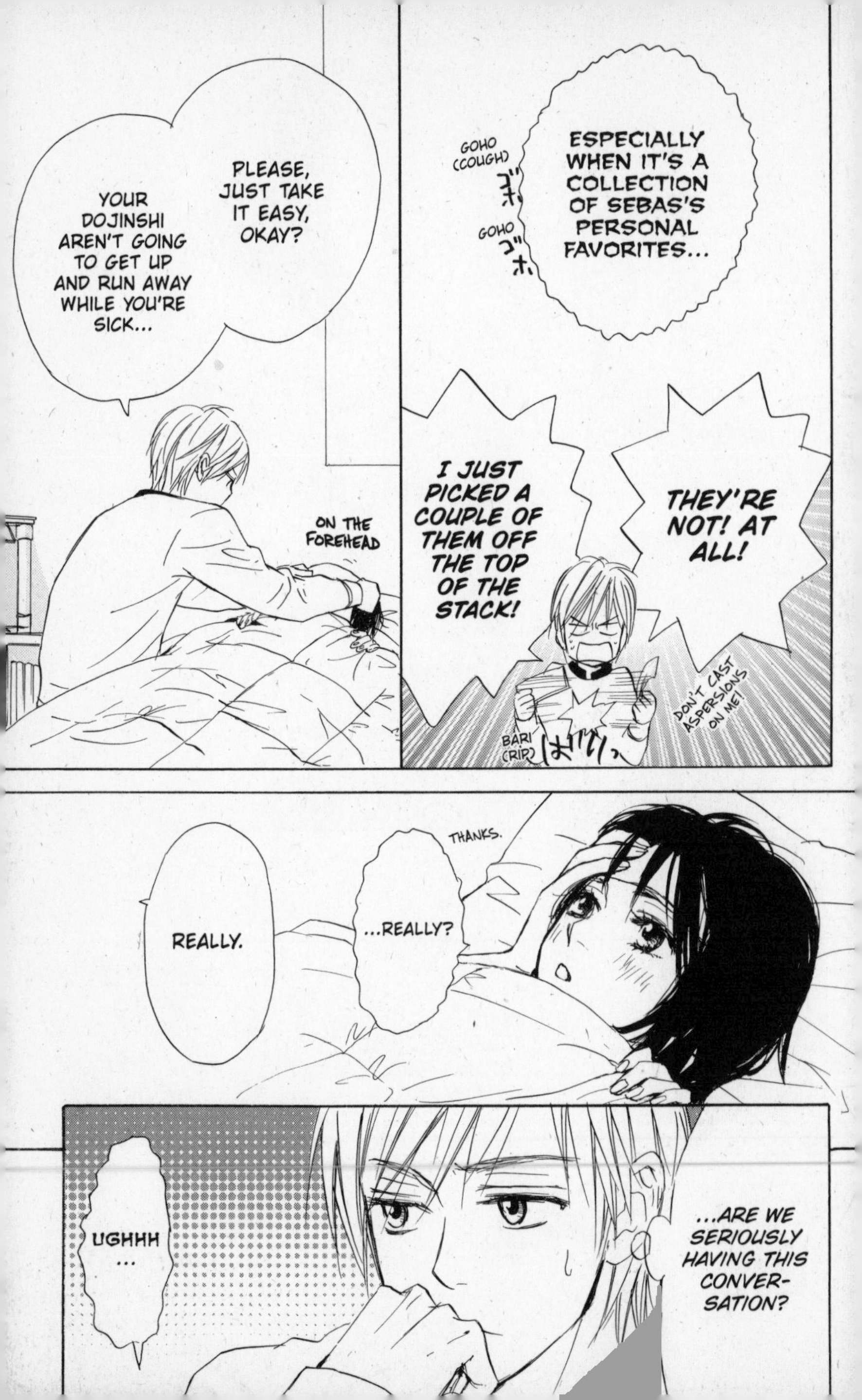
GOHO (COUGH)
GOHO
ESPECIALLY WHEN IT'S A COLLECTION OF SEBAS'S PERSONAL FAVORITES...
THEY'RE NOT! AT ALL!
I JUST PICKED A COUPLE OF THEM OFF THE TOP OF THE STACK!
DON'T CAST ASPERSIONS ON ME!
BARI (RIP)
PLEASE, JUST TAKE IT EASY, OKAY?
YOUR DOJINSHI AREN'T GOING TO GET UP AND RUN AWAY WHILE YOU'RE SICK...
ON THE FOREHEAD
THANKS.
...REALLY?
REALLY.
...ARE WE SERIOUSLY HAVING THIS CONVER-SATION?
UGHHH ...

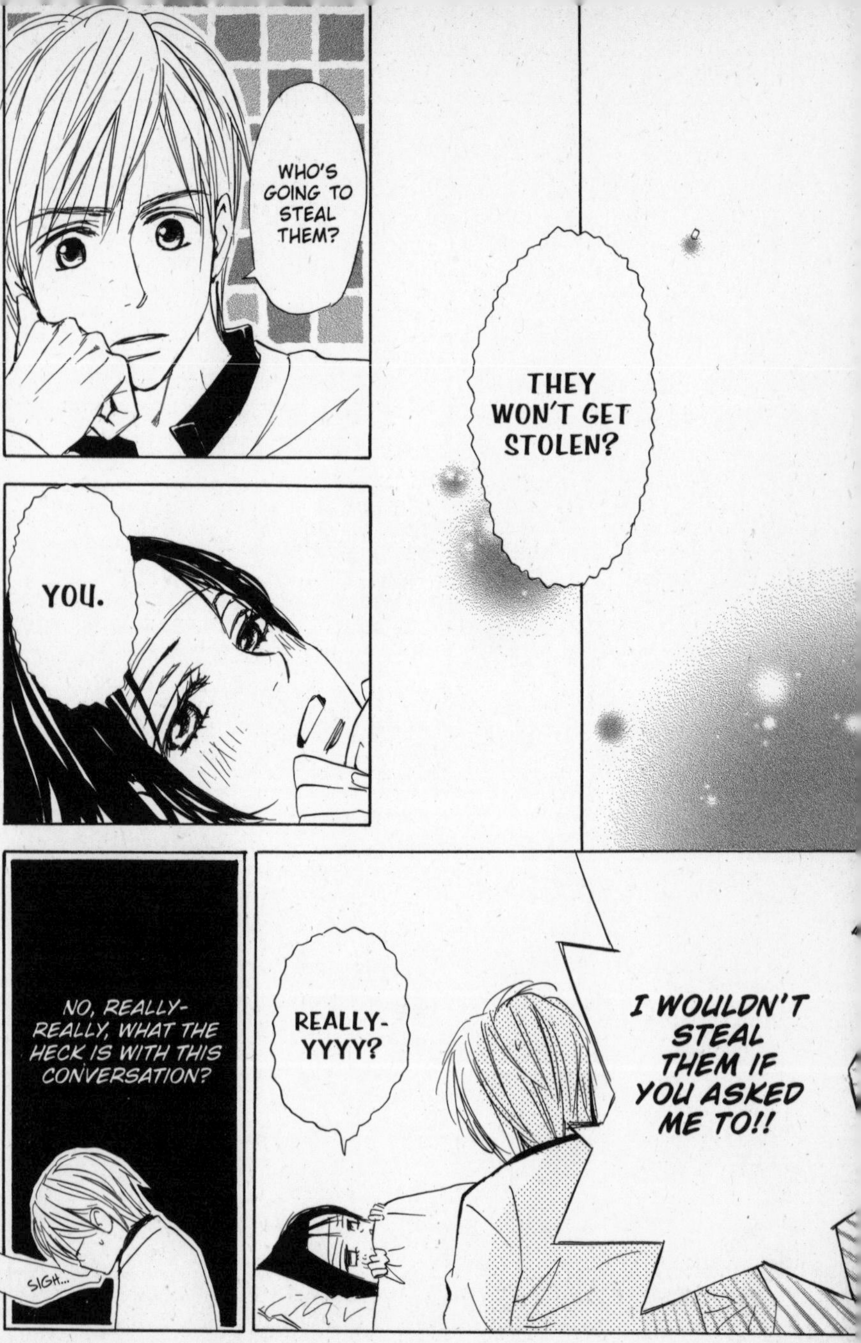
THEY WON'T GET STOLEN?
WHO'S GOING TO STEAL THEM?
YOU.
I WOULDN'T STEAL THEM IF YOU ASKED ME TO!!
REALLY-YYYY?
NO, REALLY-REALLY, WHAT THE HECK IS WITH THIS CONVERSATION?
SIGH...

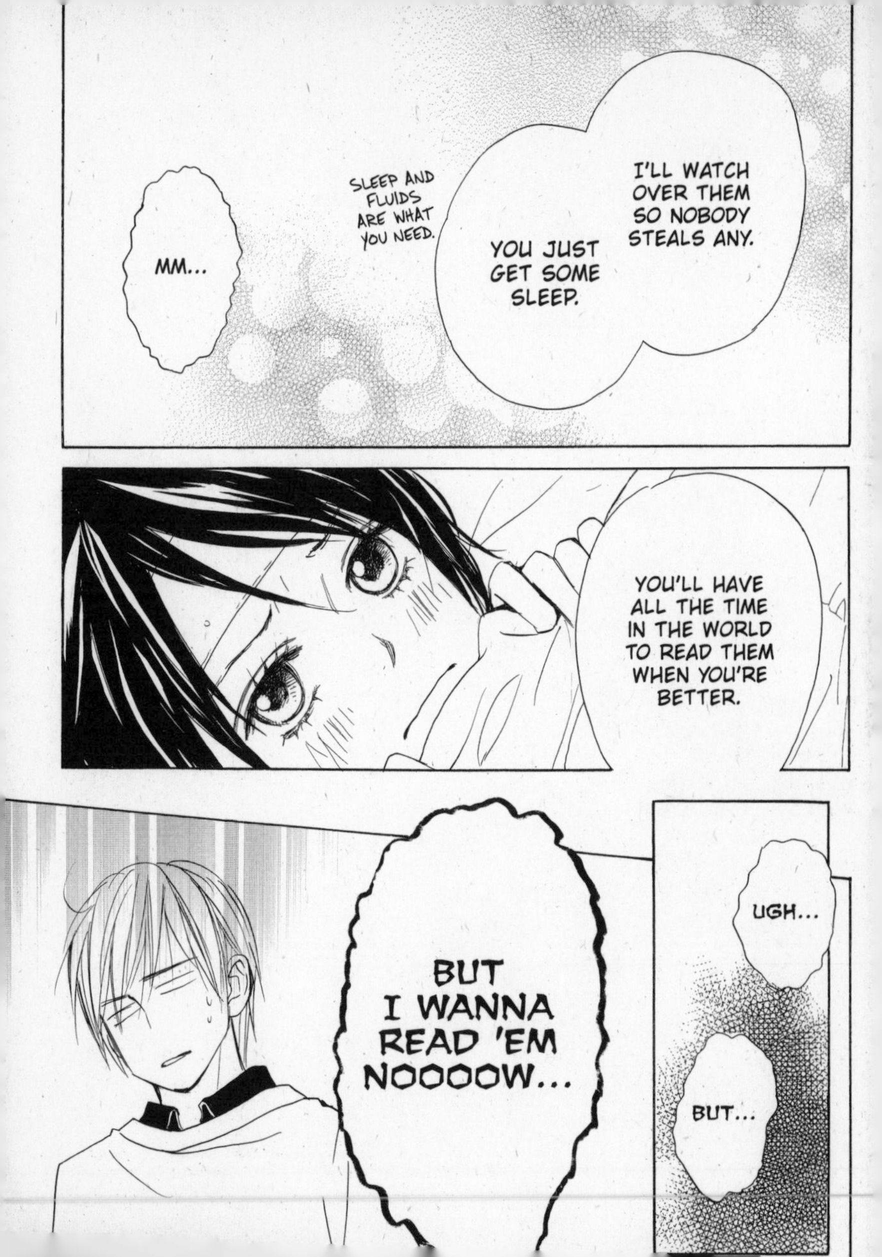
I'LL WATCH OVER THEM SO NOBODY STEALS ANY.
YOU JUST GET SOME SLEEP.
SLEEP AND FLUIDS ARE WHAT YOU NEED.
MM...
YOU'LL HAVE ALL THE TIME IN THE WORLD TO READ THEM WHEN YOU'RE BETTER.
UGH...
BUT...
BUT I WANNA READ 'EM NOOOOW...

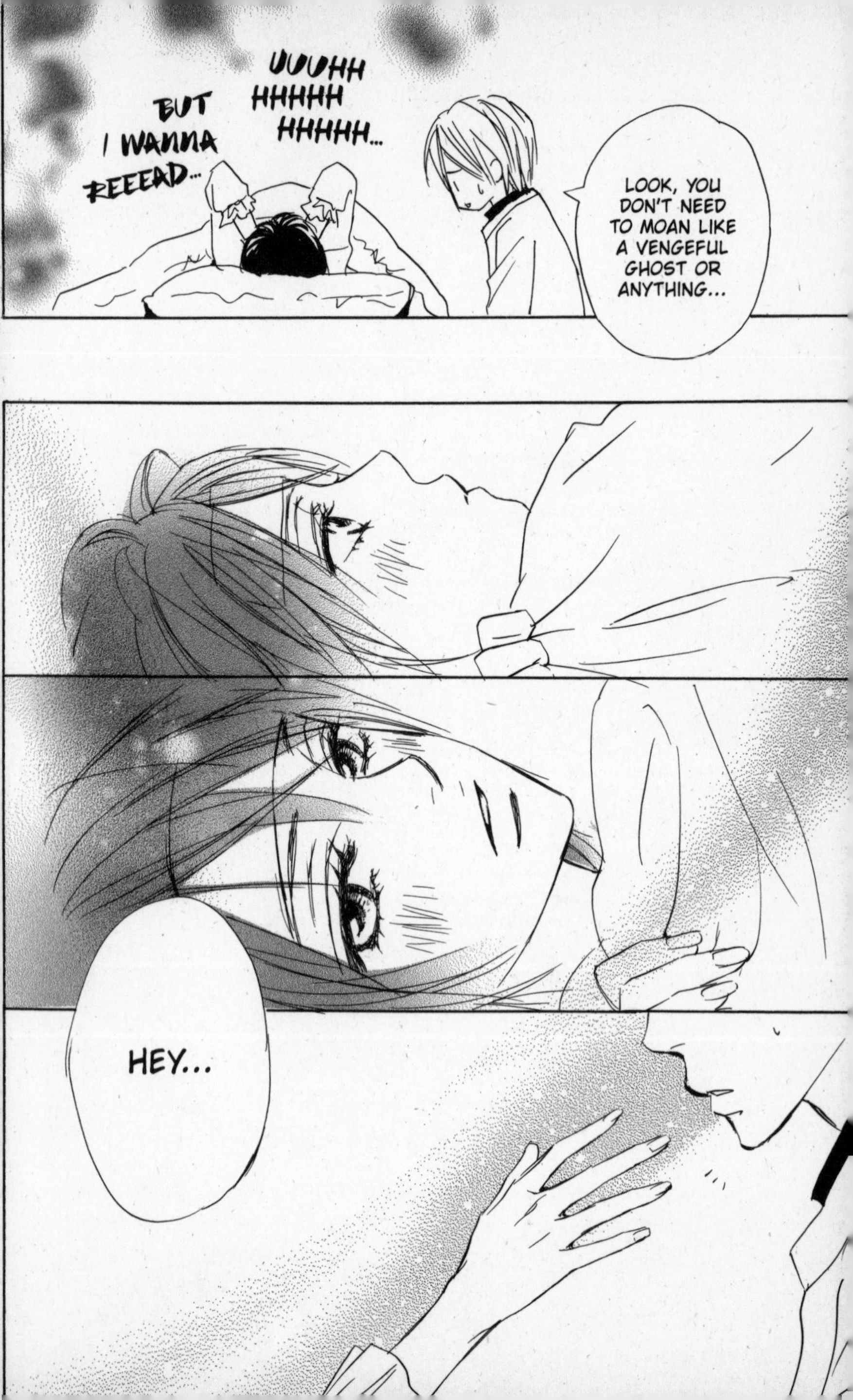
LOOK, YOU DON'T NEED TO MOAN LIKE A VENGEFUL GHOST OR ANYTHING...
UUUHH HHHHH HHHHH...
BUT I WANNA REEEAD...
HEY...

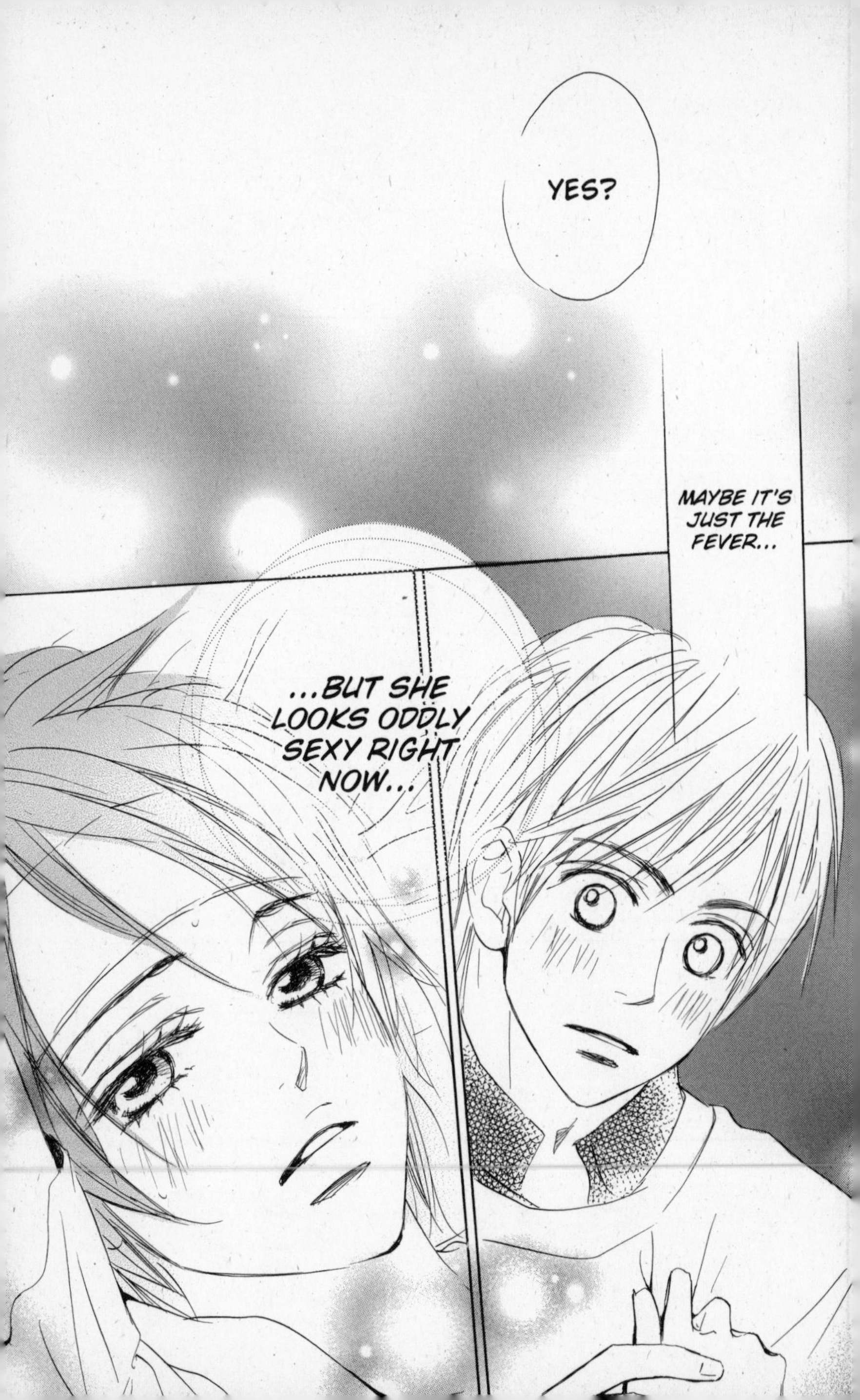
YES?
MAYBE IT'S JUST THE FEVER...
...BUT SHE LOOKS ODDLY SEXY RIGHT NOW...

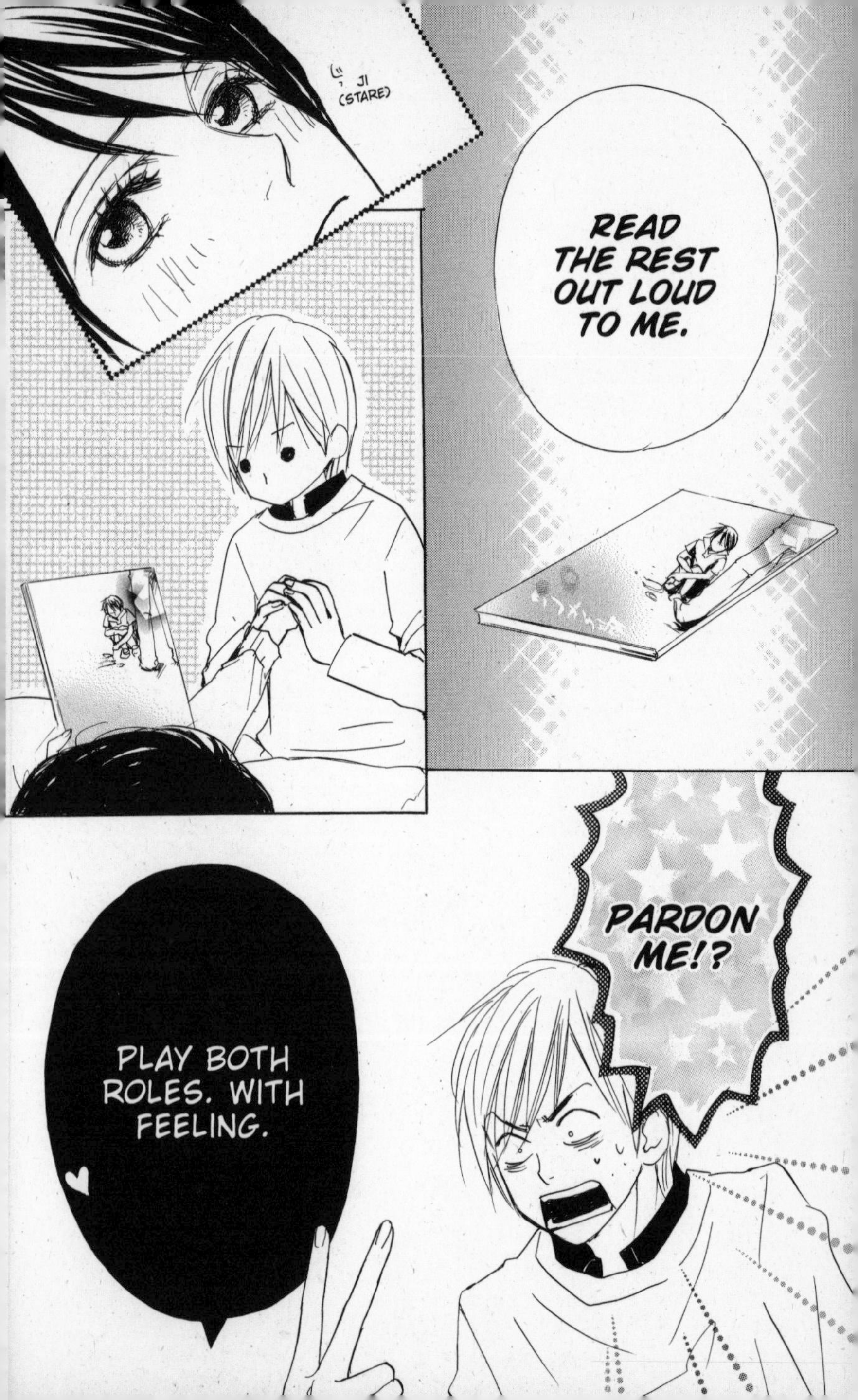
READ THE REST OUT LOUD TO ME.
JI (STARE)
PARDON ME!?
PLAY BOTH ROLES. WITH FEELING.

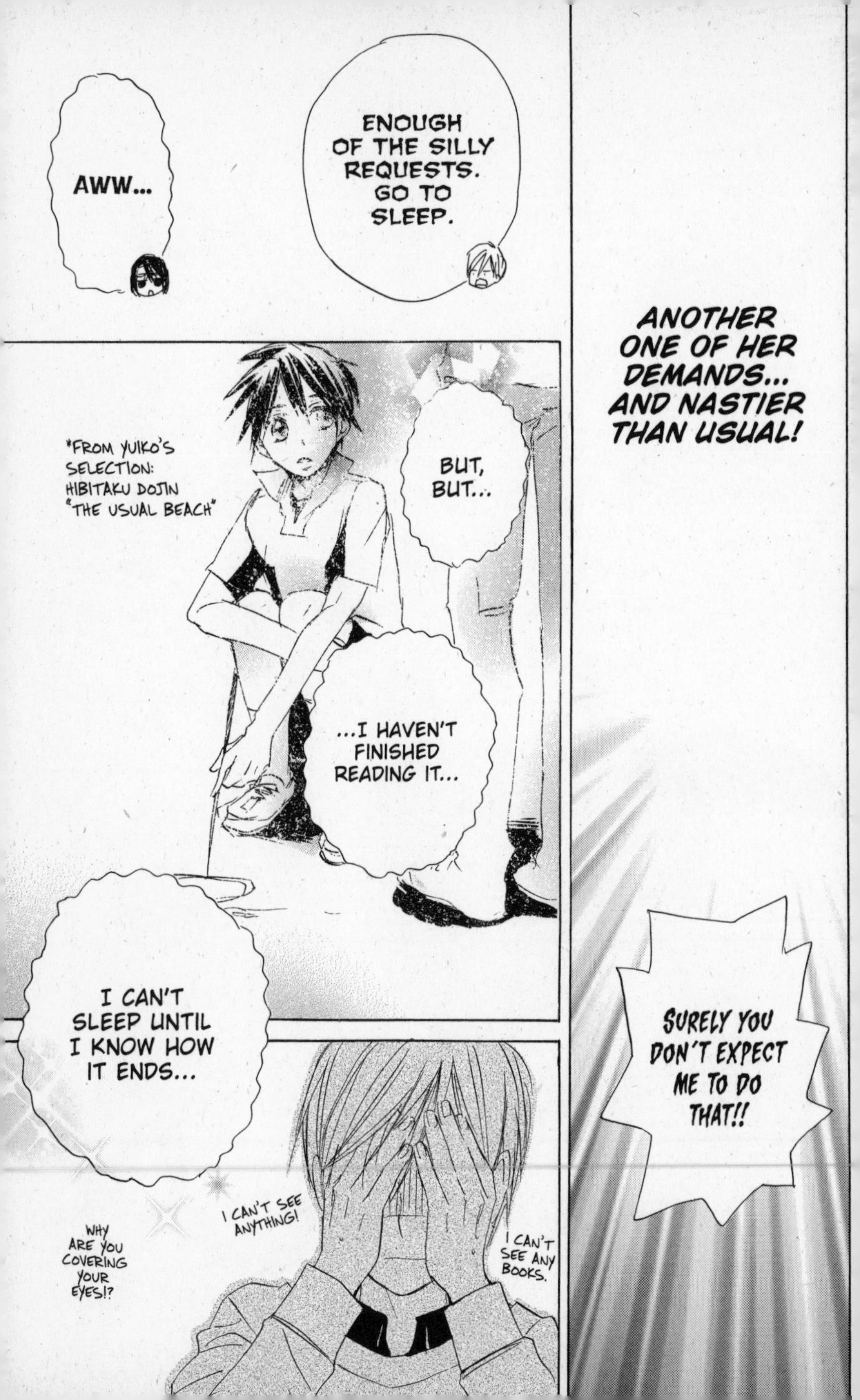
ANOTHER ONE OF HER DEMANDS... AND NASTIER THAN USUAL!
SURELY YOU DON'T EXPECT ME TO DO THAT!!
ENOUGH OF THE SILLY REQUESTS. GO TO SLEEP.
AWW...
BUT, BUT...
...I HAVEN'T FINISHED READING IT...
*FROM YUIKO'S SELECTION: HIBITAKU DOJIN "THE USUAL BEACH"
I CAN'T SLEEP UNTIL I KNOW HOW IT ENDS...
I CAN'T SEE ANY BOOKS.
I CAN'T SEE ANYTHING!
WHY ARE YOU COVERING YOUR EYES!?

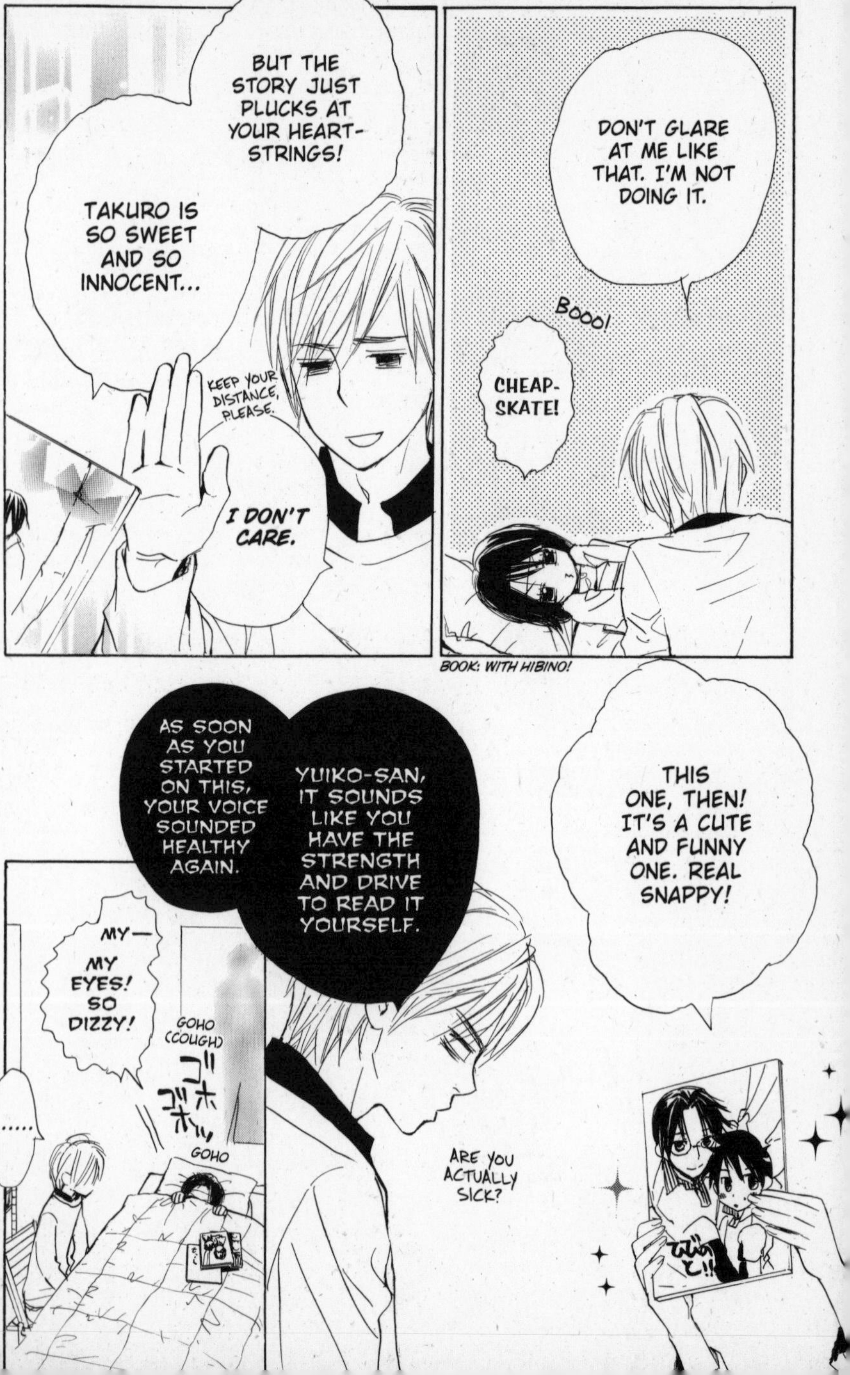
DON'T GLARE AT ME LIKE THAT. I'M NOT DOING IT.
BOOO!
CHEAP-SKATE!
BUT THE STORY JUST PLUCKS AT YOUR HEART-STRINGS!
TAKURO IS SO SWEET AND SO INNOCENT...
KEEP YOUR DISTANCE, PLEASE.
I DON'T CARE.
BOOK: WITH HIBINO!
THIS ONE, THEN! IT'S A CUTE AND FUNNY ONE. REAL SNAPPY!
YUIKO-SAN, IT SOUNDS LIKE YOU HAVE THE STRENGTH AND DRIVE TO READ IT YOURSELF.
AS SOON AS YOU STARTED ON THIS, YOUR VOICE SOUNDED HEALTHY AGAIN.
ARE YOU ACTUALLY SICK?
MY— MY EYES! SO DIZZY!
GOHO (COUGH)
ゴホゴホッ
GOHO
......

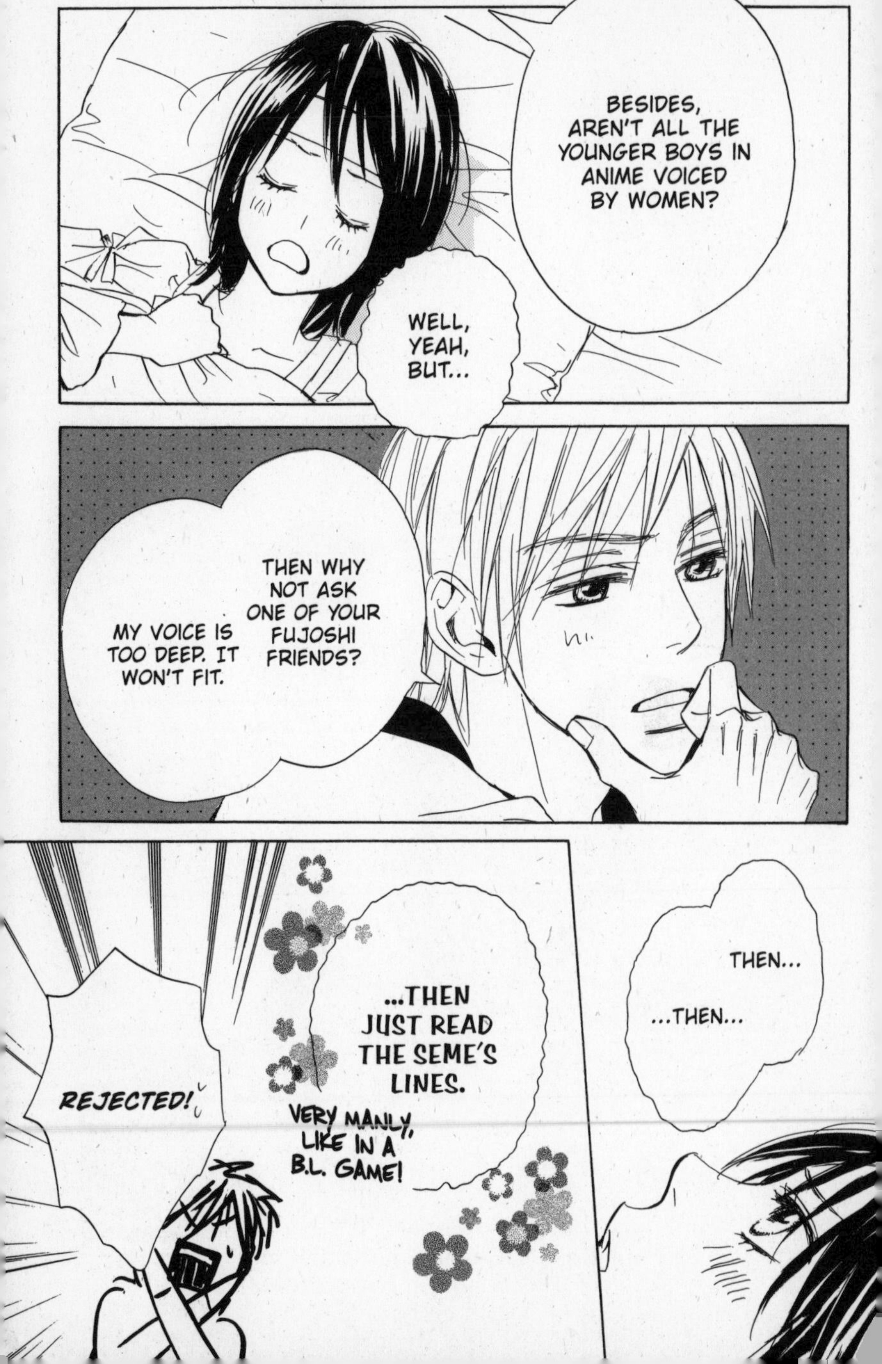
BESIDES, AREN'T ALL THE YOUNGER BOYS IN ANIME VOICED BY WOMEN?
WELL, YEAH, BUT...
THEN WHY NOT ASK ONE OF YOUR FUJOSHI FRIENDS?
MY VOICE IS TOO DEEP. IT WON'T FIT.
THEN...
...THEN...
...THEN JUST READ THE SEME'S LINES.
VERY MANLY, LIKE IN A B.L. GAME!
REJECTED!

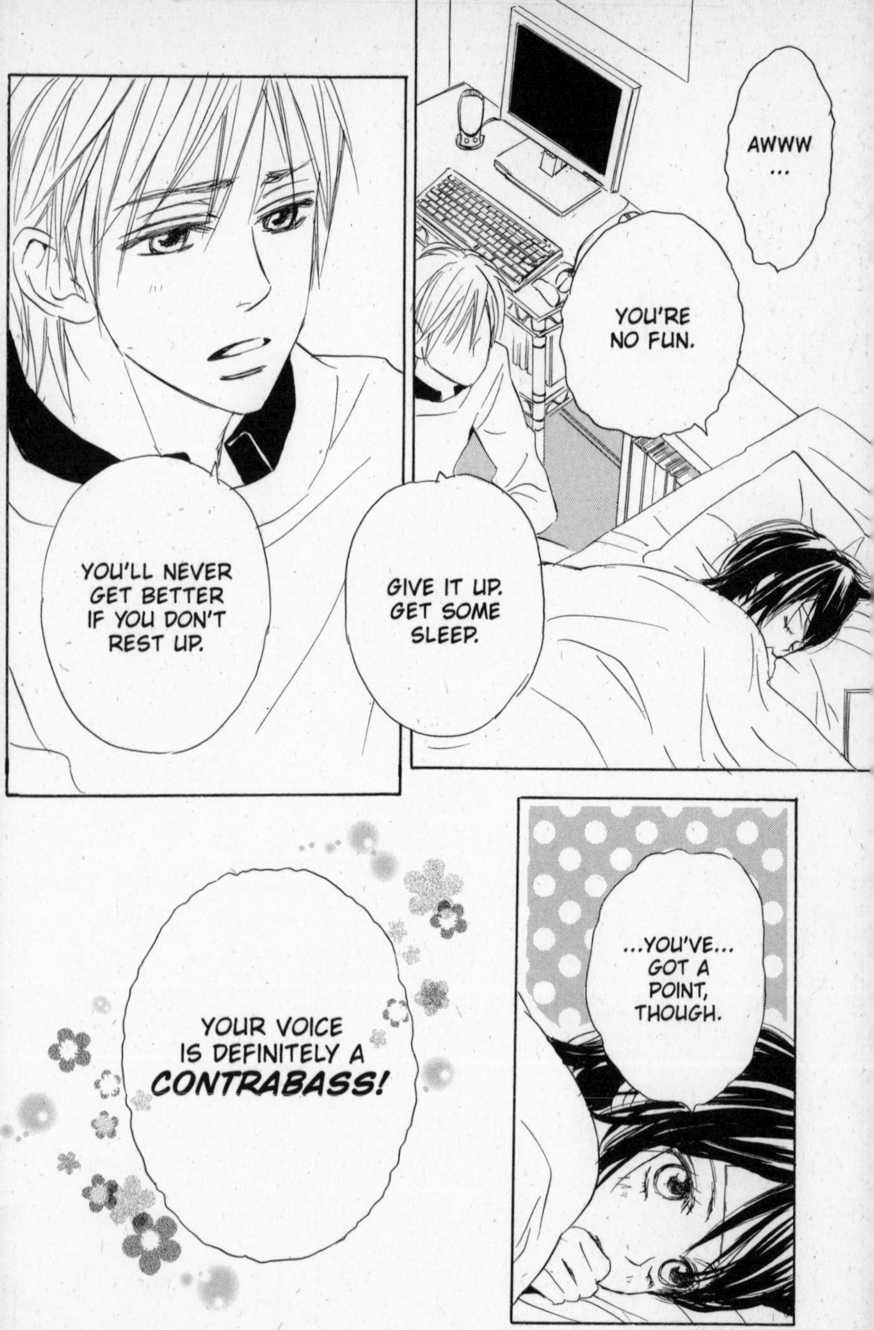
AWWW ...
YOU'RE NO FUN.
GIVE IT UP. GET SOME SLEEP.
YOU'LL NEVER GET BETTER IF YOU DON'T REST UP.
...YOU'VE... GOT A POINT, THOUGH.
YOUR VOICE IS DEFINITELY A **CONTRABASS!**

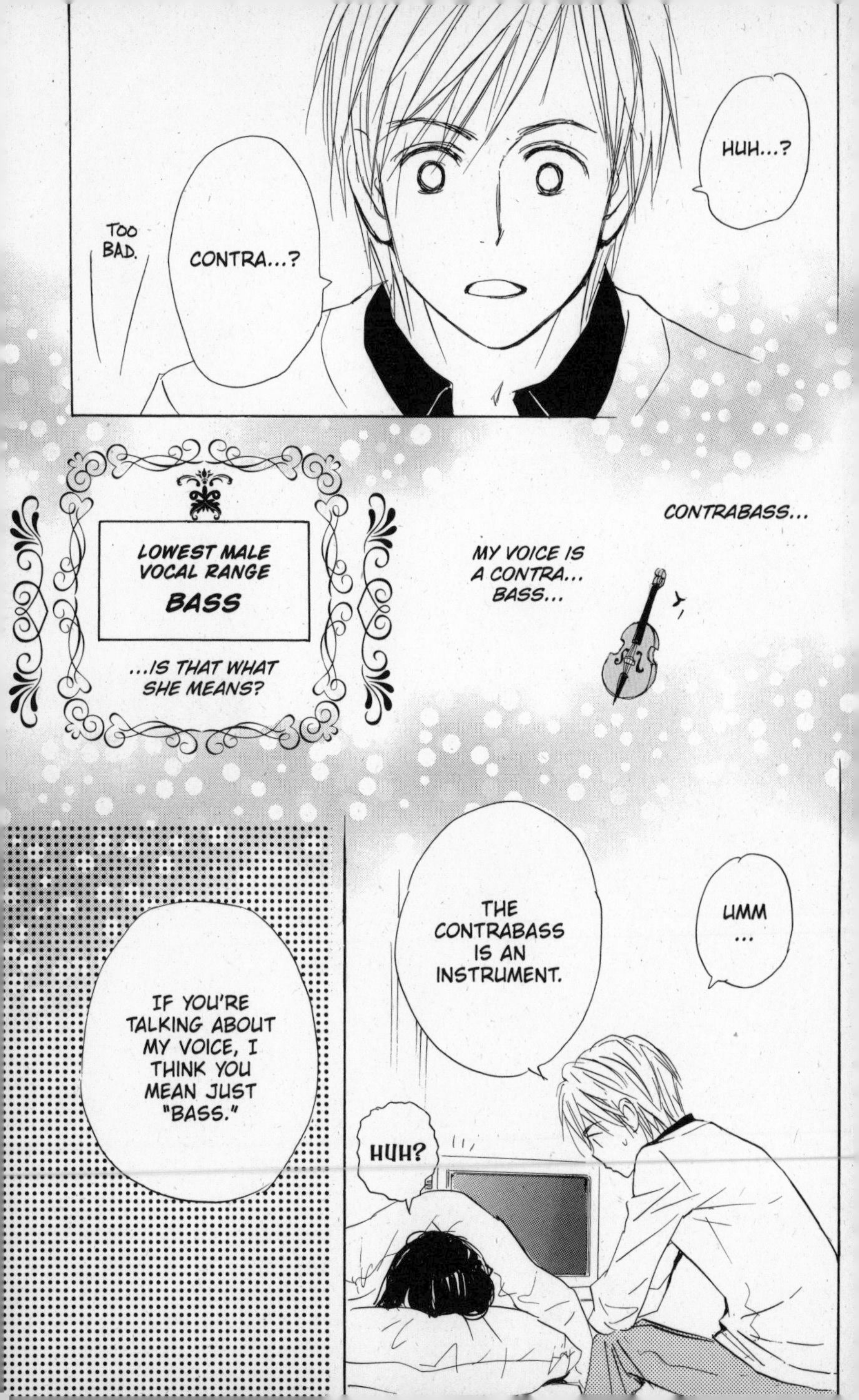
HUH...?
CONTRA...?
TOO BAD.
CONTRABASS...
MY VOICE IS A CONTRA... BASS...
LOWEST MALE VOCAL RANGE
BASS
...IS THAT WHAT SHE MEANS?
UMM ...
THE CONTRABASS IS AN INSTRUMENT.
HUH?
IF YOU'RE TALKING ABOUT MY VOICE, I THINK YOU MEAN JUST "BASS."

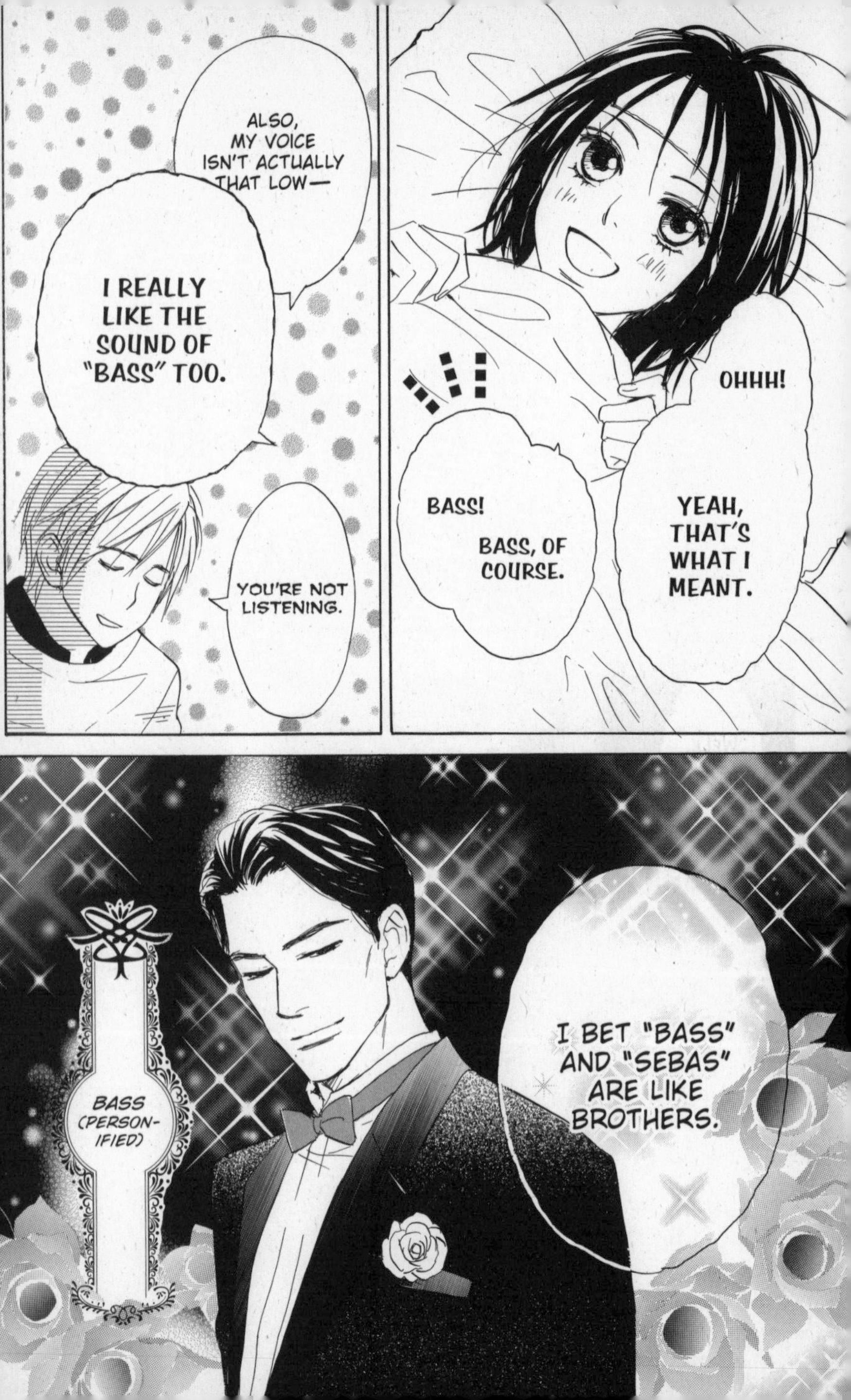
OHHH! YEAH, THAT'S WHAT I MEANT.
BASS! BASS, OF COURSE.
ALSO, MY VOICE ISN'T ACTUALLY THAT LOW—
I REALLY LIKE THE SOUND OF "BASS" TOO.
YOU'RE NOT LISTENING.
I BET "BASS" AND "SEBAS" ARE LIKE BROTHERS.
BASS (PERSON-IFIED)

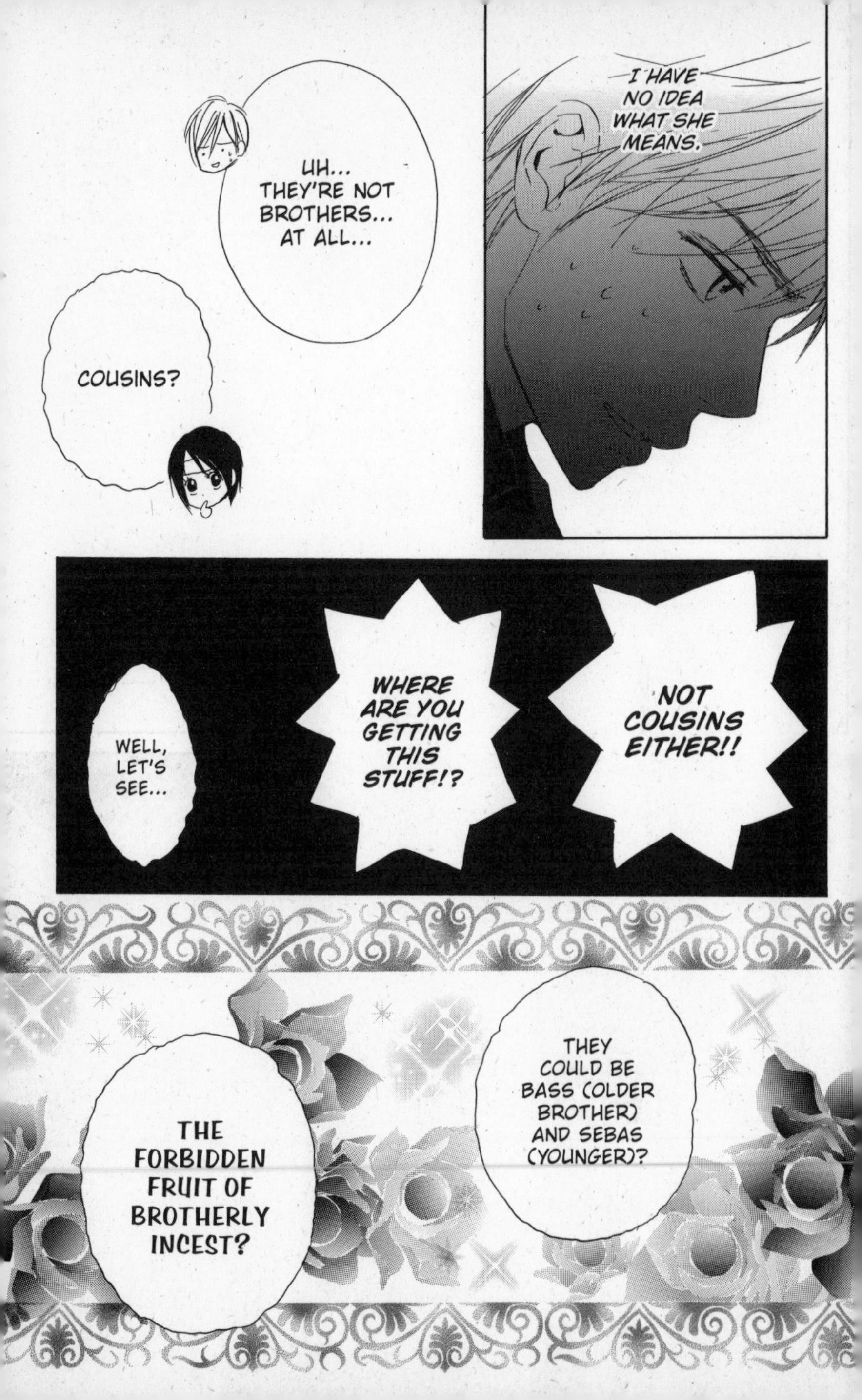
I HAVE NO IDEA WHAT SHE MEANS.
UH... THEY'RE NOT BROTHERS... AT ALL...
COUSINS?
NOT COUSINS EITHER!!
WHERE ARE YOU GETTING THIS STUFF!?
WELL, LET'S SEE...
THEY COULD BE BASS (OLDER BROTHER) AND SEBAS (YOUNGER)?
THE FORBIDDEN FRUIT OF BROTHERLY INCEST?

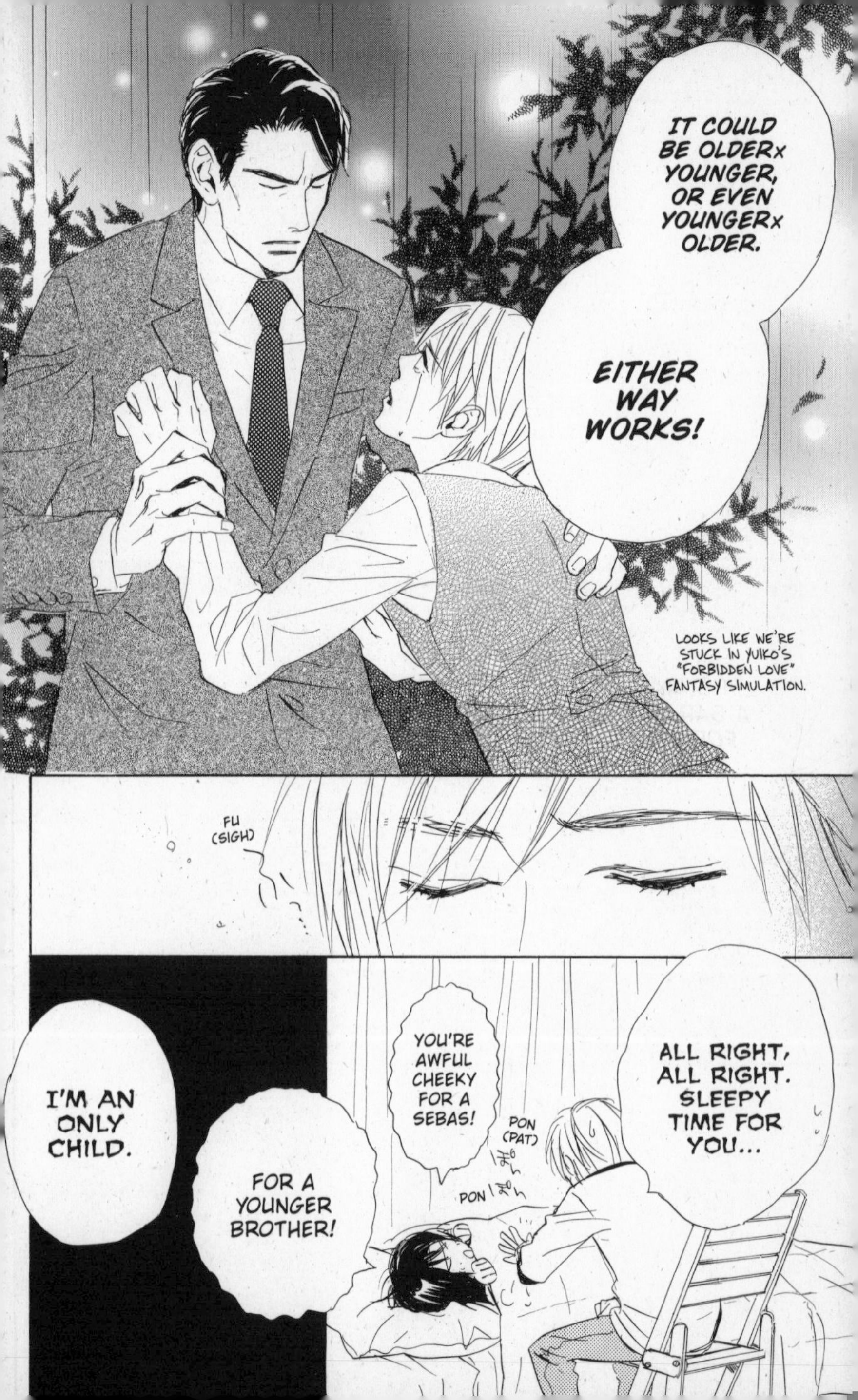

IT COULD BE OLDERx YOUNGER, OR EVEN YOUNGERx OLDER.
EITHER WAY WORKS!
LOOKS LIKE WE'RE STUCK IN YUIKO'S "FORBIDDEN LOVE" FANTASY SIMULATION.
FU (SIGH)
ALL RIGHT, ALL RIGHT. SLEEPY TIME FOR YOU...
PON (PAT)
ぽん
PON
ぽん
YOU'RE AWFUL CHEEKY FOR A SEBAS!
FOR A YOUNGER BROTHER!
I'M AN ONLY CHILD.

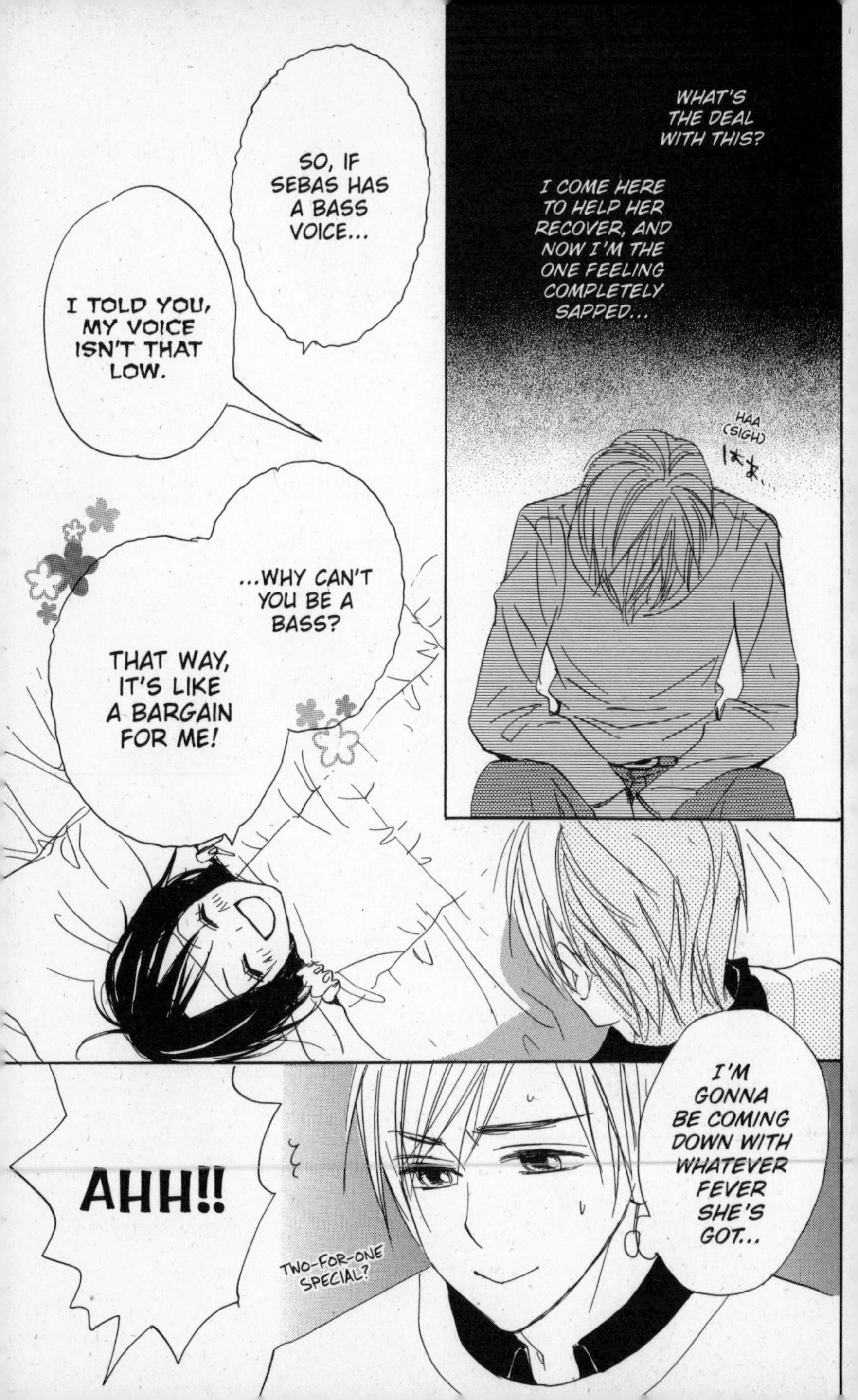
WHAT'S THE DEAL WITH THIS?
I COME HERE TO HELP HER RECOVER, AND NOW I'M THE ONE FEELING COMPLETELY SAPPED...
HAA (SIGH)
SO, IF SEBAS HAS A BASS VOICE...
I TOLD YOU, MY VOICE ISN'T THAT LOW.
...WHY CAN'T YOU BE A BASS?
THAT WAY, IT'S LIKE A BARGAIN FOR ME!
I'M GONNA BE COMING DOWN WITH WHATEVER FEVER SHE'S GOT...
TWO-FOR-ONE SPECIAL?
AHH!!

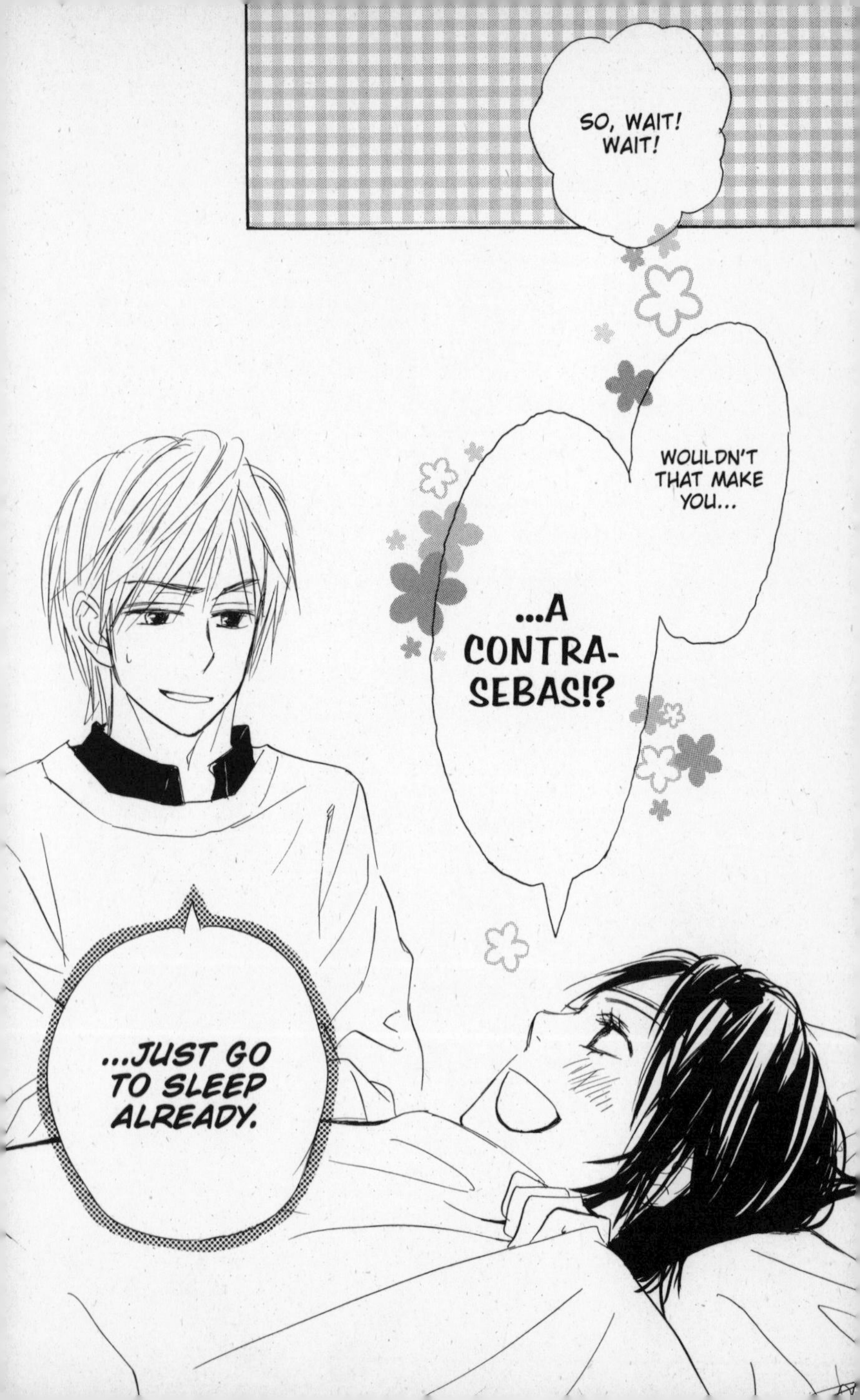
SO, WAIT! WAIT!
WOULDN'T THAT MAKE YOU...
...A CONTRA-SEBAS!?
...JUST GO TO SLEEP ALREADY.

FUJOSHI NEWS

vol.09

SURPRISE! INTERVIEW WITH THE FUJOSHI NEXT DOOR ①

WHAT KIND OF FUJOSHI LIFE DO YOU LEAD? WE CONDUCTED INTERVIEWS WITH WOMEN ON THE STREET!

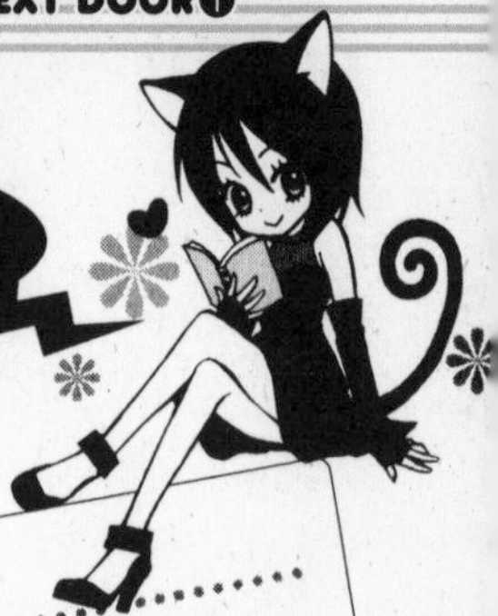

SURPRISE! INTERVIEW WITH THE FUJOSHI NEXT DOOR ①

♥FUJOSHI No.001♥ B.L. LOVER

SAITAMA PREFECTURE, C.N.-SAN

B.L. LOVER ♥

AGE: 21
OCCUPATION: STUDENT
MONTHLY HOBBY COSTS: ¥50,000 (ALMOST ALL OF MY PAYCHECK GOES TO THE LATEST B.L. DOJIN)
MOE FETISH: SHALLOW, WIMPY SEME

[TYPICAL ACTIVITIES]
READING THROUGH ORIGINAL B.L. DOJIN (GOING IN AND BUYING EVERY ONE OF THE NEW TITLES IN THE STORE, REGARDLESS OF AUTHOR OR TITLE, IS THE HEIGHT OF LUXURY.)

[TYPICAL EVENTS]
DOJINSHI RETAIL EVENTS

[SPECIAL POWER]
THE ABILITY TO INSTANTLY CLASSIFY ANY OBJECT (NOT JUST A PERSON) AS "SEME" OR "UKE"

[RECENT TROUBLES]
SEEING EVERY MAN AROUND ME AS AN UKE

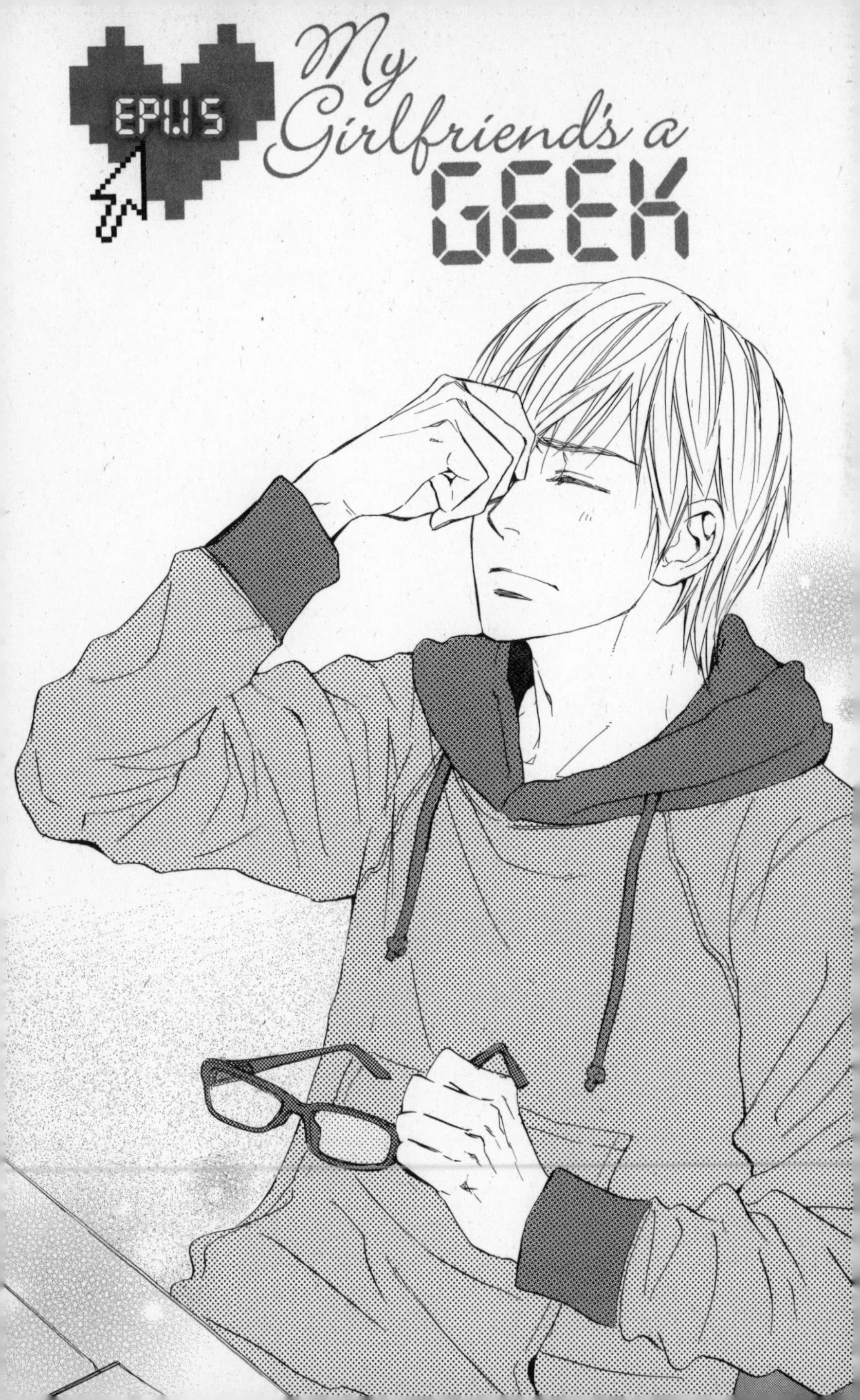
EPI.15
My Girlfriend's a
GEEK

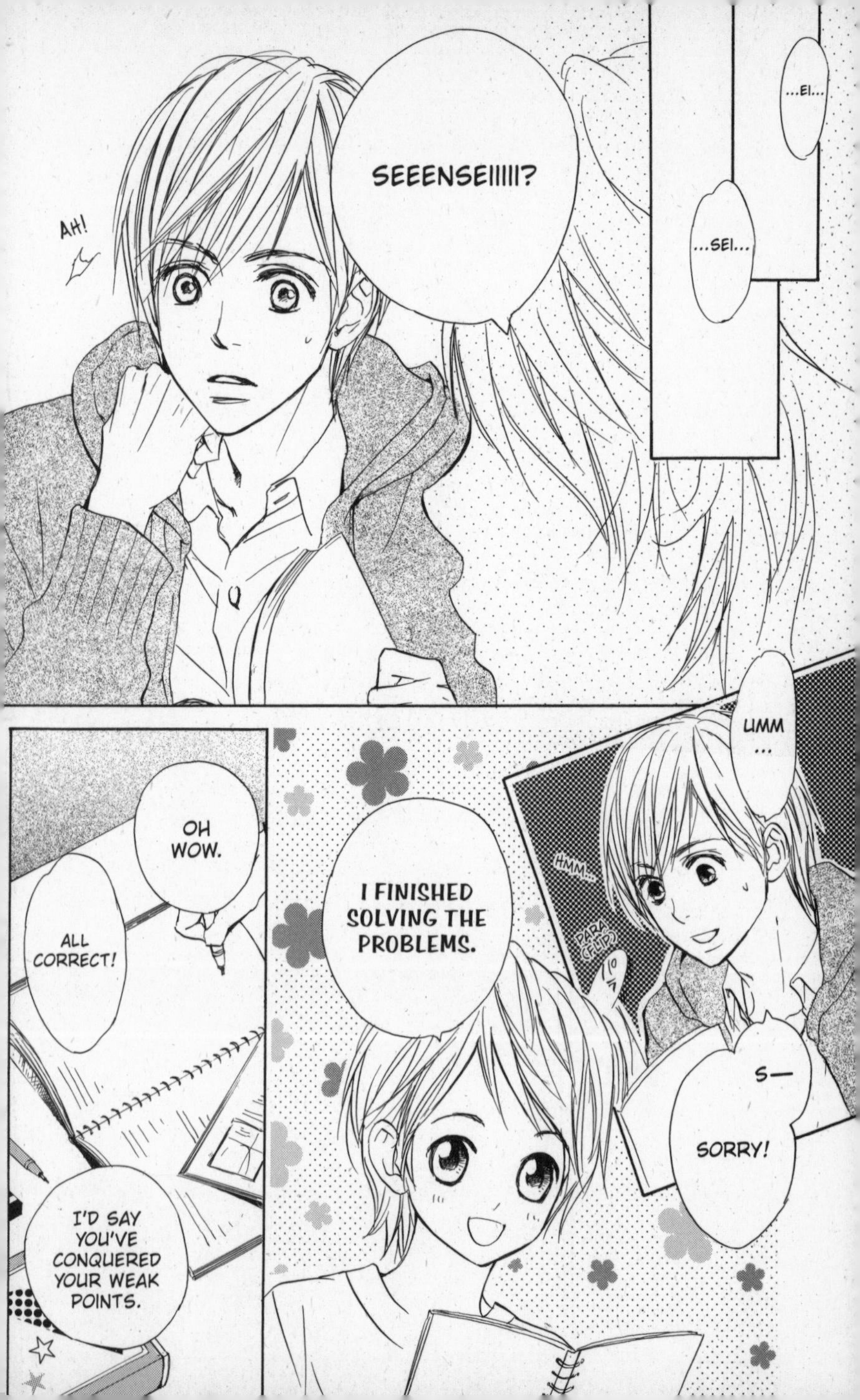
...EI...
...SEI...
SEEENSEIIIIII?
AH!
UMM ...
HMM...
PARA (FLIP)
I FINISHED SOLVING THE PROBLEMS.
S—
SORRY!
OH WOW.
ALL CORRECT!
I'D SAY YOU'VE CONQUERED YOUR WEAK POINTS.

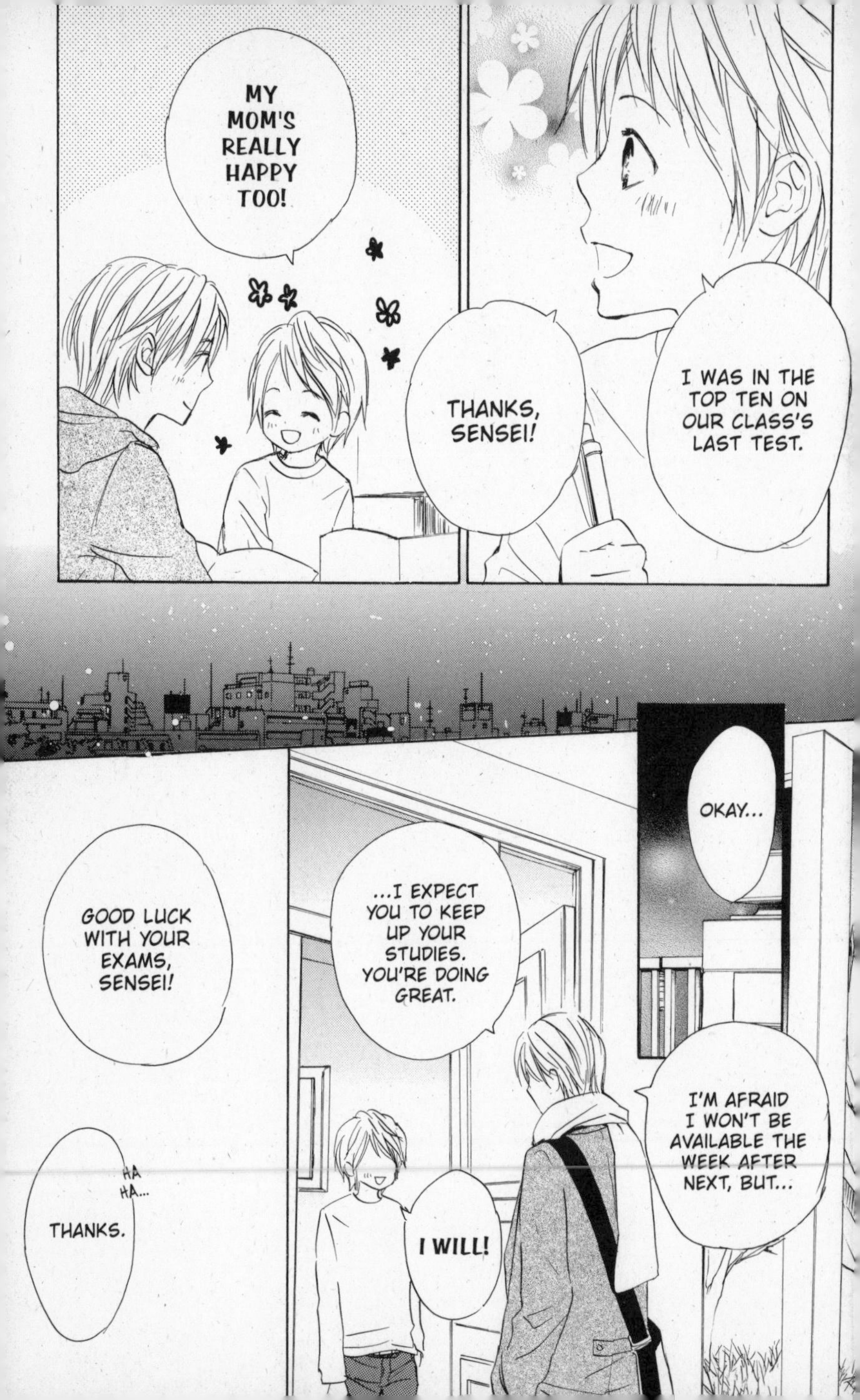
I WAS IN THE TOP TEN ON OUR CLASS'S LAST TEST.
THANKS, SENSEI!
MY MOM'S REALLY HAPPY TOO!
OKAY...
I'M AFRAID I WON'T BE AVAILABLE THE WEEK AFTER NEXT, BUT...
...I EXPECT YOU TO KEEP UP YOUR STUDIES. YOU'RE DOING GREAT.
I WILL!
GOOD LUCK WITH YOUR EXAMS, SENSEI!
HA HA...
THANKS.

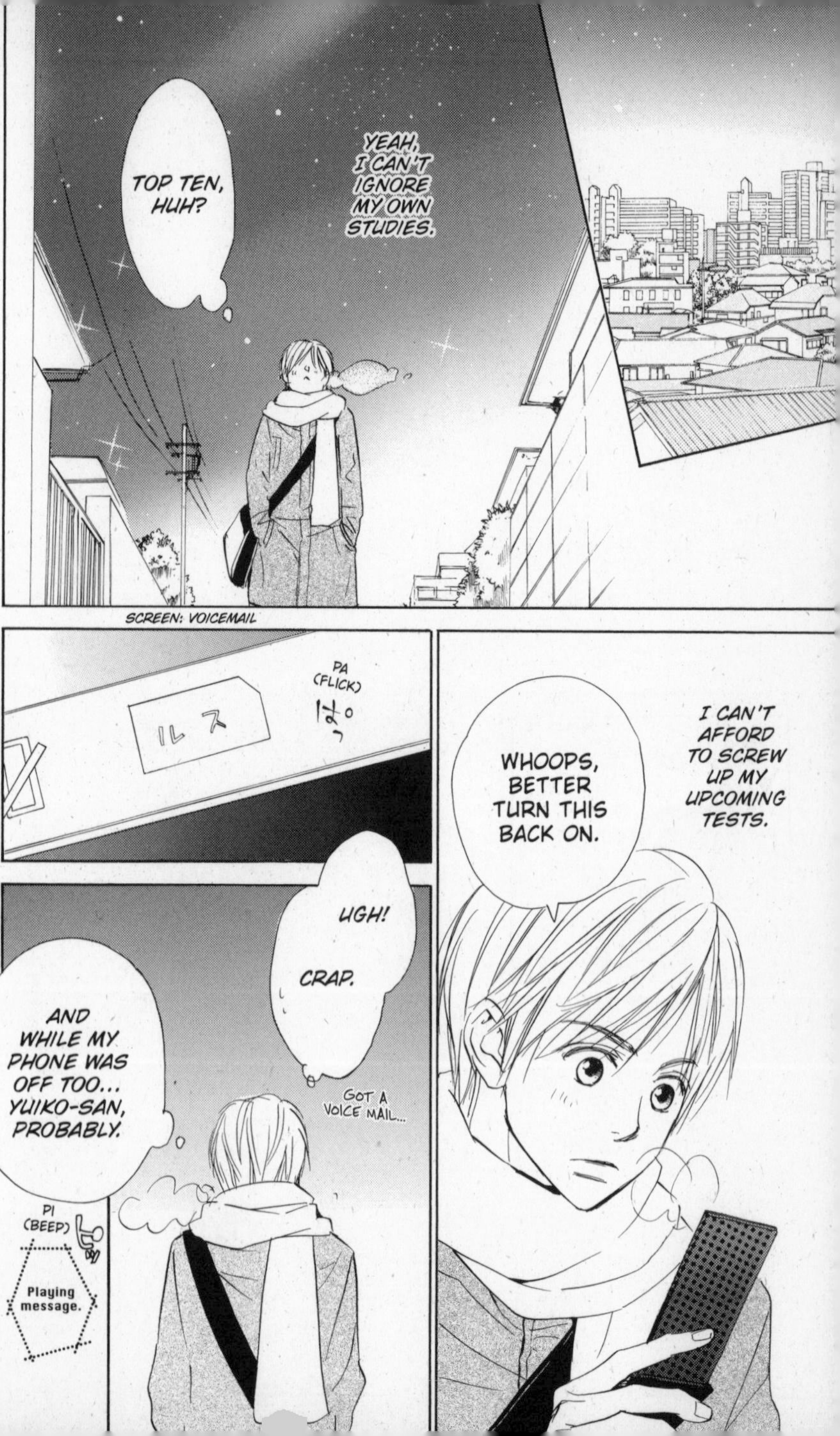
YEAH, I CAN'T IGNORE MY OWN STUDIES.
TOP TEN, HUH?
I CAN'T AFFORD TO SCREW UP MY UPCOMING TESTS.
WHOOPS, BETTER TURN THIS BACK ON.
PA (FLICK)
はっ
ルス
SCREEN: VOICEMAIL
UGH!
CRAP.
GOT A VOICE MAIL...
AND WHILE MY PHONE WAS OFF TOO... YUIKO-SAN, PROBABLY.
PI (BEEP)
Playing message.

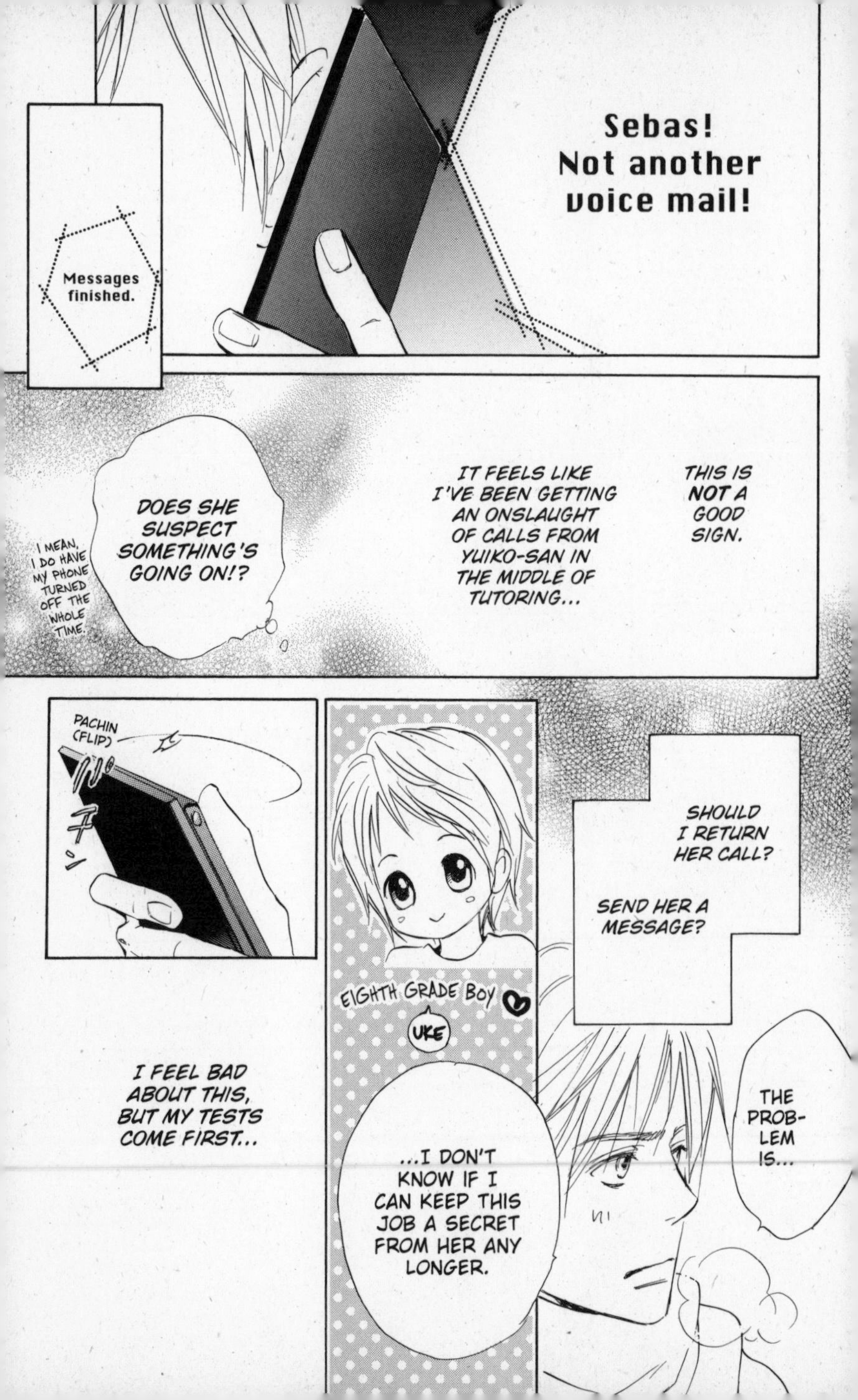

Sebas! Not another voice mail!
Messages finished.
THIS IS NOT A GOOD SIGN.
IT FEELS LIKE I'VE BEEN GETTING AN ONSLAUGHT OF CALLS FROM YUIKO-SAN IN THE MIDDLE OF TUTORING...
DOES SHE SUSPECT SOMETHING'S GOING ON!?
I MEAN, I DO HAVE MY PHONE TURNED OFF THE WHOLE TIME.
SHOULD I RETURN HER CALL?
SEND HER A MESSAGE?
THE PROB-LEM IS...
...I DON'T KNOW IF I CAN KEEP THIS JOB A SECRET FROM HER ANY LONGER.
EIGHTH GRADE BOY
UKE
PACHIN (FLIP)
I FEEL BAD ABOUT THIS, BUT MY TESTS COME FIRST...

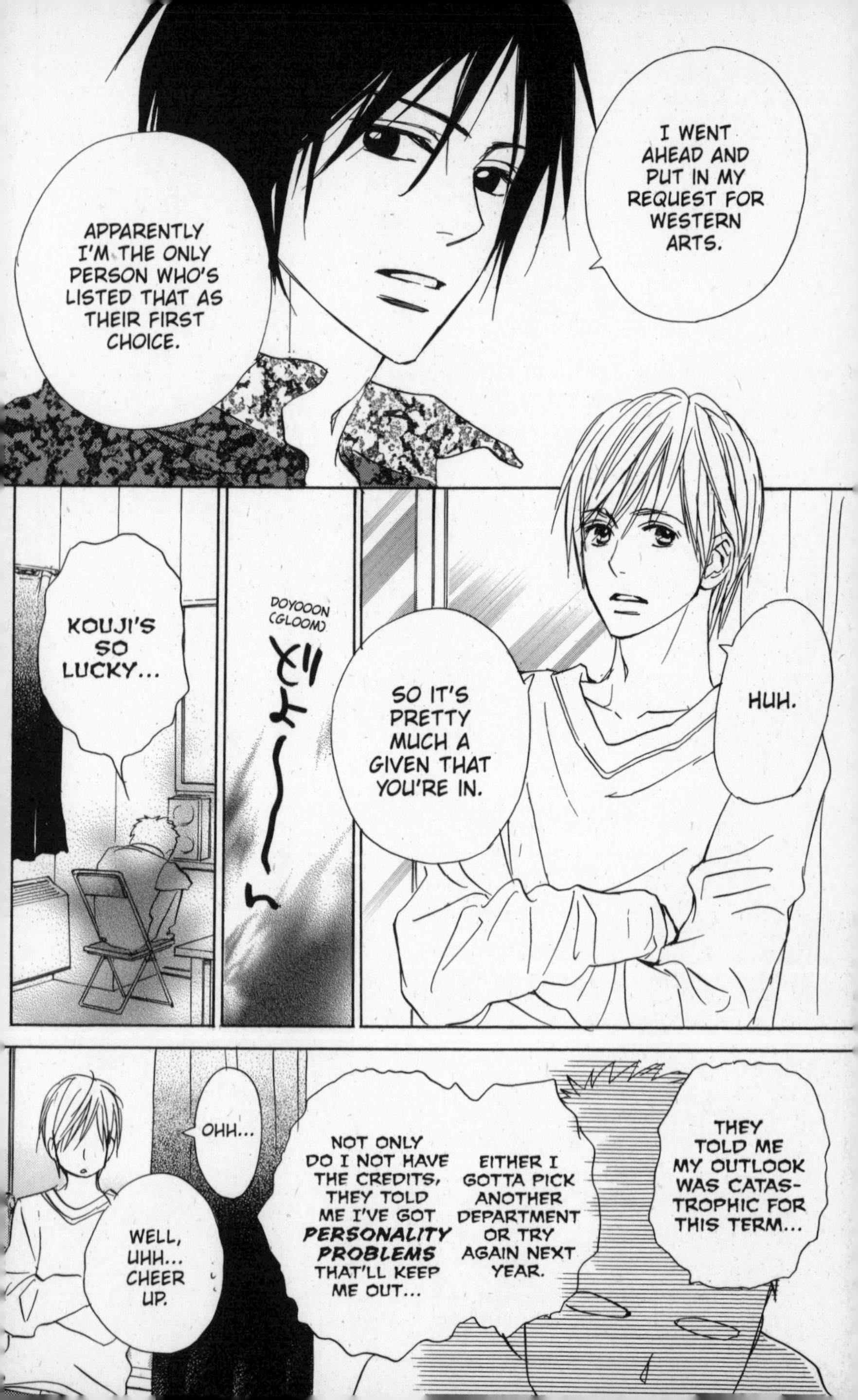
I WENT AHEAD AND PUT IN MY REQUEST FOR WESTERN ARTS.
APPARENTLY I'M THE ONLY PERSON WHO'S LISTED THAT AS THEIR FIRST CHOICE.
HUH.
SO IT'S PRETTY MUCH A GIVEN THAT YOU'RE IN.
DOYOOON (GLOOM)
どよーん
KOUJI'S SO LUCKY...
THEY TOLD ME MY OUTLOOK WAS CATAS-TROPHIC FOR THIS TERM...
EITHER I GOTTA PICK ANOTHER DEPARTMENT OR TRY AGAIN NEXT YEAR.
NOT ONLY DO I NOT HAVE THE CREDITS, THEY TOLD ME I'VE GOT ***PERSONALITY PROBLEMS*** THAT'LL KEEP ME OUT...
OHH...
WELL, UHH... CHEER UP.

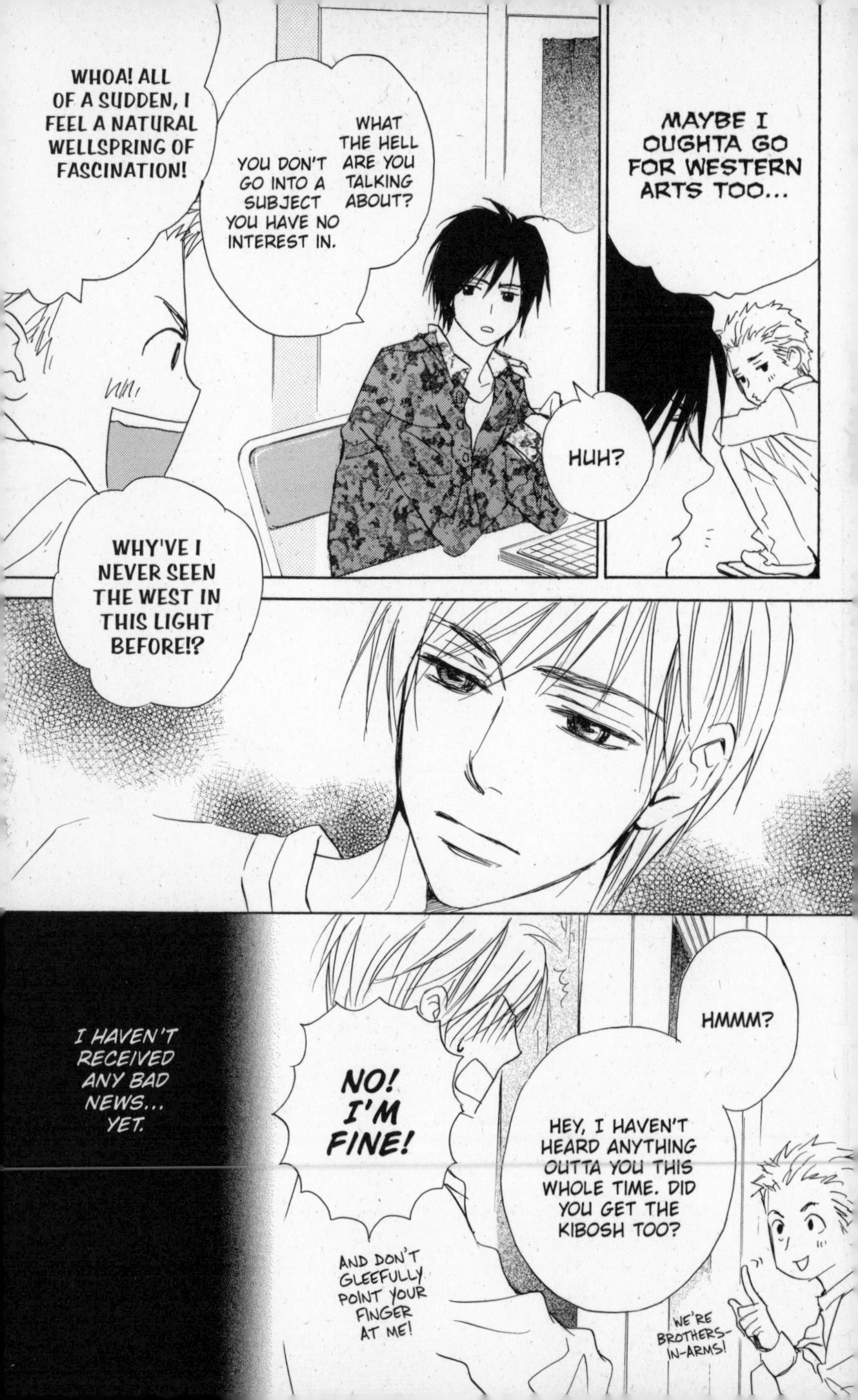
MAYBE I OUGHTA GO FOR WESTERN ARTS TOO...
HUH?
WHOA! ALL OF A SUDDEN, I FEEL A NATURAL WELLSPRING OF FASCINATION!
WHAT THE HELL ARE YOU TALKING ABOUT?
YOU DON'T GO INTO A SUBJECT YOU HAVE NO INTEREST IN.
WHY'VE I NEVER SEEN THE WEST IN THIS LIGHT BEFORE!?
HMMM?
HEY, I HAVEN'T HEARD ANYTHING OUTTA YOU THIS WHOLE TIME. DID YOU GET THE KIBOSH TOO?
WE'RE BROTHERS-IN-ARMS!
NO! I'M FINE!
AND DON'T GLEEFULLY POINT YOUR FINGER AT ME!
I HAVEN'T RECEIVED ANY BAD NEWS... YET.

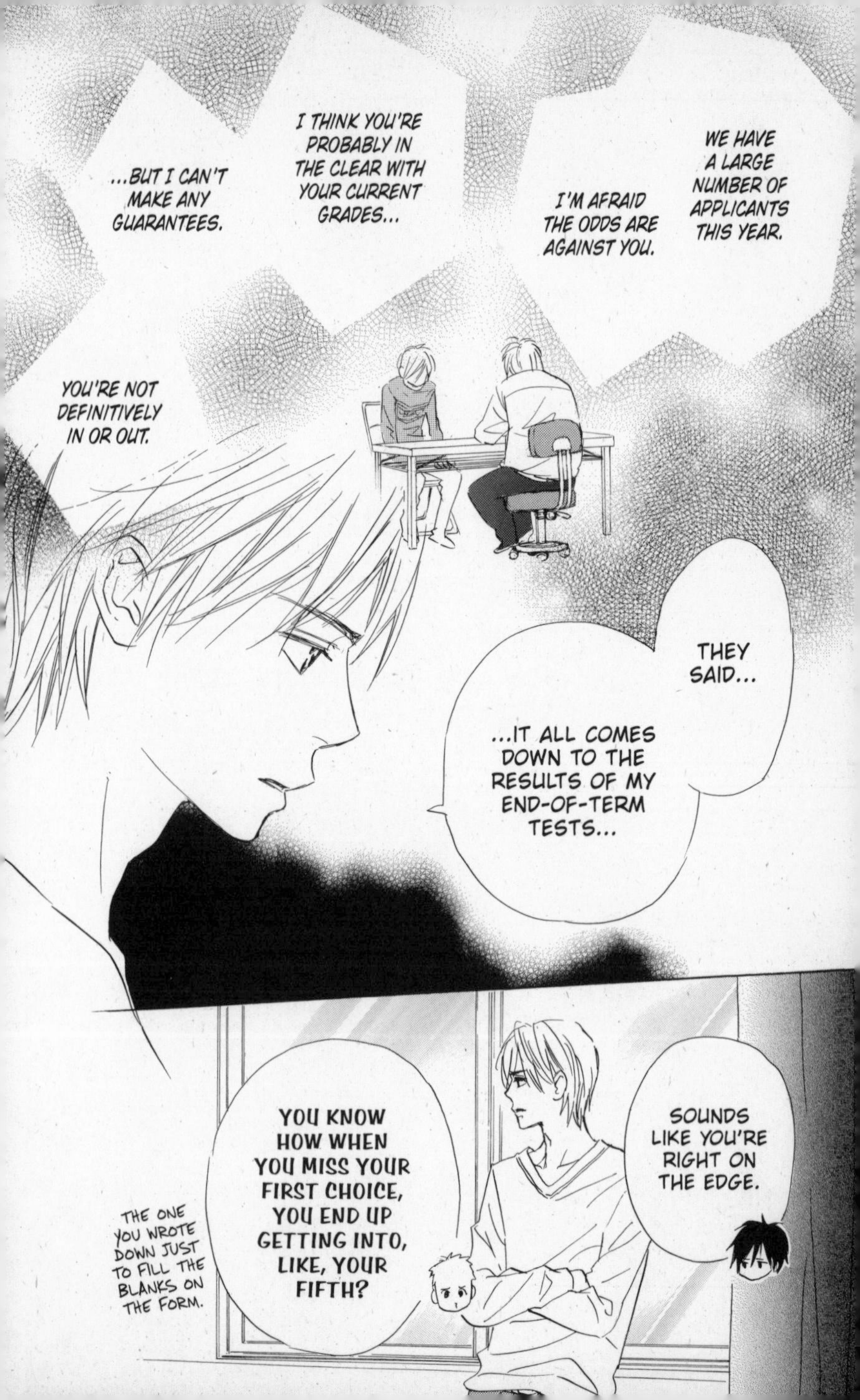
WE HAVE A LARGE NUMBER OF APPLICANTS THIS YEAR.
I'M AFRAID THE ODDS ARE AGAINST YOU.
I THINK YOU'RE PROBABLY IN THE CLEAR WITH YOUR CURRENT GRADES...
...BUT I CAN'T MAKE ANY GUARANTEES.
YOU'RE NOT DEFINITIVELY IN OR OUT.
THEY SAID...
...IT ALL COMES DOWN TO THE RESULTS OF MY END-OF-TERM TESTS...
SOUNDS LIKE YOU'RE RIGHT ON THE EDGE.
YOU KNOW HOW WHEN YOU MISS YOUR FIRST CHOICE, YOU END UP GETTING INTO, LIKE, YOUR FIFTH?
THE ONE YOU WROTE DOWN JUST TO FILL THE BLANKS ON THE FORM.

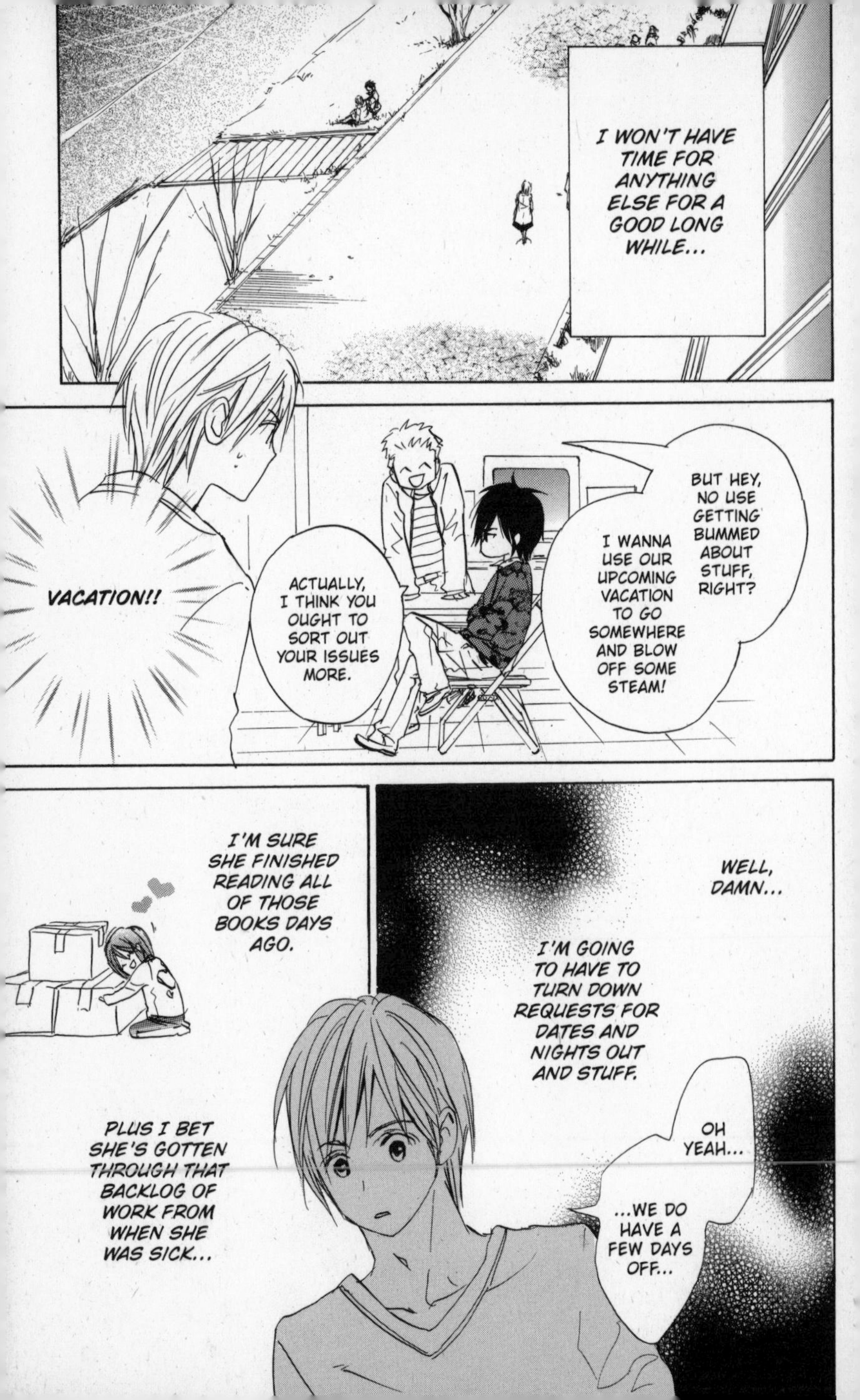
I WON'T HAVE TIME FOR ANYTHING ELSE FOR A GOOD LONG WHILE...
BUT HEY, NO USE GETTING BUMMED ABOUT STUFF, RIGHT?
I WANNA USE OUR UPCOMING VACATION TO GO SOMEWHERE AND BLOW OFF SOME STEAM!
ACTUALLY, I THINK YOU OUGHT TO SORT OUT YOUR ISSUES MORE.
VACATION!!
WELL, DAMN...
I'M GOING TO HAVE TO TURN DOWN REQUESTS FOR DATES AND NIGHTS OUT AND STUFF.
OH YEAH...
...WE DO HAVE A FEW DAYS OFF...
I'M SURE SHE FINISHED READING ALL OF THOSE BOOKS DAYS AGO.
PLUS I BET SHE'S GOTTEN THROUGH THAT BACKLOG OF WORK FROM WHEN SHE WAS SICK...

Someone got me a ticket
to an ESRoma event!!
\(≧▽≦)/
Which means I'm off to
my holy land! ♡♡♡
I might not be able to see
you during the holiday...
Sorry!!
But you never know when I
might launch a sneak attack.

YIKES.

*I'M ACTUALLY
FEELING RELIEF
AT A MESSAGE
SAYING, "I
WON'T BE ABLE
TO SEE YOU."*

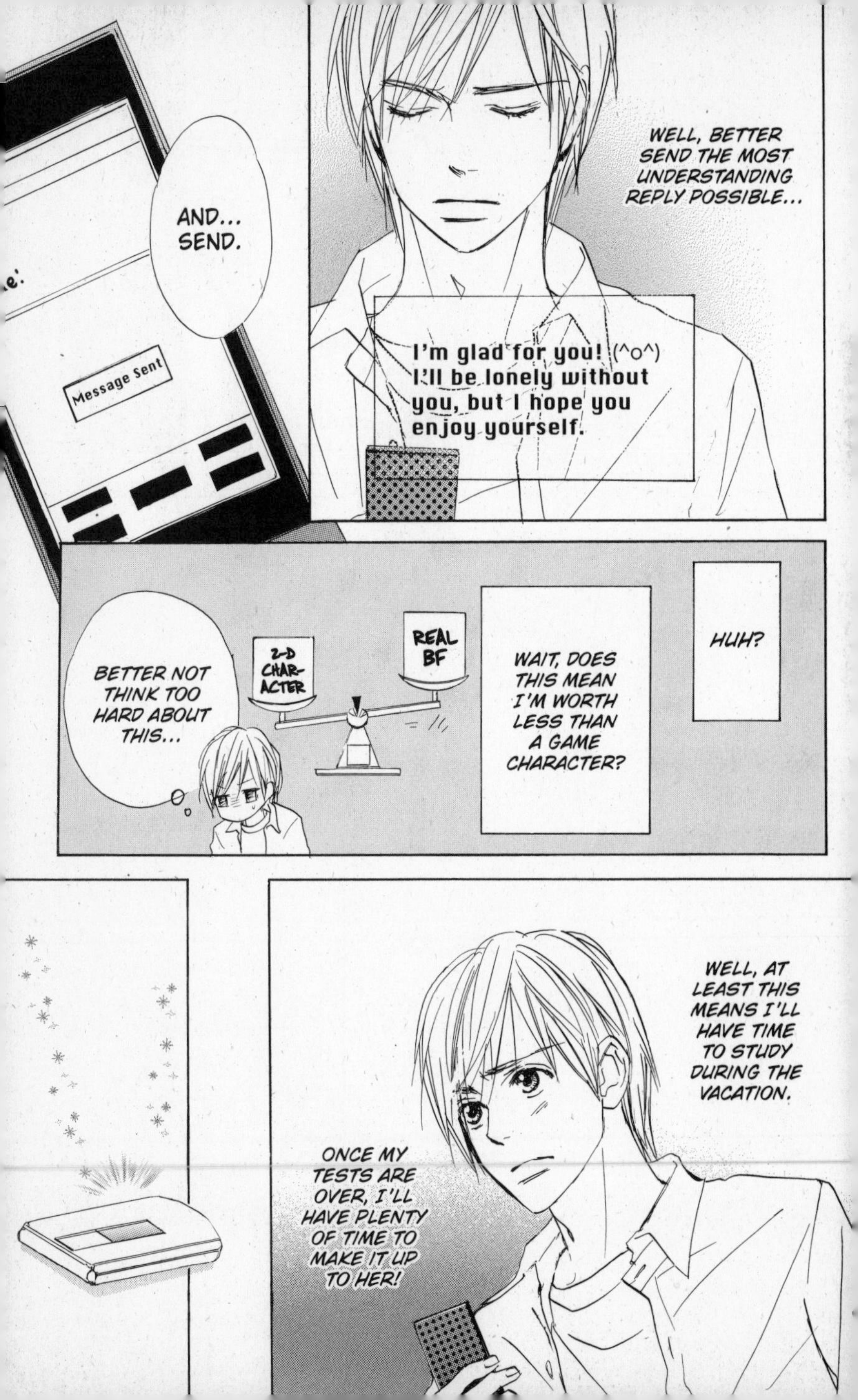
WELL, BETTER SEND THE MOST UNDERSTANDING REPLY POSSIBLE...
I'm glad for you! (^o^) I'll be lonely without you, but I hope you enjoy yourself.
AND... SEND.
Message Sent
HUH?
WAIT, DOES THIS MEAN I'M WORTH LESS THAN A GAME CHARACTER?
REAL BF
2-D CHARACTER
BETTER NOT THINK TOO HARD ABOUT THIS...
WELL, AT LEAST THIS MEANS I'LL HAVE TIME TO STUDY DURING THE VACATION.
ONCE MY TESTS ARE OVER, I'LL HAVE PLENTY OF TIME TO MAKE IT UP TO HER!

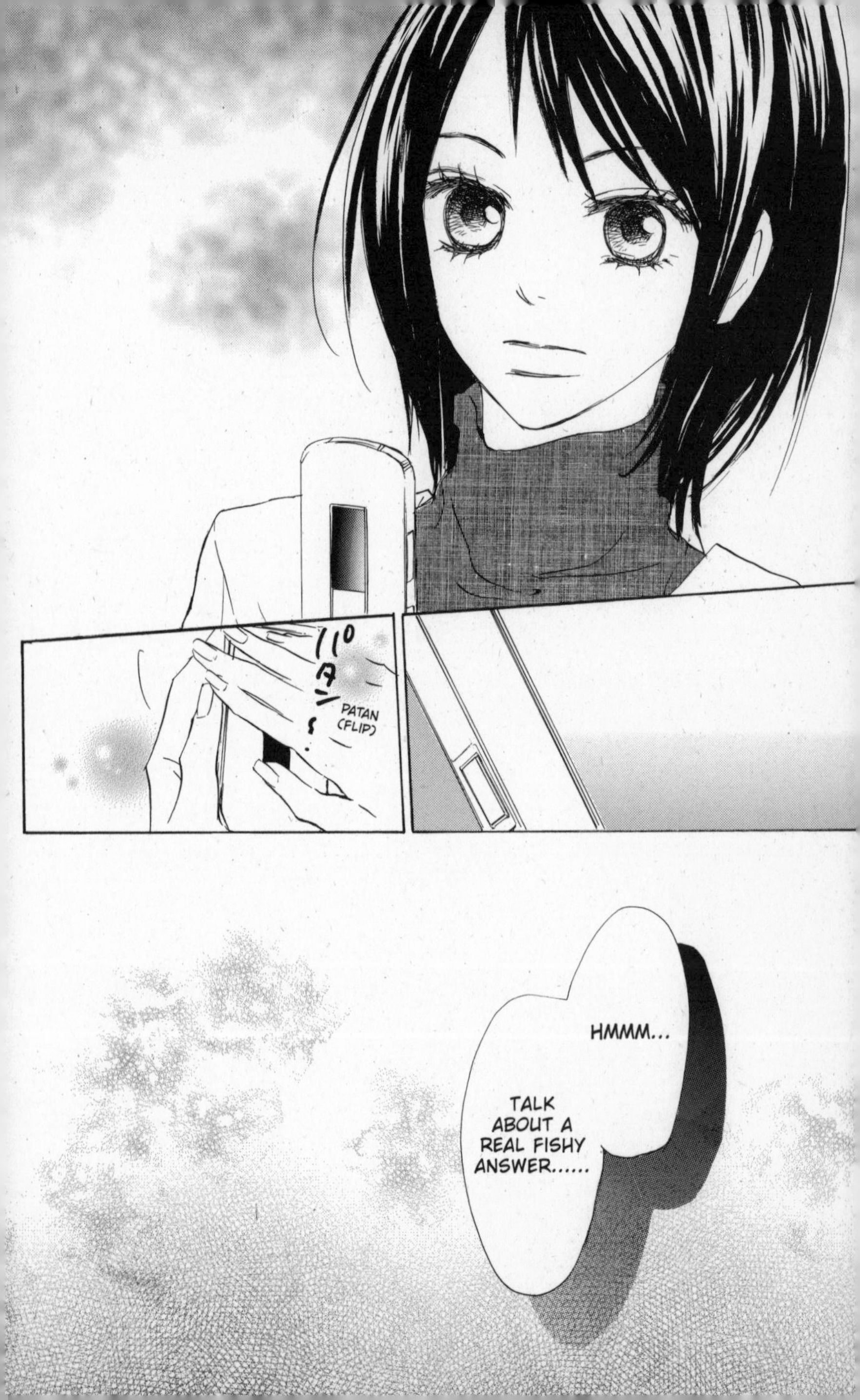
PATAN (FLIP)
HMMM...
TALK ABOUT A REAL FISHY ANSWER......

FUJOSHI NEWS

vol.10

SURPRISE! INTERVIEW WITH THE FUJOSHI NEXT DOOR②

SURPRISE! INTERVIEW WITH THE FUJOSHI NEXT DOOR ②

♥FUJOSHI No.002♥ GAME LOVER

TOKYO, T.O.-SAN

GAME LOVER ♥

AGE: 24
OCCUPATION: BEAUTICIAN
MONTHLY HOBBY COSTS: ¥30,000
(THREE GAMES A MONTH ON AVERAGE)
MOE FETISH: SHOTA BOYS WITH ANIMAL EARS

[TYPICAL ACTIVITIES]
HOLING UP INSIDE ON MY DAYS OFF AND HAVING MARATHON GAMING SESSIONS (I PLAY GAMES UNTIL I PASS OUT. I LOVE SIMULATION RPGs THAT LAST FOR AGES.)

[TYPICAL EVENTS]
LIVE APPEARANCES AND PERFORMANCES OF GIRLY-GAME VOICE ACTORS

[SPECIAL POWER]
I'M A STYLIST, SO I CAN RECREATE VIDEO GAME CHARACTER HAIRSTYLES ON MY OWN.

[RECENT TROUBLES]
SINCE I HAVE ALMOST EVERY CONSOLE AND CAN'T BRING MYSELF TO GET RID OF ANY, I'M RUNNING OUT OF SPACE.

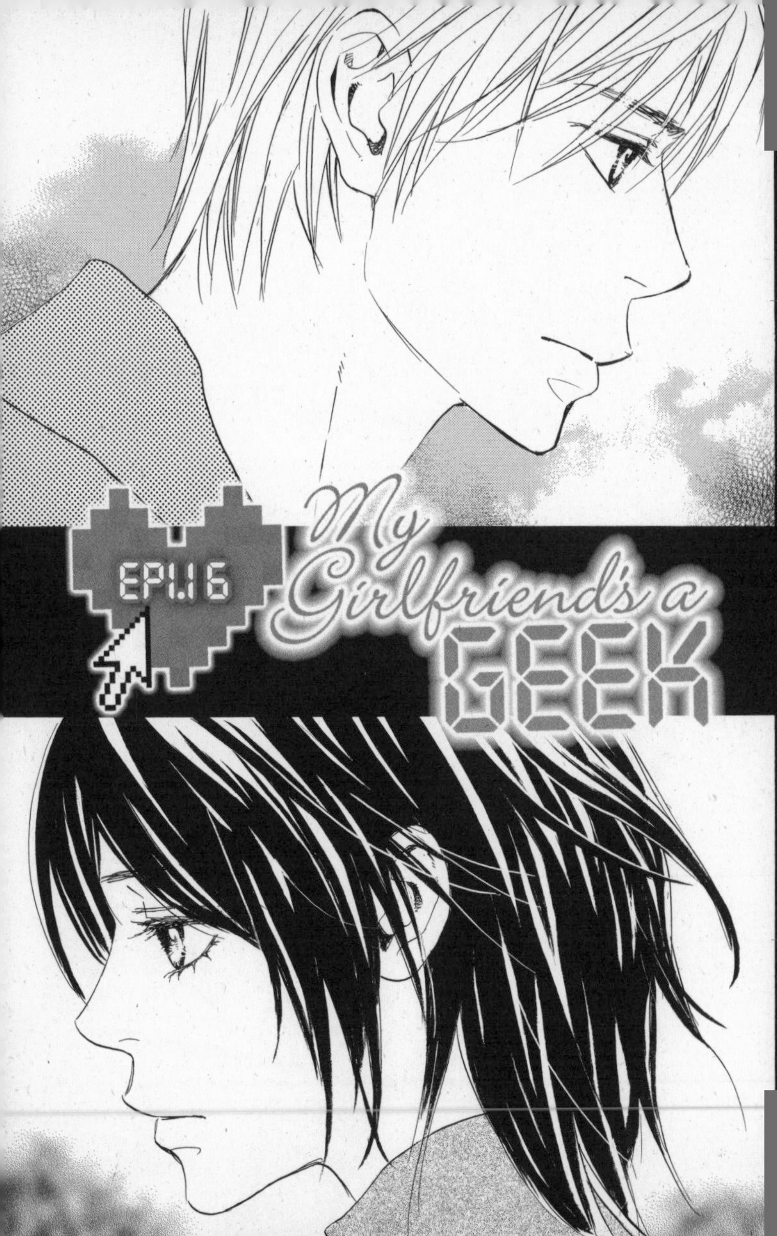
EPI.16
My Girlfriend's a GEEK

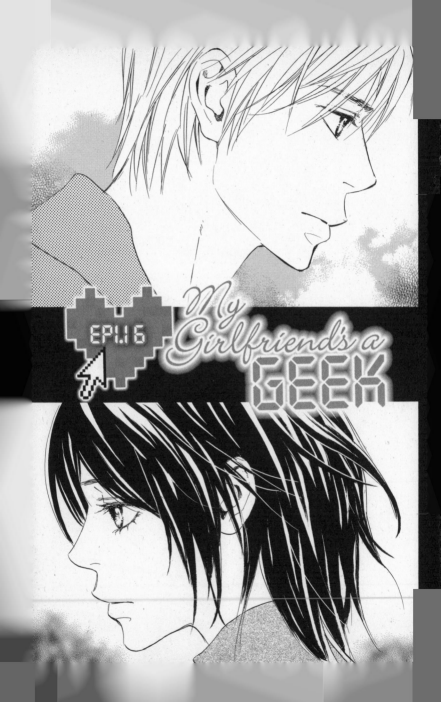

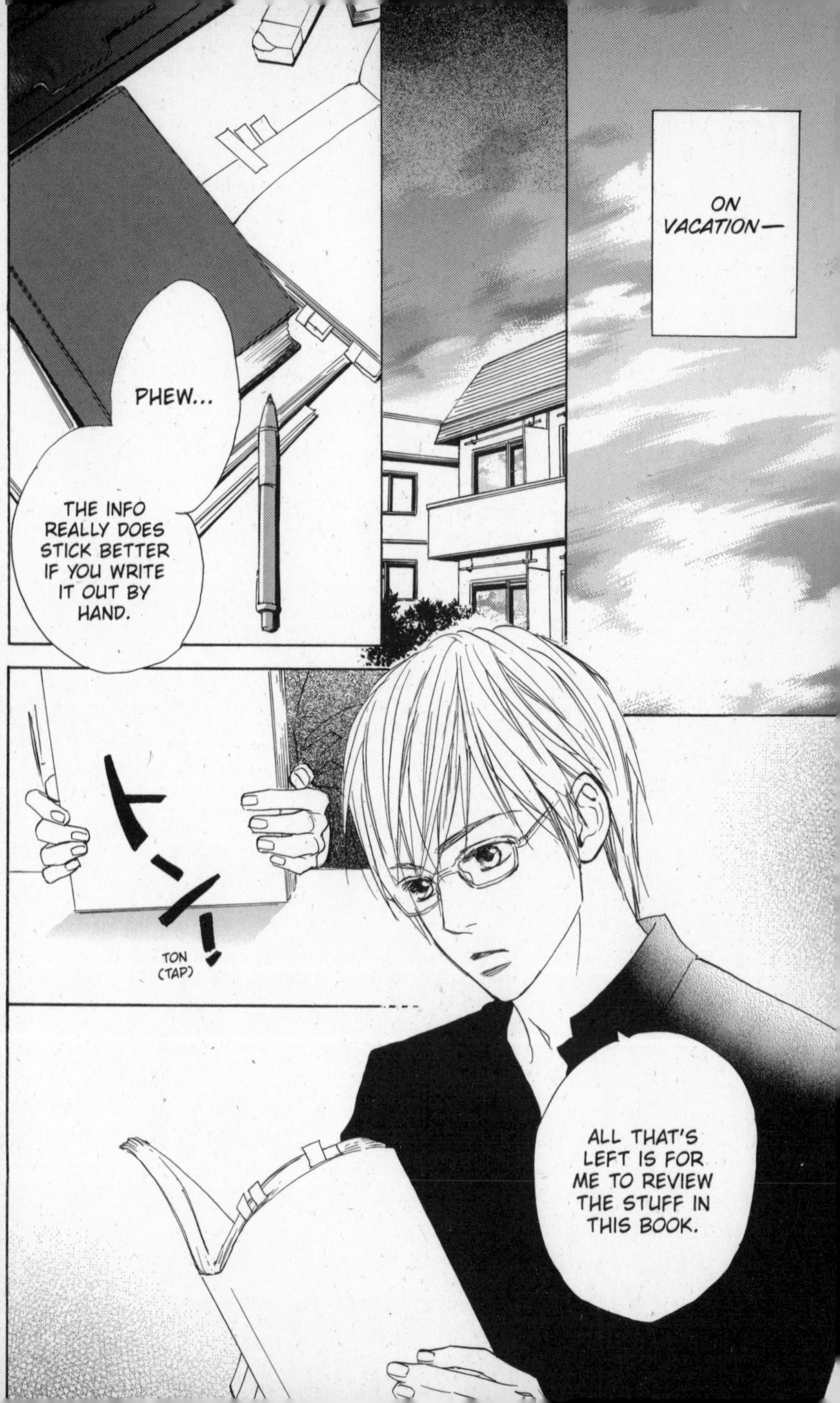
ON VACATION—
PHEW...
THE INFO REALLY DOES STICK BETTER IF YOU WRITE IT OUT BY HAND.
TON (TAP)
ALL THAT'S LEFT IS FOR ME TO REVIEW THE STUFF IN THIS BOOK.

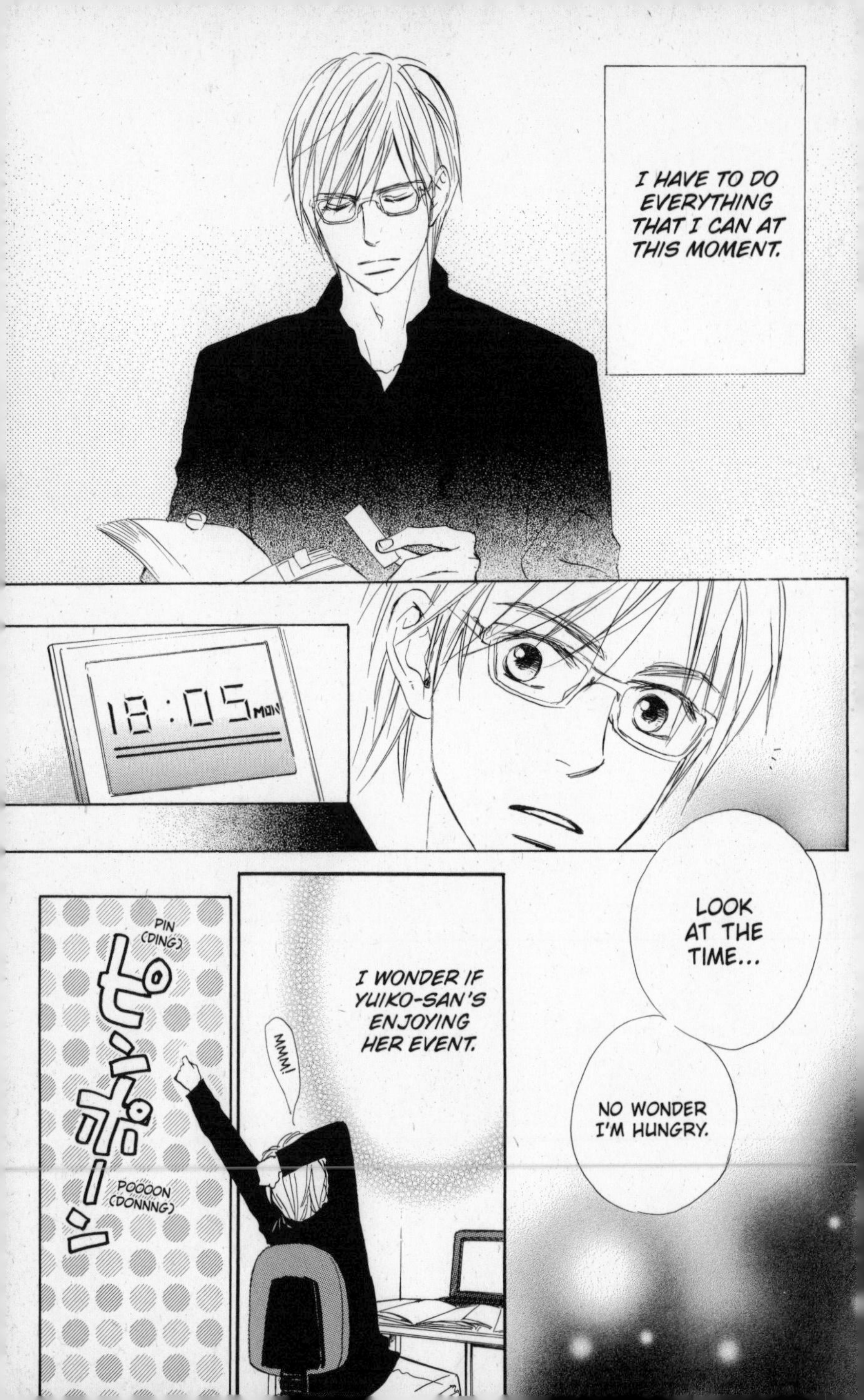
I HAVE TO DO EVERYTHING THAT I CAN AT THIS MOMENT.
18:05 MON
LOOK AT THE TIME...
NO WONDER I'M HUNGRY.
I WONDER IF YUIKO-SAN'S ENJOYING HER EVENT.
MMM!
ピンポーン
PIN (DING)
POOOON (DONNNG)

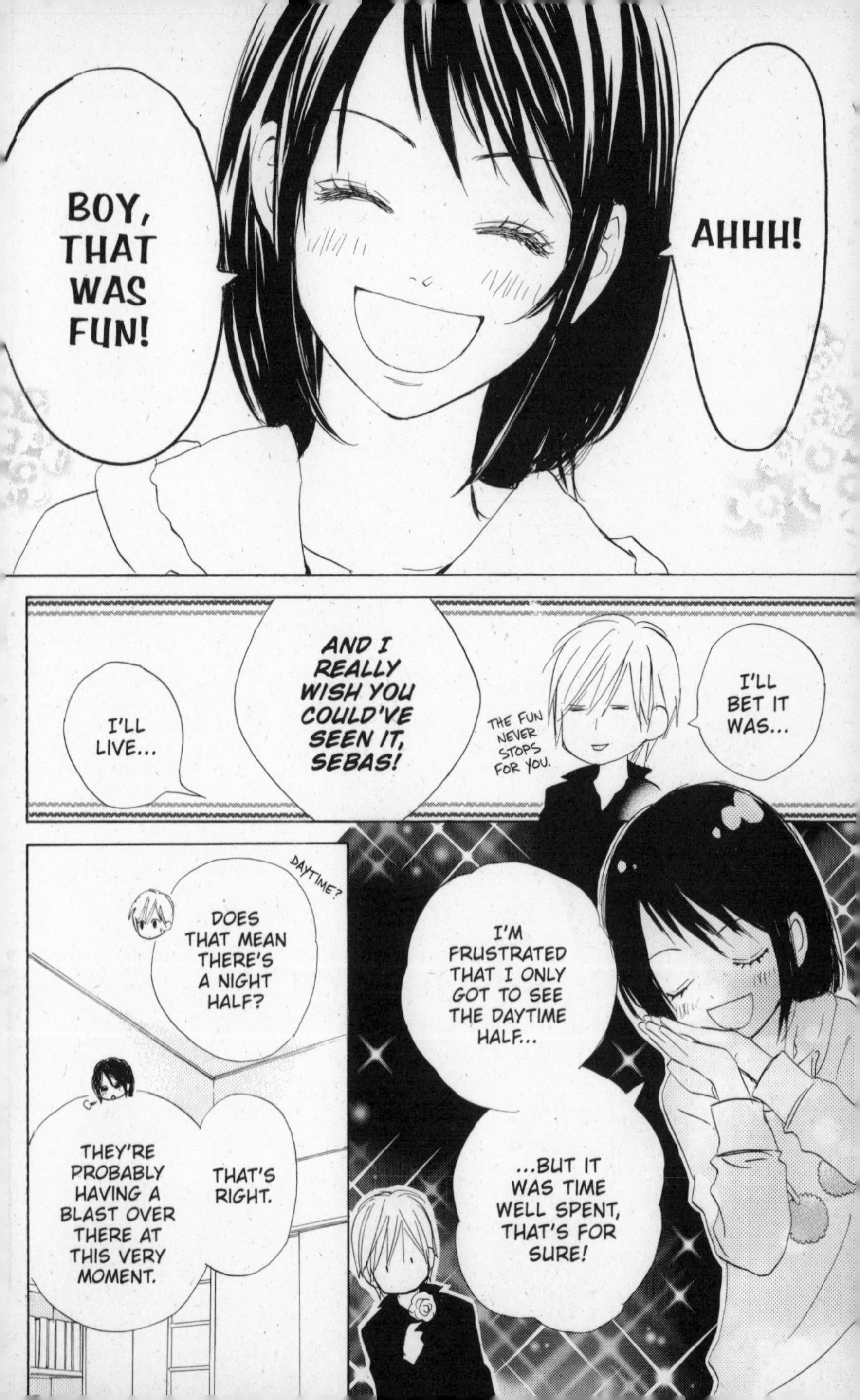
AHHH!
BOY, THAT WAS FUN!
I'LL BET IT WAS...
THE FUN NEVER STOPS FOR YOU.
AND I REALLY WISH YOU COULD'VE SEEN IT, SEBAS!
I'LL LIVE...
I'M FRUSTRATED THAT I ONLY GOT TO SEE THE DAYTIME HALF...
...BUT IT WAS TIME WELL SPENT, THAT'S FOR SURE!
DAYTIME?
DOES THAT MEAN THERE'S A NIGHT HALF?
THAT'S RIGHT.
THEY'RE PROBABLY HAVING A BLAST OVER THERE AT THIS VERY MOMENT.

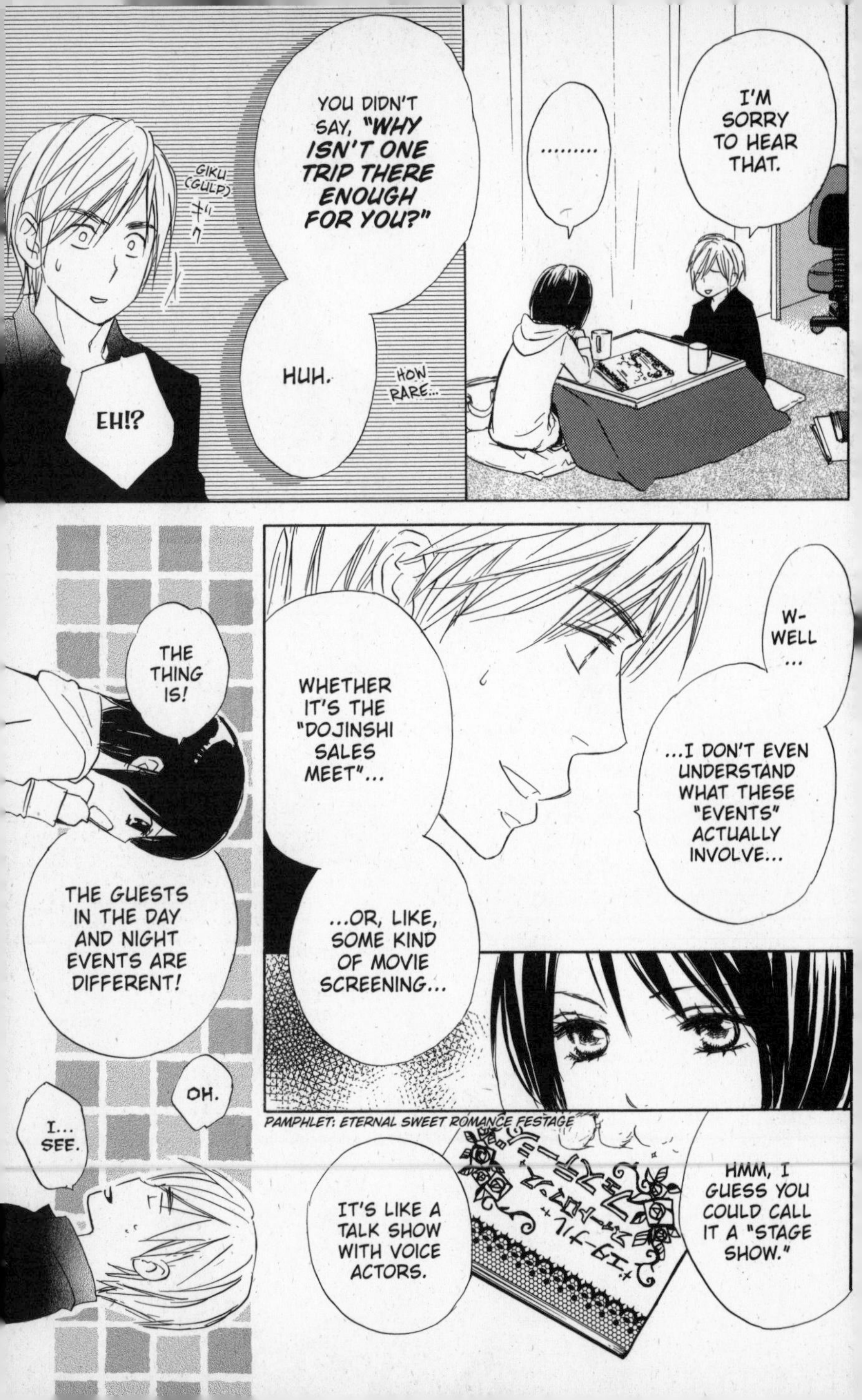
I'M SORRY TO HEAR THAT.
....
YOU DIDN'T SAY, "WHY ISN'T ONE TRIP THERE ENOUGH FOR YOU?"
GIKU (GULP)
HUH.
HOW RARE...
EH!?
W-WELL...
...I DON'T EVEN UNDERSTAND WHAT THESE "EVENTS" ACTUALLY INVOLVE...
WHETHER IT'S THE "DOJINSHI SALES MEET"...
...OR, LIKE, SOME KIND OF MOVIE SCREENING...
PAMPHLET: ETERNAL SWEET ROMANCE FESTAGE
HMM, I GUESS YOU COULD CALL IT A "STAGE SHOW."
IT'S LIKE A TALK SHOW WITH VOICE ACTORS.
THE THING IS!
THE GUESTS IN THE DAY AND NIGHT EVENTS ARE DIFFERENT!
OH.
I... SEE.

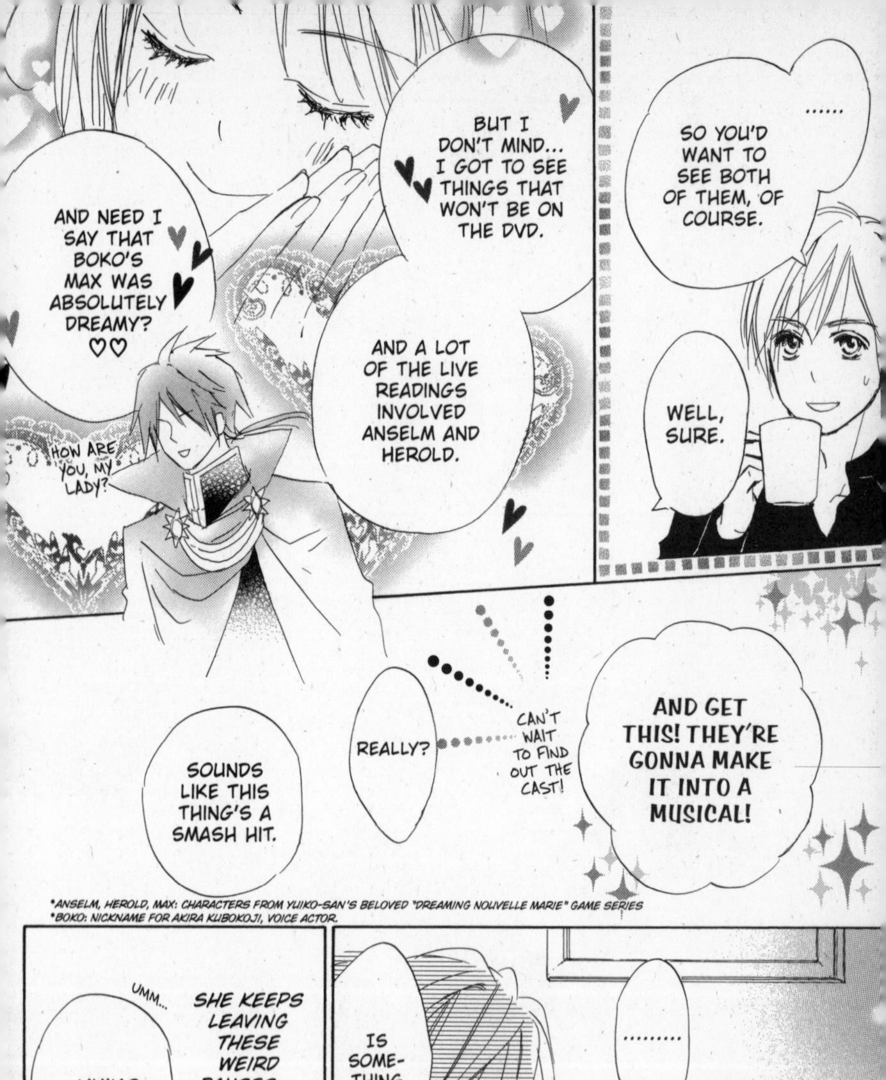
......
SO YOU'D WANT TO SEE BOTH OF THEM, OF COURSE.
WELL, SURE.
BUT I DON'T MIND... I GOT TO SEE THINGS THAT WON'T BE ON THE DVD.
AND NEED I SAY THAT BOKO'S MAX WAS ABSOLUTELY DREAMY? ♡♡
AND A LOT OF THE LIVE READINGS INVOLVED ANSELM AND HEROLD.
HOW ARE YOU, MY LADY?
AND GET THIS! THEY'RE GONNA MAKE IT INTO A MUSICAL!
CAN'T WAIT TO FIND OUT THE CAST!
REALLY?
SOUNDS LIKE THIS THING'S A SMASH HIT.

*ANSELM, HEROLD, MAX: CHARACTERS FROM YUIKO-SAN'S BELOVED "DREAMING NOUVELLE MARIE" GAME SERIES
*BOKO: NICKNAME FOR AKIRA KUBOKOJI, VOICE ACTOR.

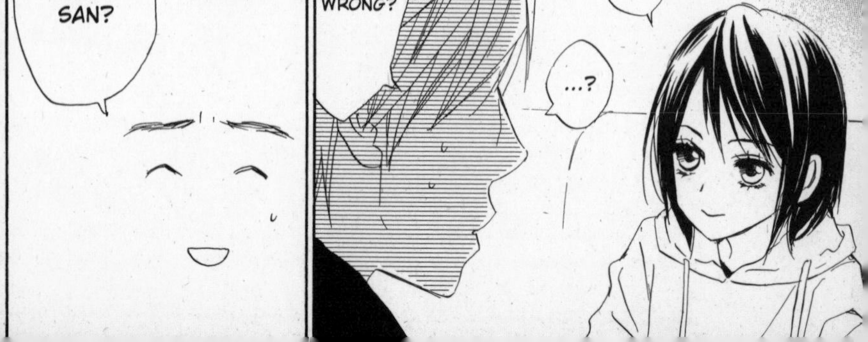
....
IS SOME-THING WRONG?
...?
SHE KEEPS LEAVING THESE WEIRD PAUSES...
UMM...
...YUIKO-SAN?

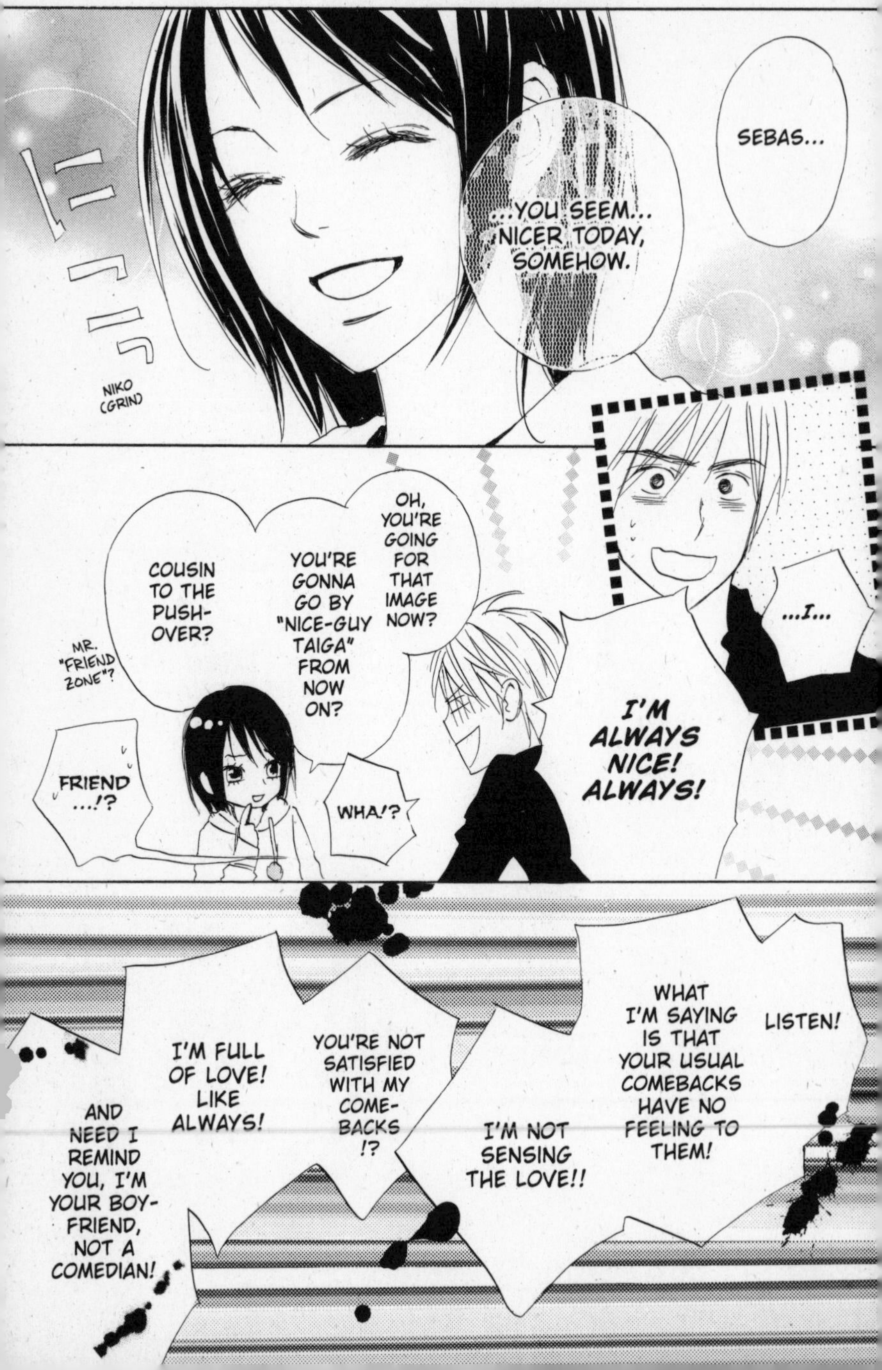
SEBAS...
...YOU SEEM... NICER TODAY, SOMEHOW.
NIKO (GRIN)
...I...
I'M ALWAYS NICE! ALWAYS!
OH, YOU'RE GOING FOR THAT IMAGE NOW?
YOU'RE GONNA GO BY "NICE-GUY TAIGA" FROM NOW ON?
COUSIN TO THE PUSH-OVER?
MR. "FRIEND ZONE"?
WHA!?
FRIEND ...!?
LISTEN!
WHAT I'M SAYING IS THAT YOUR USUAL COMEBACKS HAVE NO FEELING TO THEM!
I'M NOT SENSING THE LOVE!!
YOU'RE NOT SATISFIED WITH MY COME-BACKS !?
I'M FULL OF LOVE! LIKE ALWAYS!
AND NEED I REMIND YOU, I'M YOUR BOY-FRIEND, NOT A COMEDIAN!

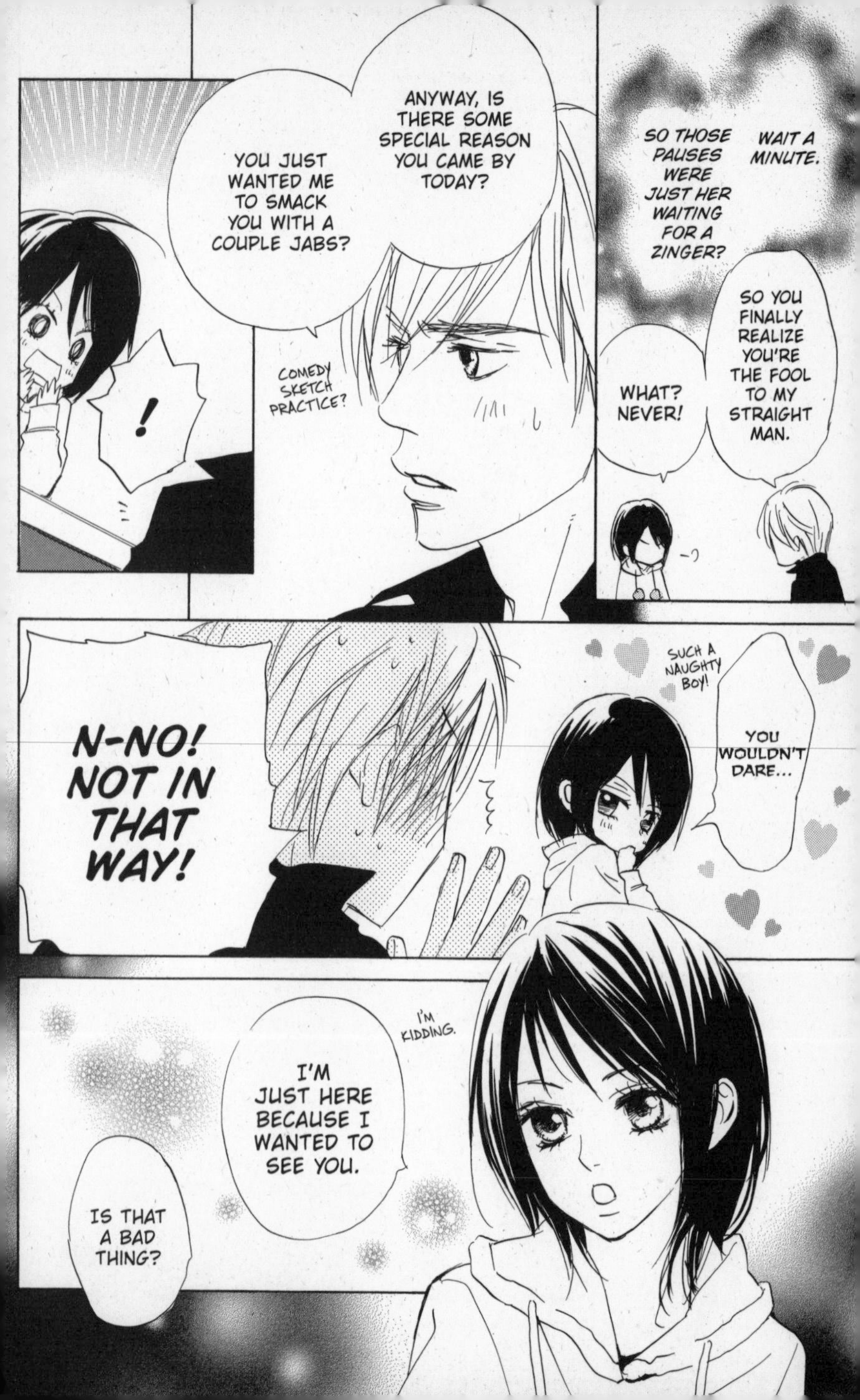
WAIT A MINUTE.
SO THOSE PAUSES WERE JUST HER WAITING FOR A ZINGER?
SO YOU FINALLY REALIZE YOU'RE THE FOOL TO MY STRAIGHT MAN.
WHAT? NEVER!
ANYWAY, IS THERE SOME SPECIAL REASON YOU CAME BY TODAY?
YOU JUST WANTED ME TO SMACK YOU WITH A COUPLE JABS?
COMEDY SKETCH PRACTICE?
!
SUCH A NAUGHTY BOY!
YOU WOULDN'T DARE...
N-NO! NOT IN THAT WAY!
I'M KIDDING.
I'M JUST HERE BECAUSE I WANTED TO SEE YOU.
IS THAT A BAD THING?

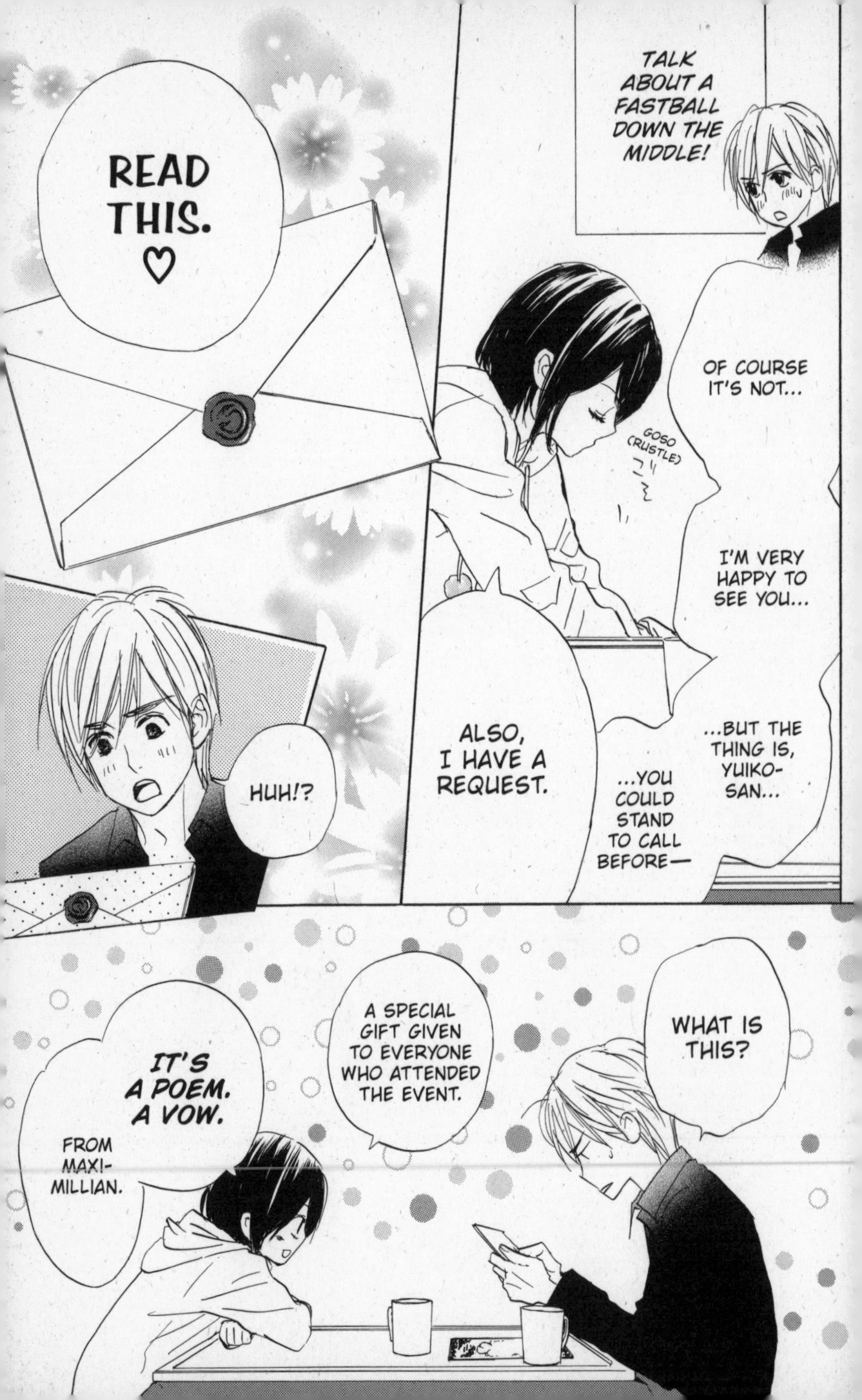
TALK ABOUT A FASTBALL DOWN THE MIDDLE!
OF COURSE IT'S NOT...
GOSO (RUSTLE)
I'M VERY HAPPY TO SEE YOU...
...BUT THE THING IS, YUIKO-SAN...
...YOU COULD STAND TO CALL BEFORE—
ALSO, I HAVE A REQUEST.
READ THIS. ♡
HUH!?
WHAT IS THIS?
A SPECIAL GIFT GIVEN TO EVERYONE WHO ATTENDED THE EVENT.
IT'S A POEM. A VOW.
FROM MAXI-MILLIAN.

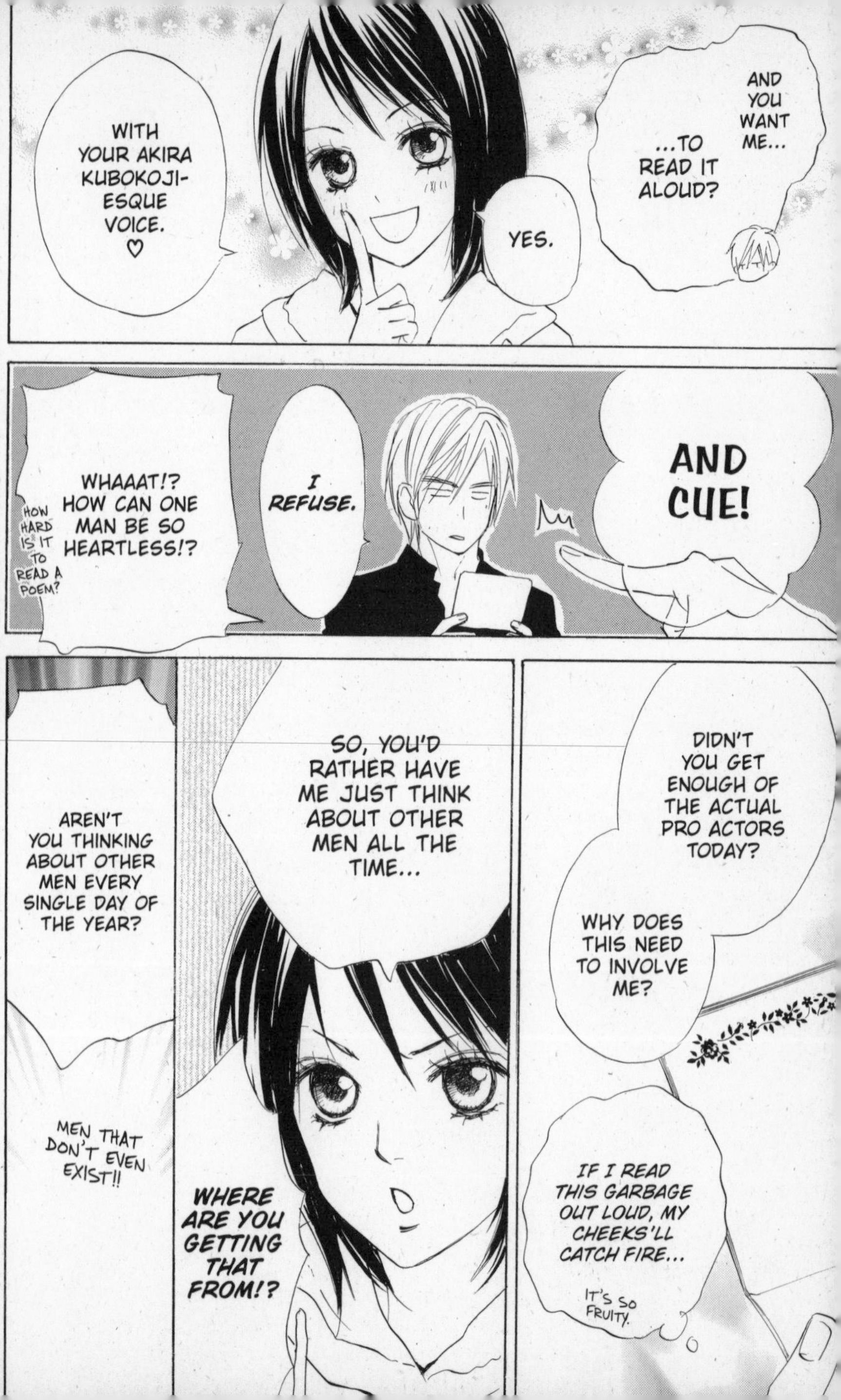
AND YOU WANT ME...
...TO READ IT ALOUD?
YES.
WITH YOUR AKIRA KUBOKOJI-ESQUE VOICE. ♡
AND CUE!
I REFUSE.
WHAAAT!? HOW CAN ONE MAN BE SO HEARTLESS!?
HOW HARD IS IT TO READ A POEM?
DIDN'T YOU GET ENOUGH OF THE ACTUAL PRO ACTORS TODAY?
WHY DOES THIS NEED TO INVOLVE ME?
IF I READ THIS GARBAGE OUT LOUD, MY CHEEKS'LL CATCH FIRE...
IT'S SO FRUITY.
SO, YOU'D RATHER HAVE ME JUST THINK ABOUT OTHER MEN ALL THE TIME...
WHERE ARE YOU GETTING THAT FROM!?
AREN'T YOU THINKING ABOUT OTHER MEN EVERY SINGLE DAY OF THE YEAR?
MEN THAT DON'T EVEN EXIST!!

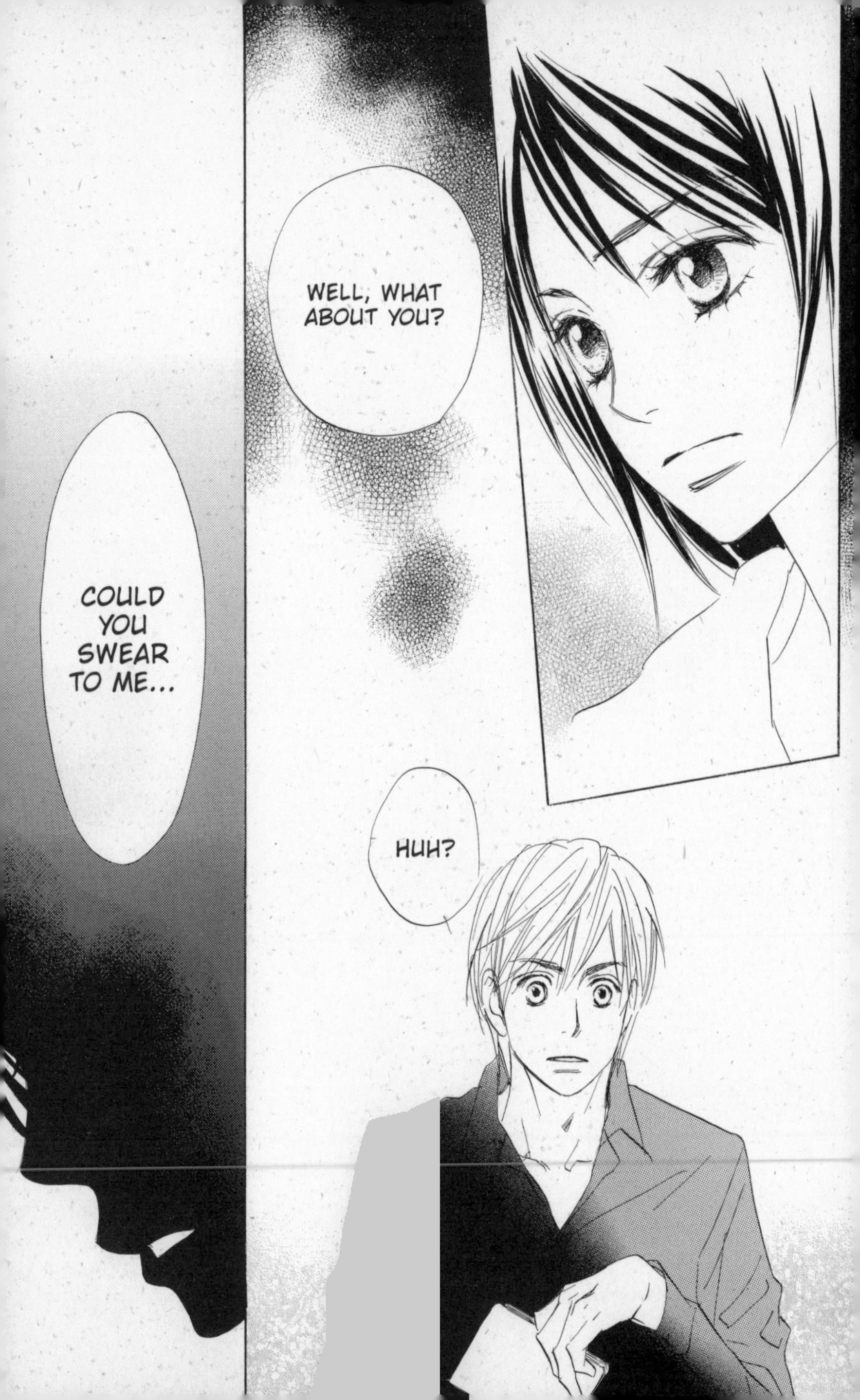
WELL, WHAT ABOUT YOU?
HUH?
COULD YOU SWEAR TO ME...

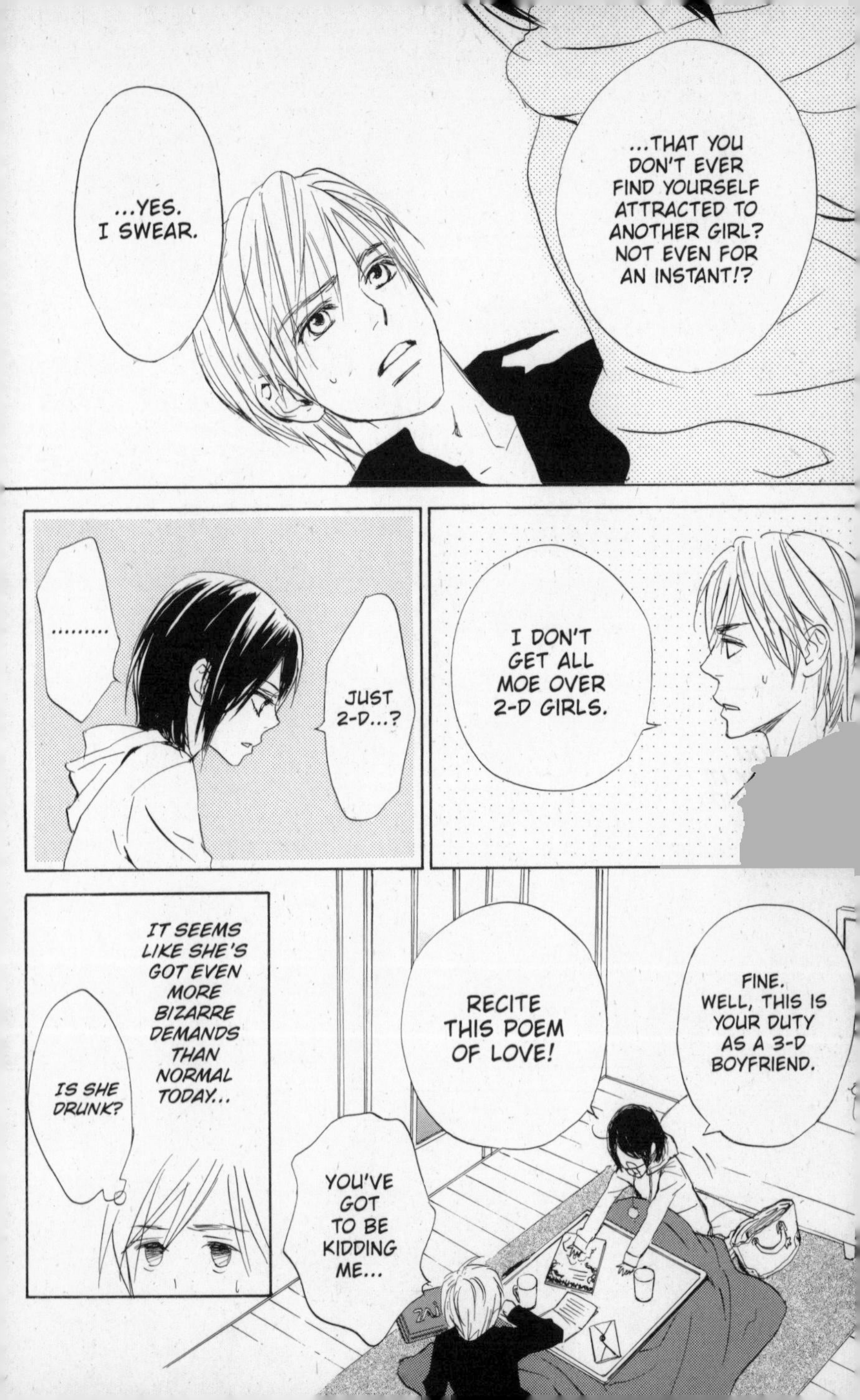
...THAT YOU DON'T EVER FIND YOURSELF ATTRACTED TO ANOTHER GIRL? NOT EVEN FOR AN INSTANT!?
...YES. I SWEAR.
I DON'T GET ALL MOE OVER 2-D GIRLS.
JUST 2-D...?
....
FINE. WELL, THIS IS YOUR DUTY AS A 3-D BOYFRIEND.
RECITE THIS POEM OF LOVE!
YOU'VE GOT TO BE KIDDING ME...
IT SEEMS LIKE SHE'S GOT EVEN MORE BIZARRE DEMANDS THAN NORMAL TODAY...
IS SHE DRUNK?

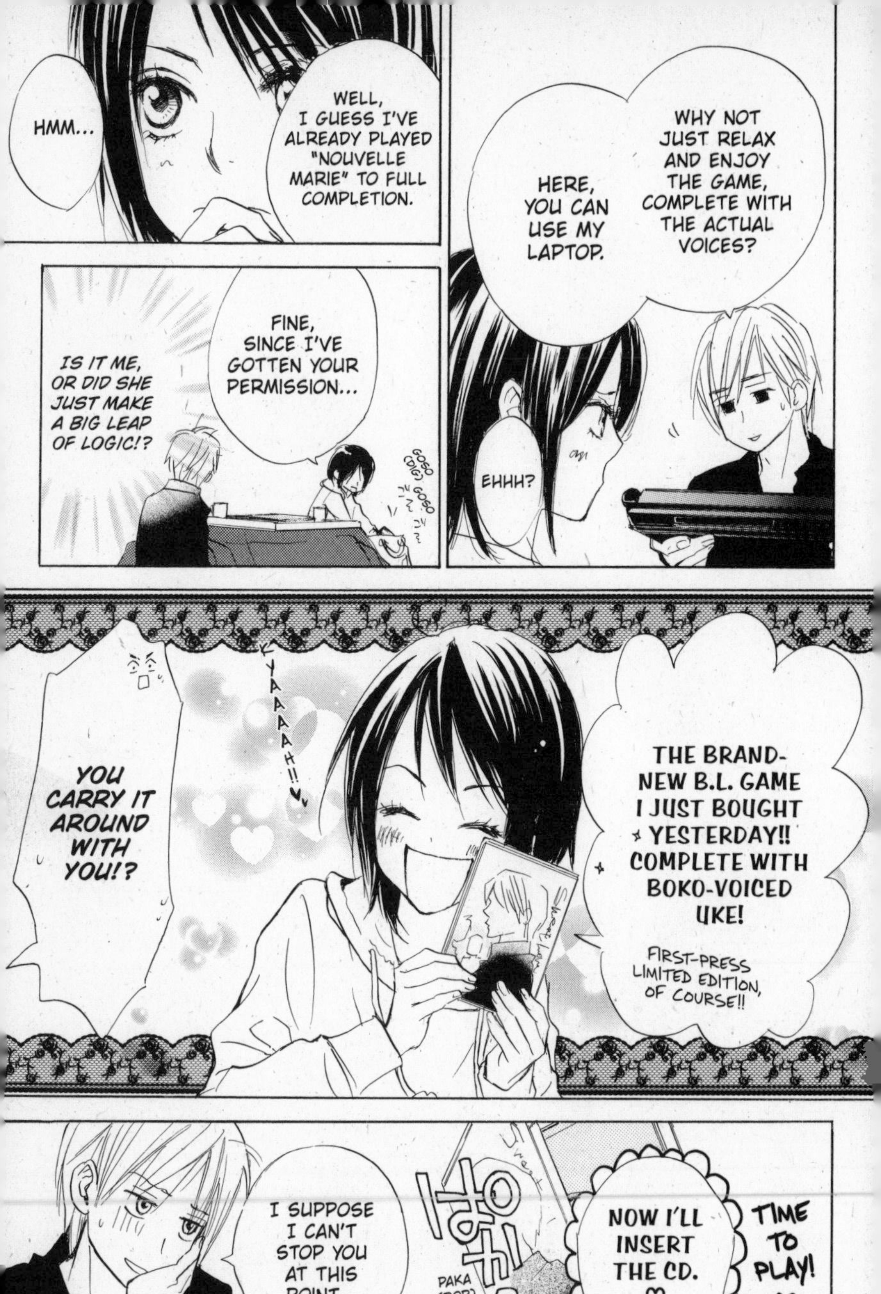
WHY NOT JUST RELAX AND ENJOY THE GAME, COMPLETE WITH THE ACTUAL VOICES?
HERE, YOU CAN USE MY LAPTOP.
EHHH?
WELL, I GUESS I'VE ALREADY PLAYED "NOUVELLE MARIE" TO FULL COMPLETION.
HMM...
FINE, SINCE I'VE GOTTEN YOUR PERMISSION...
GOSO (DIG) GOSO
IS IT ME, OR DID SHE JUST MAKE A BIG LEAP OF LOGIC!?
THE BRAND-NEW B.L. GAME I JUST BOUGHT YESTERDAY!! COMPLETE WITH BOKO-VOICED UKE!
FIRST-PRESS LIMITED EDITION, OF COURSE!!
YAAAAH!!
YOU CARRY IT AROUND WITH YOU!?
TIME TO PLAY!
NOW I'LL INSERT THE CD. ♡
ぱかっ
PAKA (POP)
I SUPPOSE I CAN'T STOP YOU AT THIS POINT...

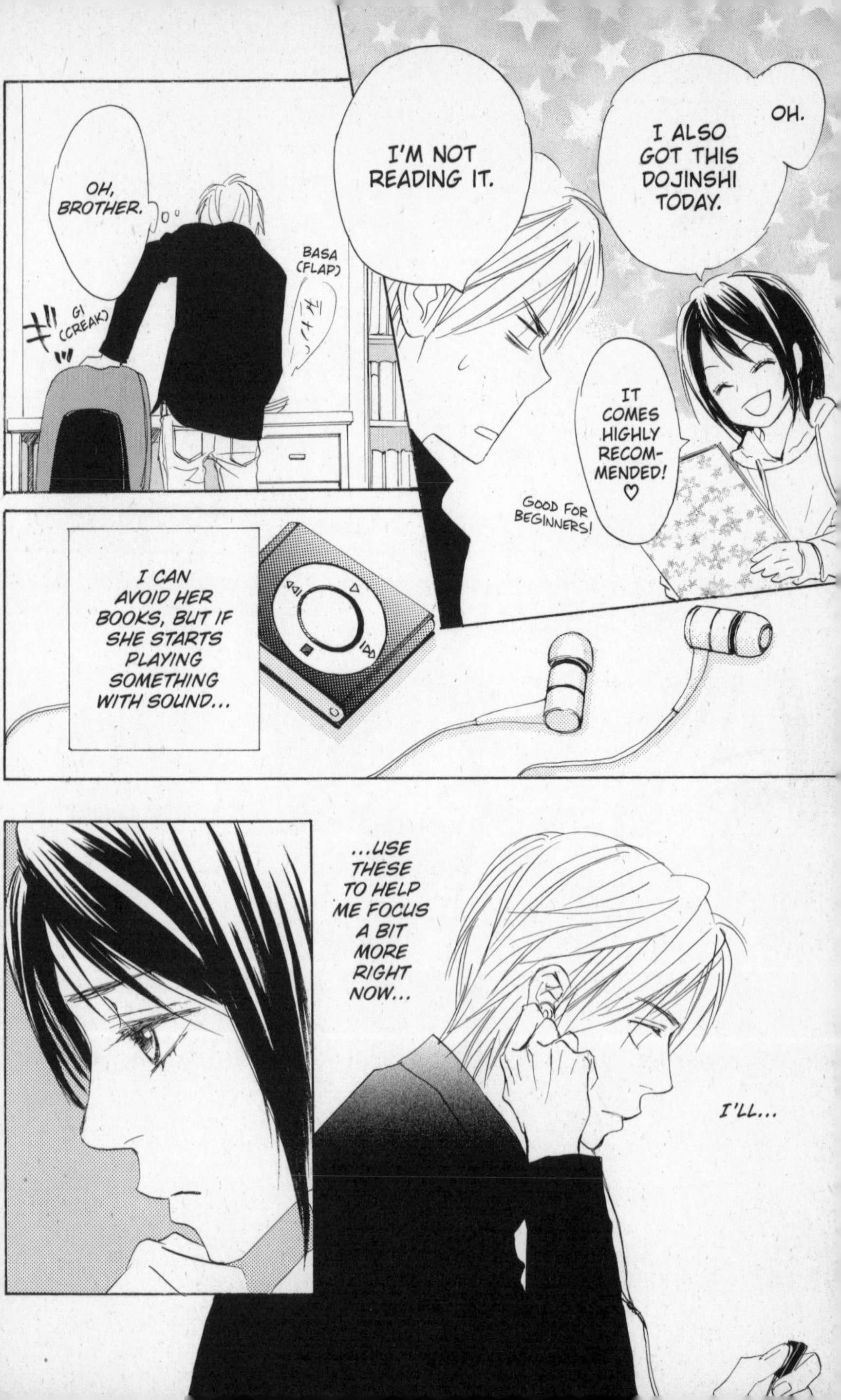
OH.
I ALSO GOT THIS DOJINSHI TODAY.
IT COMES HIGHLY RECOM-MENDED! ♡
GOOD FOR BEGINNERS!
I'M NOT READING IT.
OH, BROTHER.
BASA (FLAP)
GI (CREAK)
I CAN AVOID HER BOOKS, BUT IF SHE STARTS PLAYING SOMETHING WITH SOUND...
I'LL...
...USE THESE TO HELP ME FOCUS A BIT MORE RIGHT NOW...

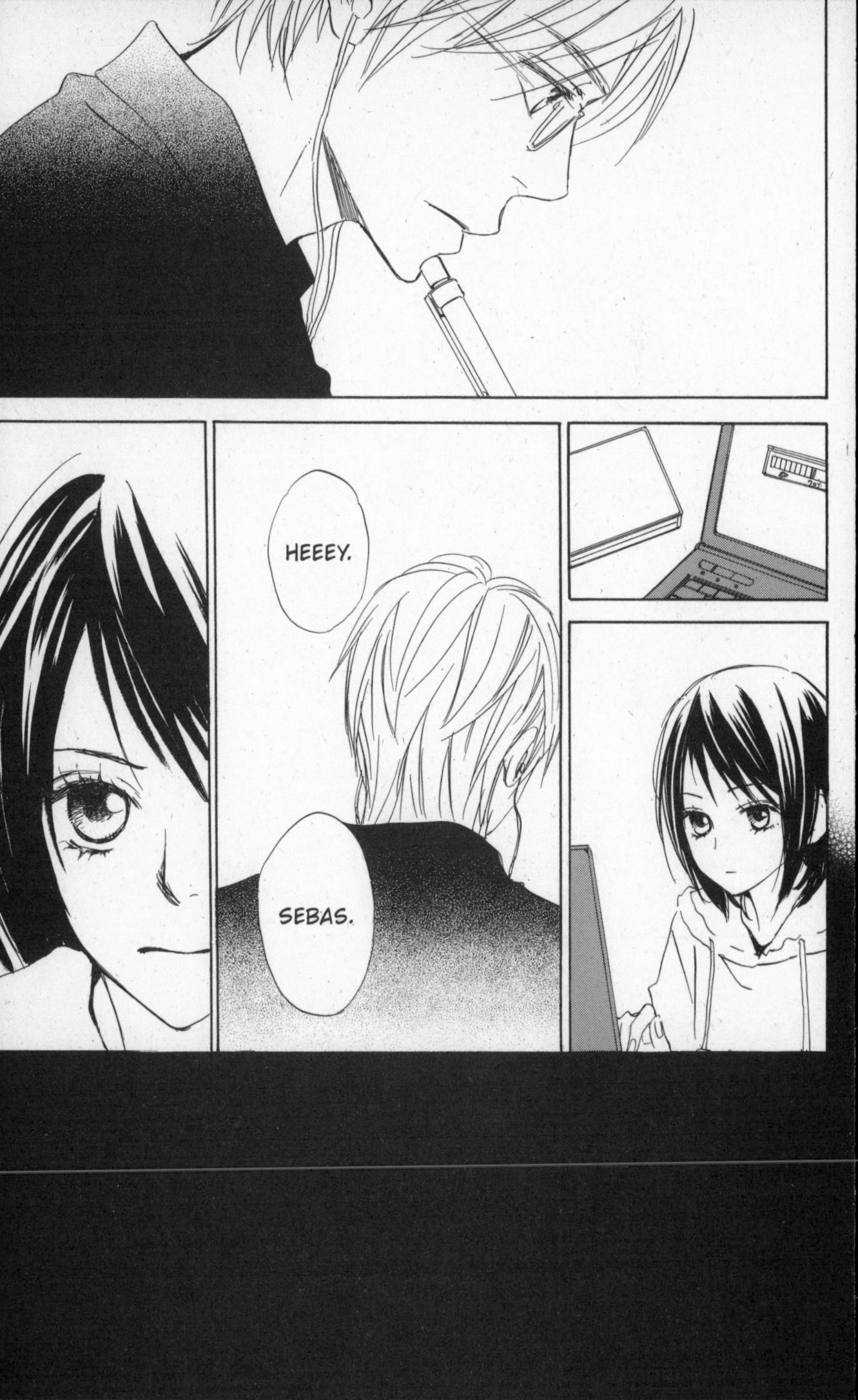
HEEEY.
SEBAS.

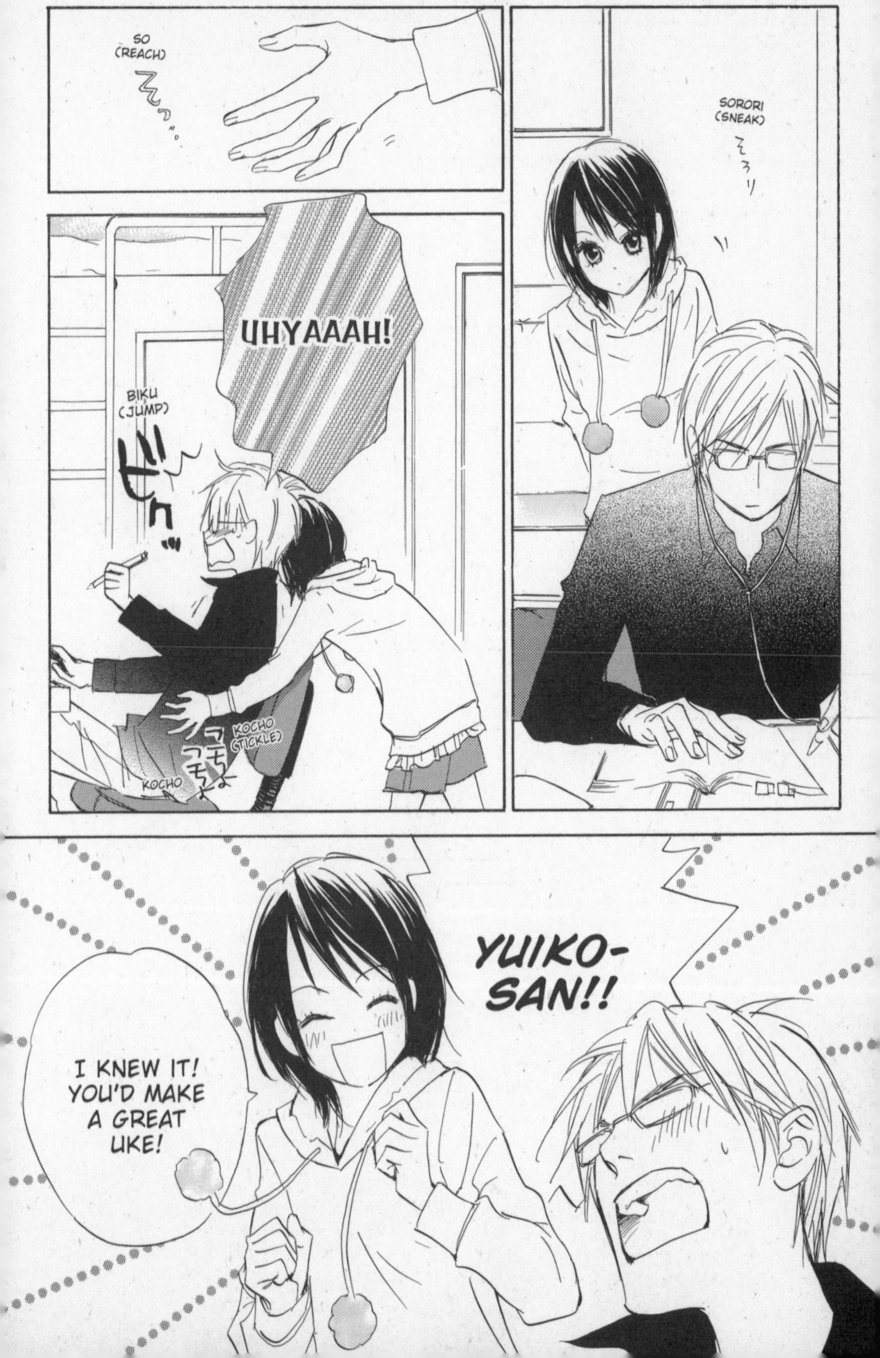
SORORI (SNEAK)
SO (REACH)
UHYAAAH!
BIKU (JUMP)
KOCHO (TICKLE)
KOCHO
YUIKO-SAN!!
I KNEW IT! YOU'D MAKE A GREAT UKE!

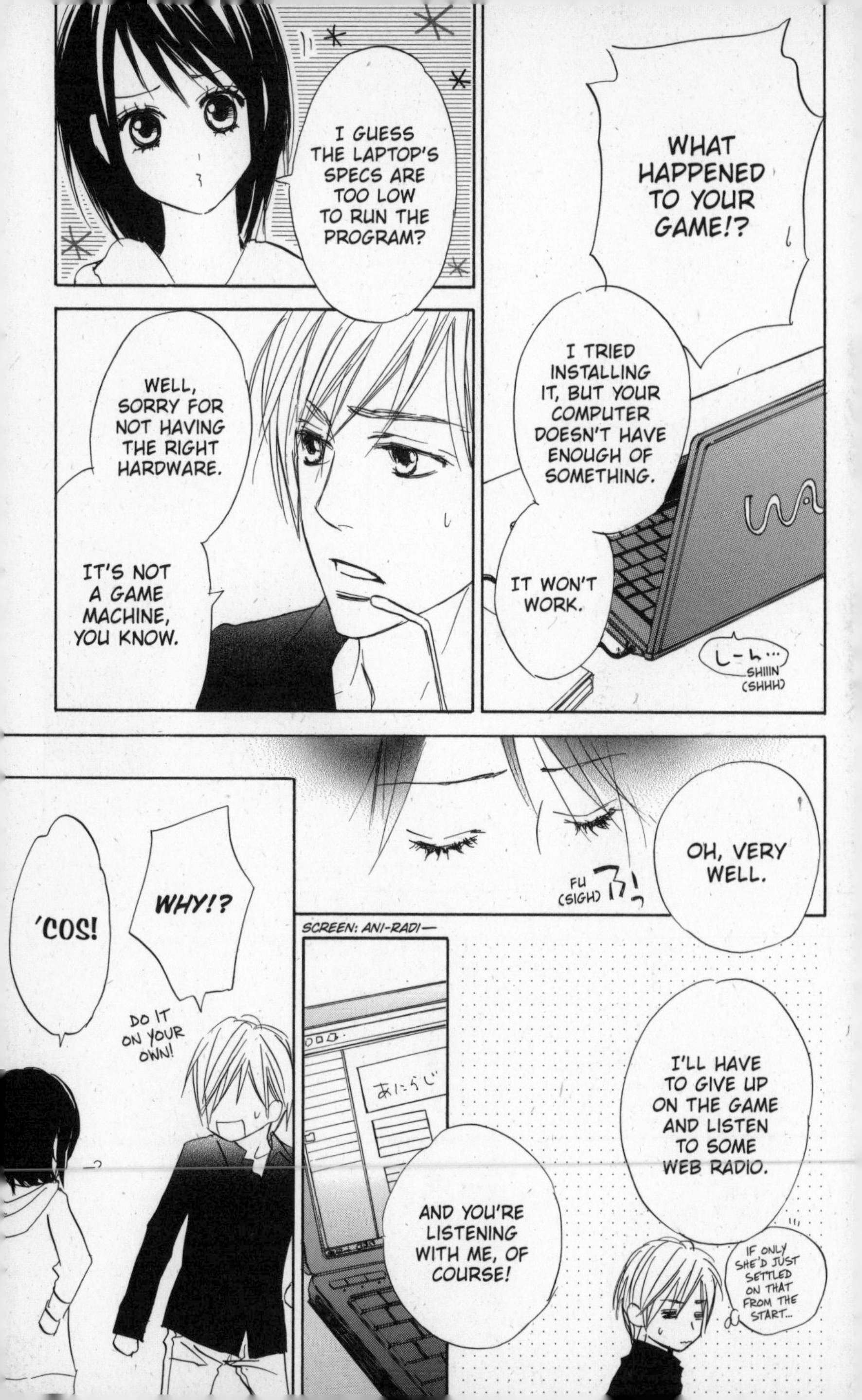
WHAT HAPPENED TO YOUR GAME!?
I TRIED INSTALLING IT, BUT YOUR COMPUTER DOESN'T HAVE ENOUGH OF SOMETHING.
IT WON'T WORK.
しーん…
SHIIIN (SHHH)
I GUESS THE LAPTOP'S SPECS ARE TOO LOW TO RUN THE PROGRAM?
WELL, SORRY FOR NOT HAVING THE RIGHT HARDWARE.
IT'S NOT A GAME MACHINE, YOU KNOW.
OH, VERY WELL.
ふっ
FU (SIGH)
I'LL HAVE TO GIVE UP ON THE GAME AND LISTEN TO SOME WEB RADIO.
SCREEN: ANI-RADI—
あにらじ
AND YOU'RE LISTENING WITH ME, OF COURSE!
IF ONLY SHE'D JUST SETTLED ON THAT FROM THE START...
WHY!?
'COS!
DO IT ON YOUR OWN!

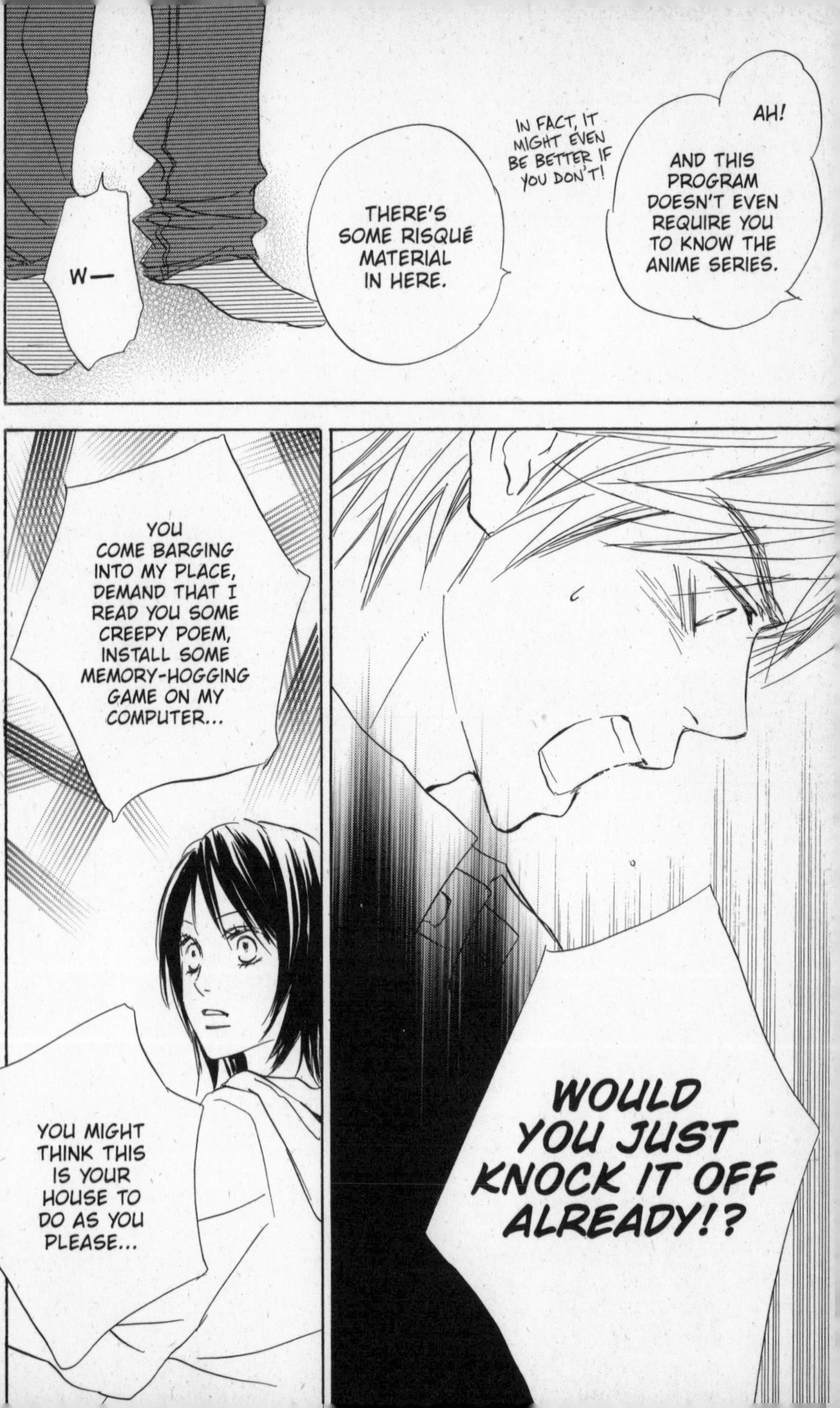
AH!
AND THIS PROGRAM DOESN'T EVEN REQUIRE YOU TO KNOW THE ANIME SERIES.
IN FACT, IT MIGHT EVEN BE BETTER IF YOU DON'T!
THERE'S SOME RISQUÉ MATERIAL IN HERE.
W—
WOULD YOU JUST KNOCK IT OFF ALREADY!?
YOU COME BARGING INTO MY PLACE, DEMAND THAT I READ YOU SOME CREEPY POEM, INSTALL SOME MEMORY-HOGGING GAME ON MY COMPUTER...
YOU MIGHT THINK THIS IS YOUR HOUSE TO DO AS YOU PLEASE...

...BUT
I'M ACTUALLY
BUSY RIGHT
NOW!

I DON'T
HAVE TIME TO
PUT UP WITH
YOUR STUPID
OTAKU CRAP!

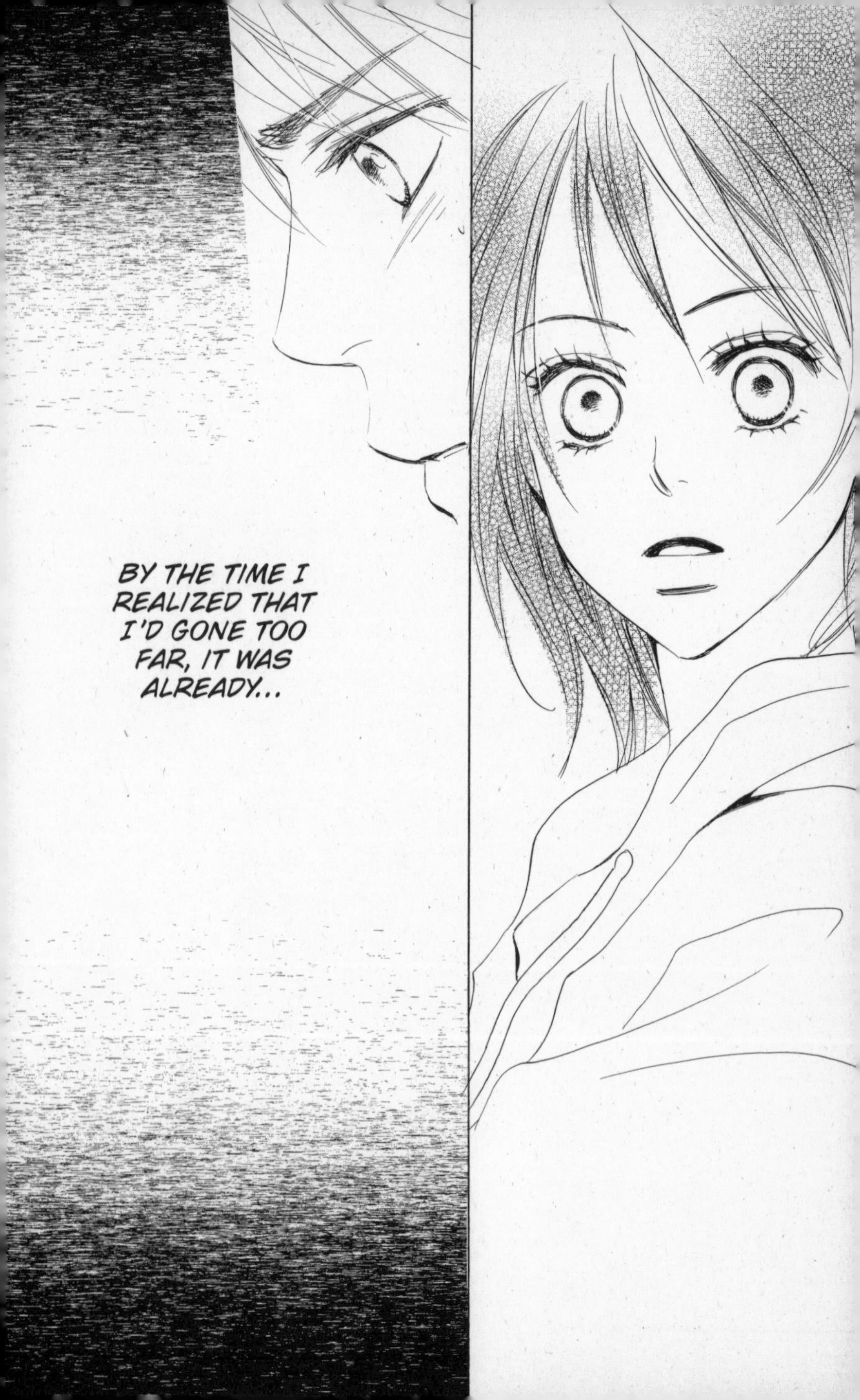
BY THE TIME I REALIZED THAT I'D GONE TOO FAR, IT WAS ALREADY...

FUJOSHI NEWS

vol.11

SURPRISE! INTERVIEW WITH THE FUJOSHI NEXT DOOR ③

SURPRISE! INTERVIEW WITH THE FUJOSHI NEXT DOOR ③

♥FUJOSHI No.003♥ VOICE ACTOR LOVER

CHIBA PREFECTURE, N.N.-SAN

VOICE ACTOR LOVER ♥

AGE: 22
OCCUPATION: TEMP WORKER
MONTHLY HOBBY COSTS: ¥50-60,000
MOE FETISH: COLLARBONES

[TYPICAL ACTIVITIES]
LISTENING TO DRAMA CDs ON MY COMMUTE; LOOKING FOR MANGA AND NOVELS THAT COULD EASILY GET THEIR OWN DRAMA CDs AND TRYING TO GUESS WHO THE CAST WILL BE

[TYPICAL EVENTS]
ANY EVENT IN WHICH VOICE ACTORS MAKE AN APPEARANCE

[SPECIAL POWER]
ABSOLUTE VOICE RECOGNITION (I CAN TELL WHICH ACTOR IS SPEAKING FROM JUST A SINGLE WORD.)

[RECENT TROUBLES]
I WATCHED AN ANIME IN WHICH ONE OF MY FAVORITE ACTORS IS PLAYING A HUSBAND, AND I IMAGINE I'M THE WIFE. IT'S SO FUN IN MY HEAD THAT I HAVE TROUBLE RETURNING TO REALITY.

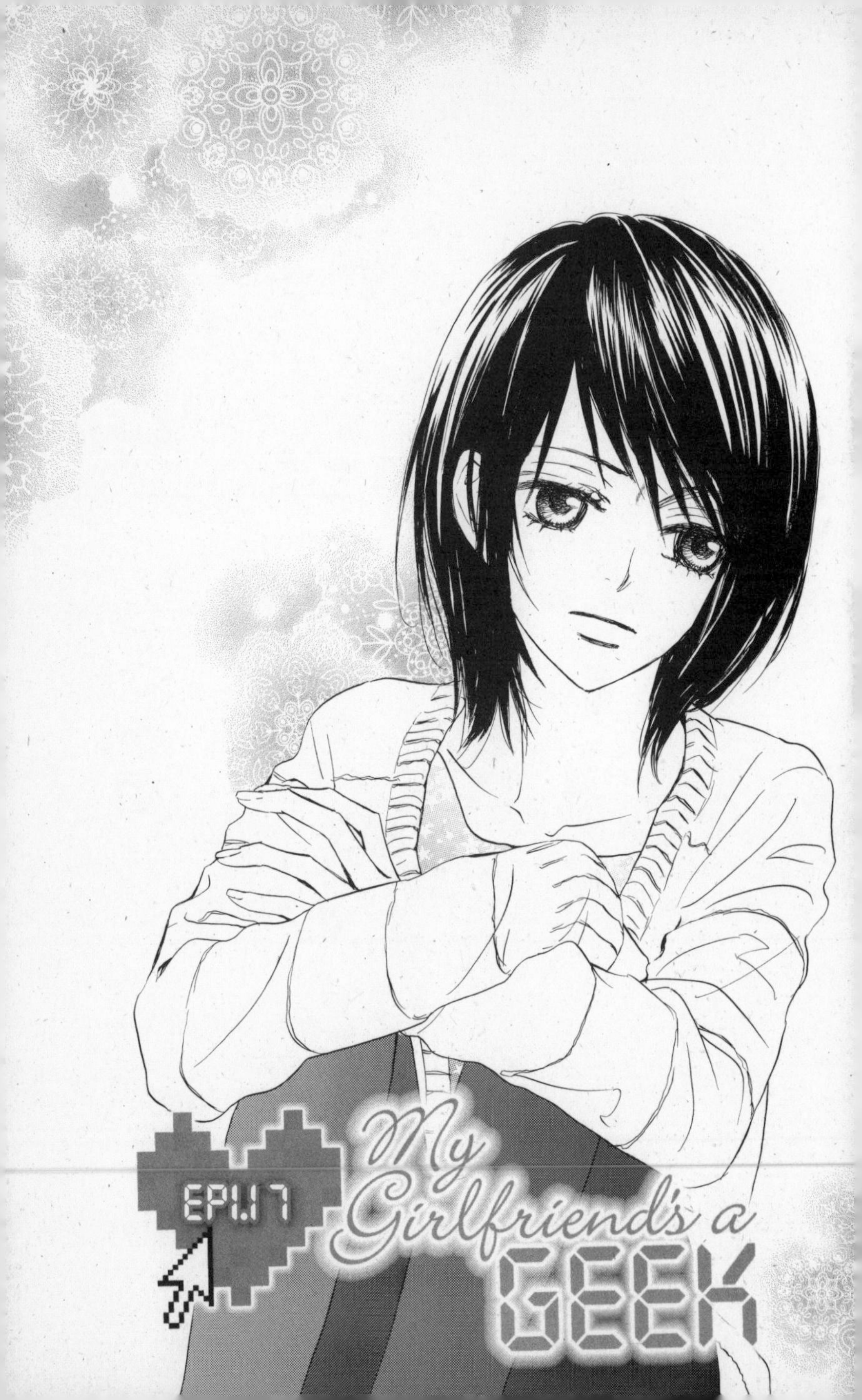
EP11.17
My Girlfriend's a GEEK

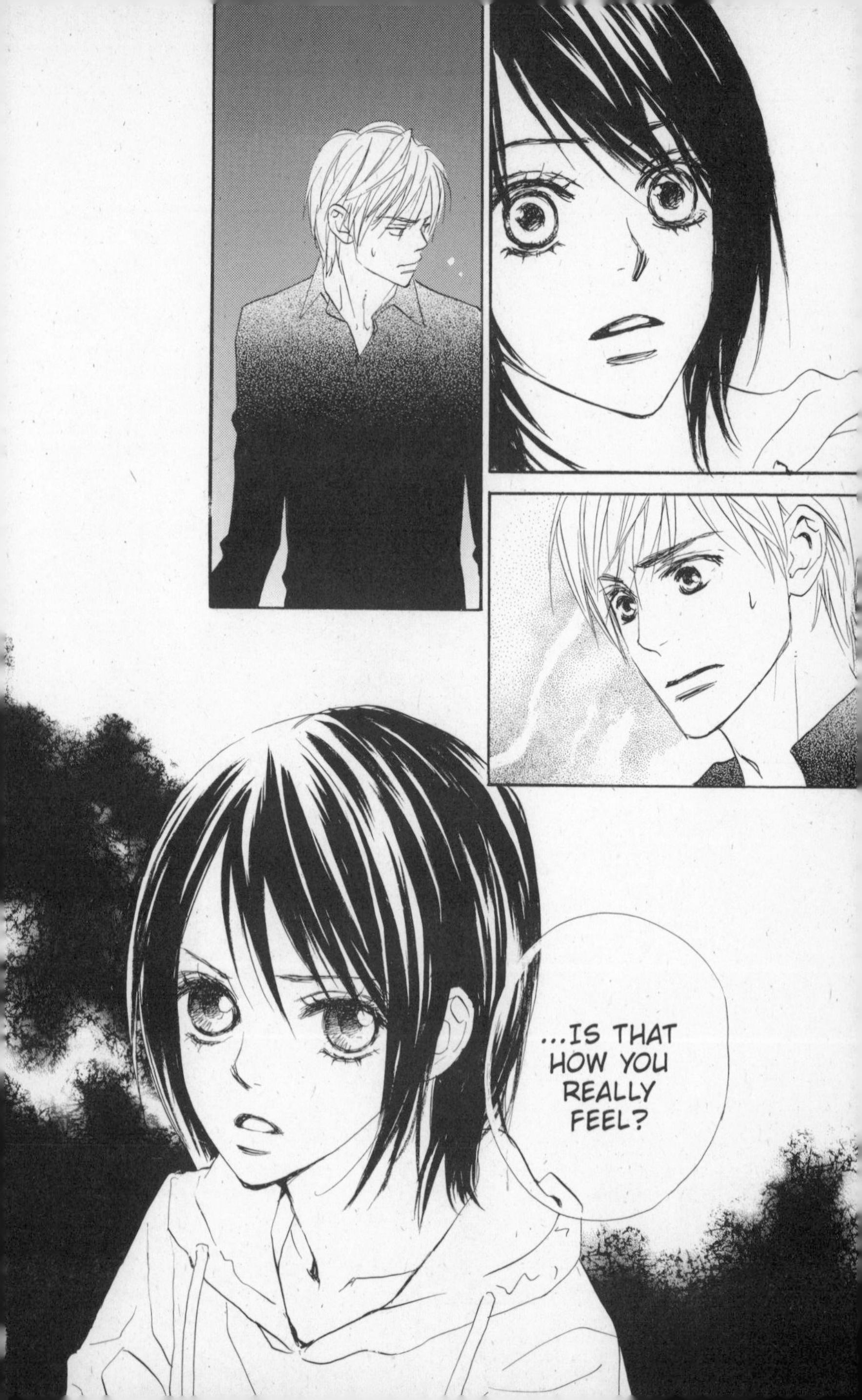
...IS THAT HOW YOU REALLY FEEL?

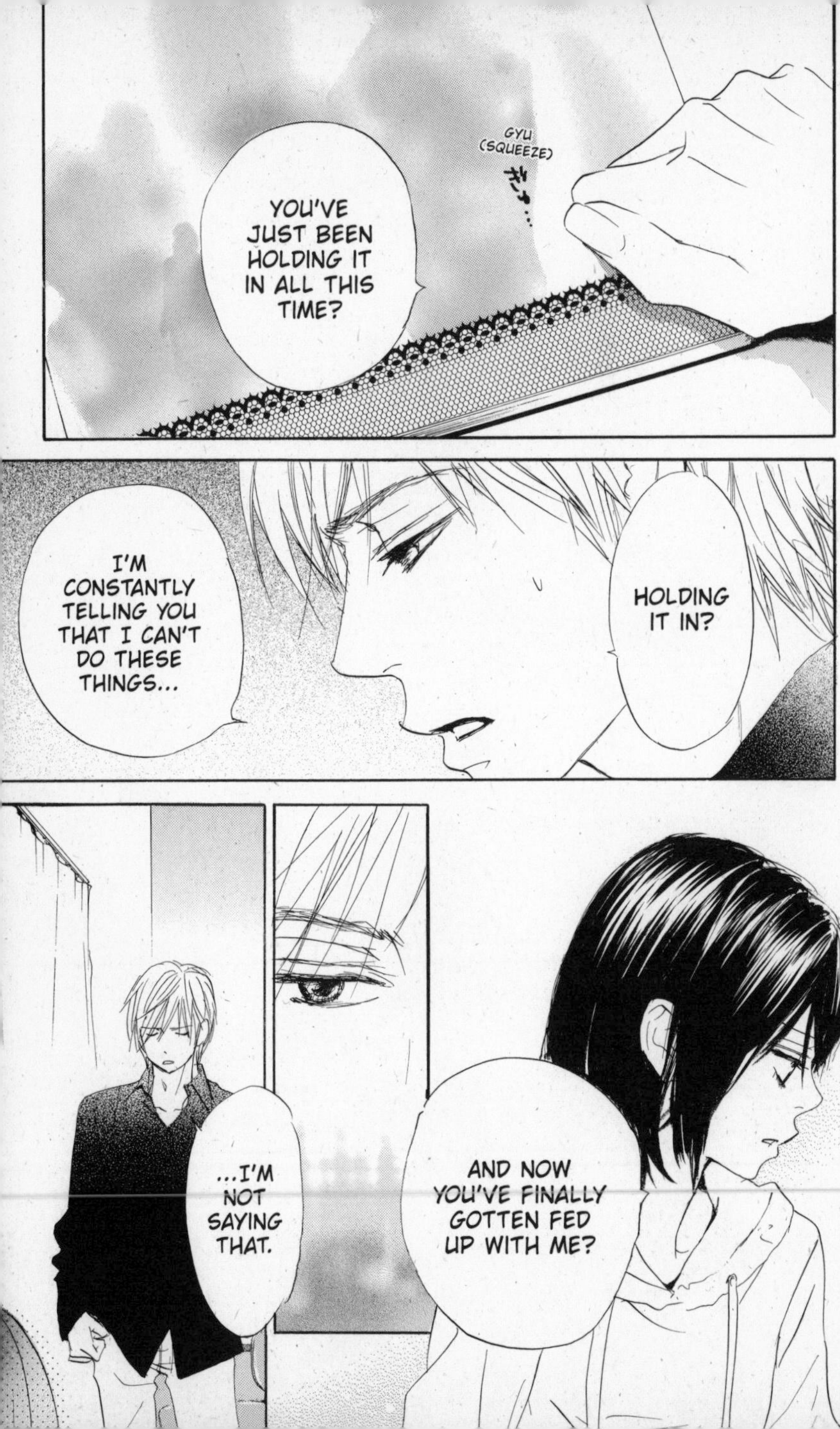
GYU (SQUEEZE)
YOU'VE JUST BEEN HOLDING IT IN ALL THIS TIME?
HOLDING IT IN?
I'M CONSTANTLY TELLING YOU THAT I CAN'T DO THESE THINGS...
AND NOW YOU'VE FINALLY GOTTEN FED UP WITH ME?
...I'M NOT SAYING THAT.

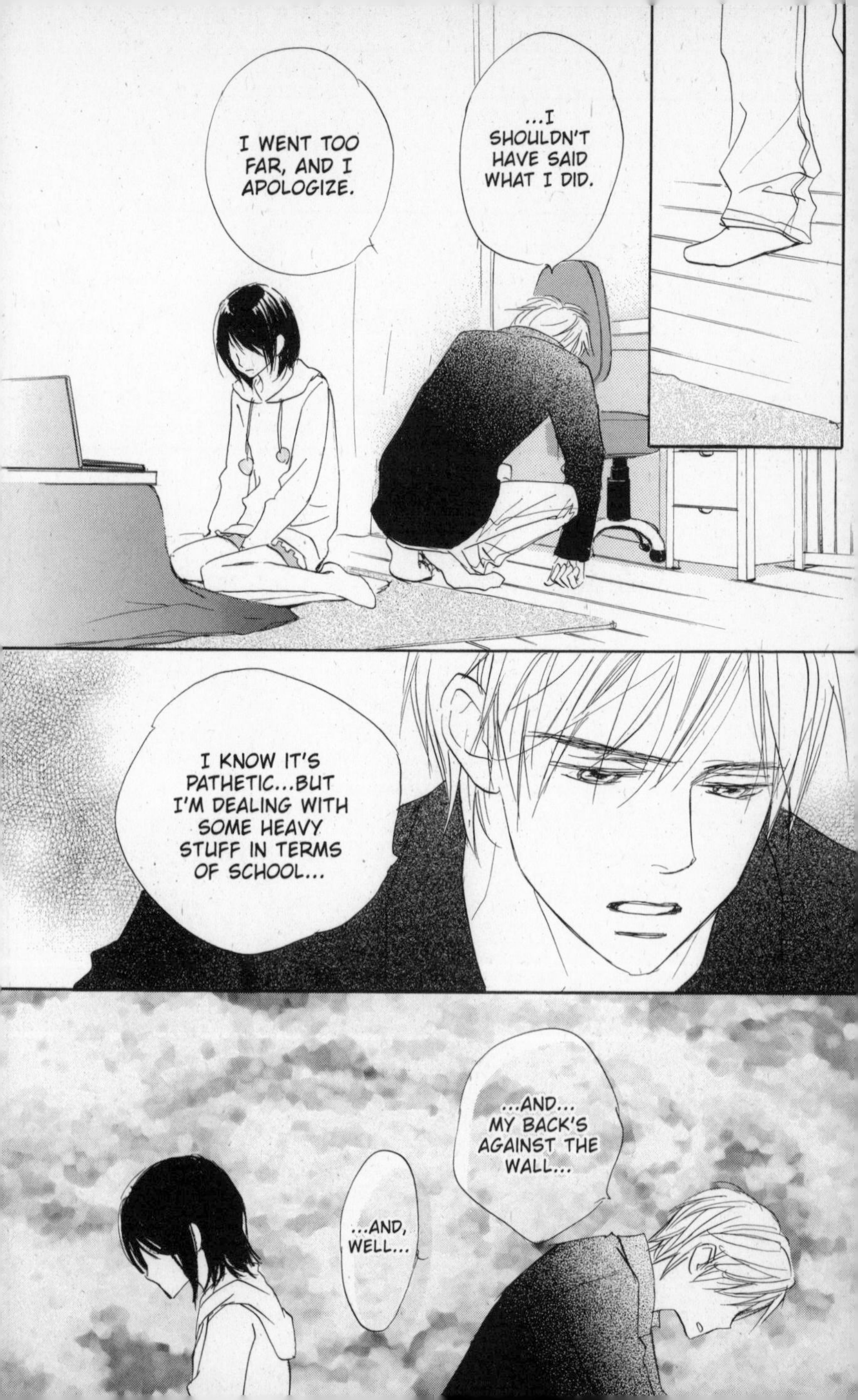
...I SHOULDN'T HAVE SAID WHAT I DID.
I WENT TOO FAR, AND I APOLOGIZE.
I KNOW IT'S PATHETIC...BUT I'M DEALING WITH SOME HEAVY STUFF IN TERMS OF SCHOOL...
...AND... MY BACK'S AGAINST THE WALL...
...AND, WELL...

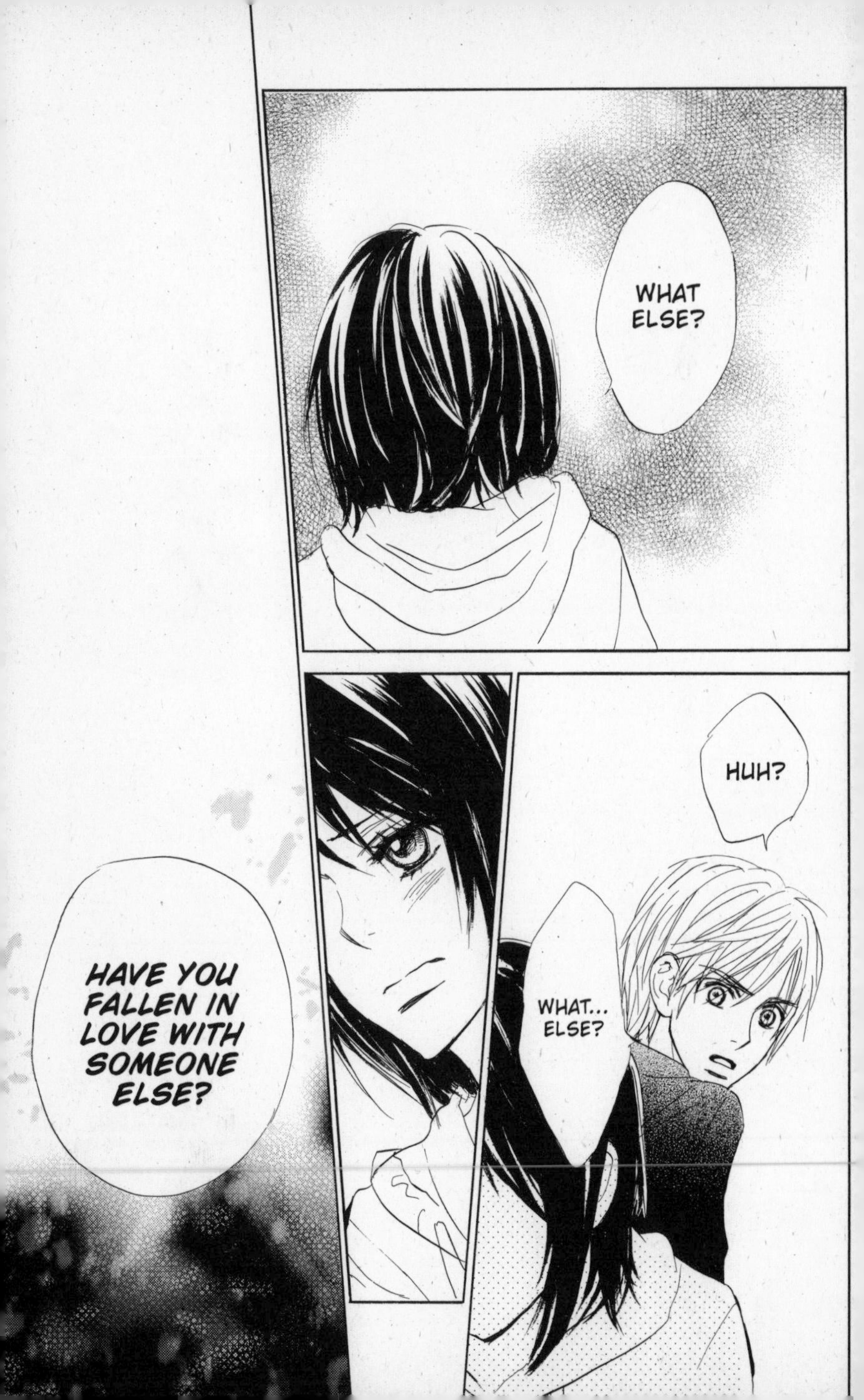
WHAT ELSE?
HUH?
WHAT... ELSE?
HAVE YOU FALLEN IN LOVE WITH SOMEONE ELSE?

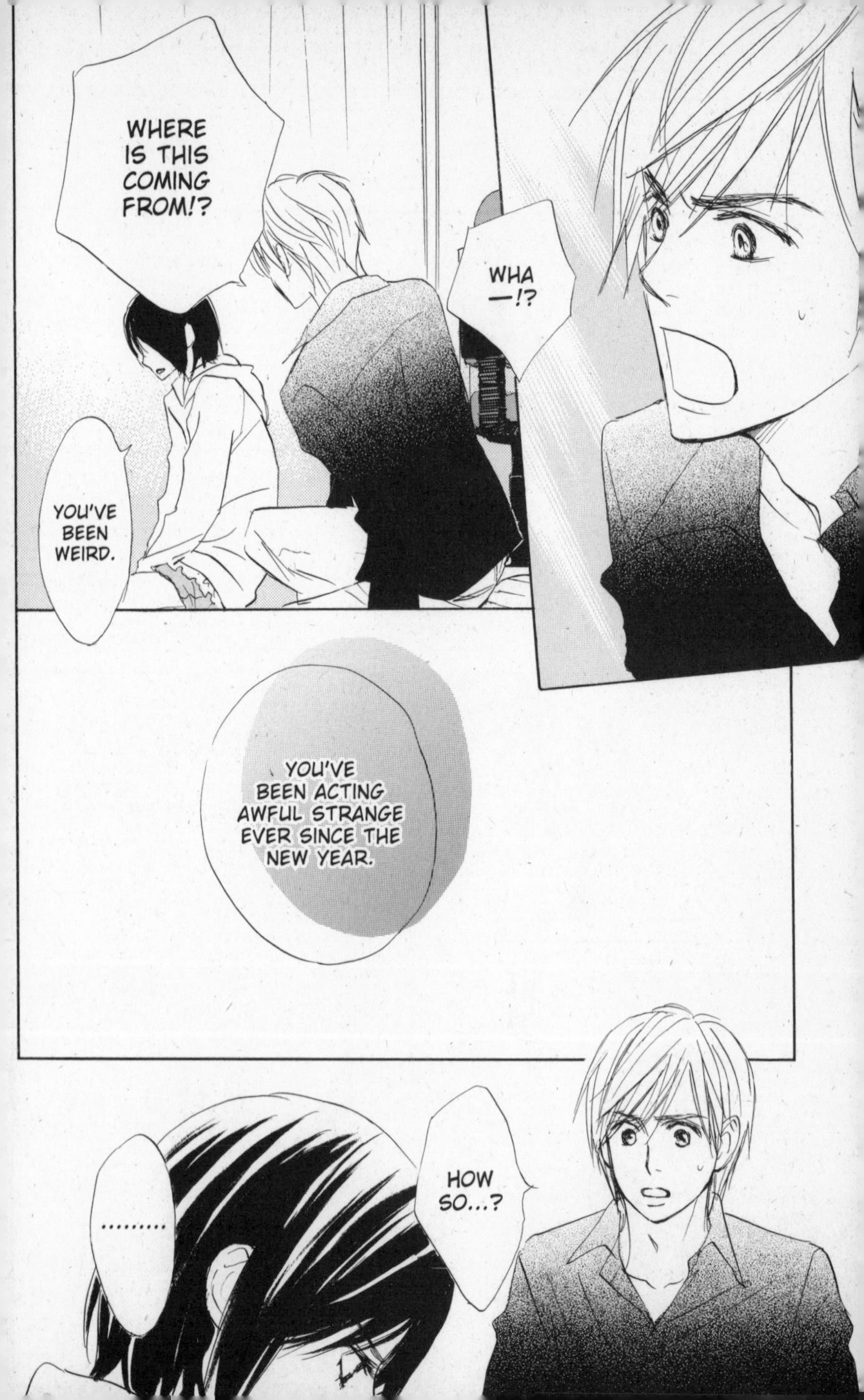
WHA—!?
WHERE IS THIS COMING FROM!?
YOU'VE BEEN WEIRD.
YOU'VE BEEN ACTING AWFUL STRANGE EVER SINCE THE NEW YEAR.
HOW SO...?
....

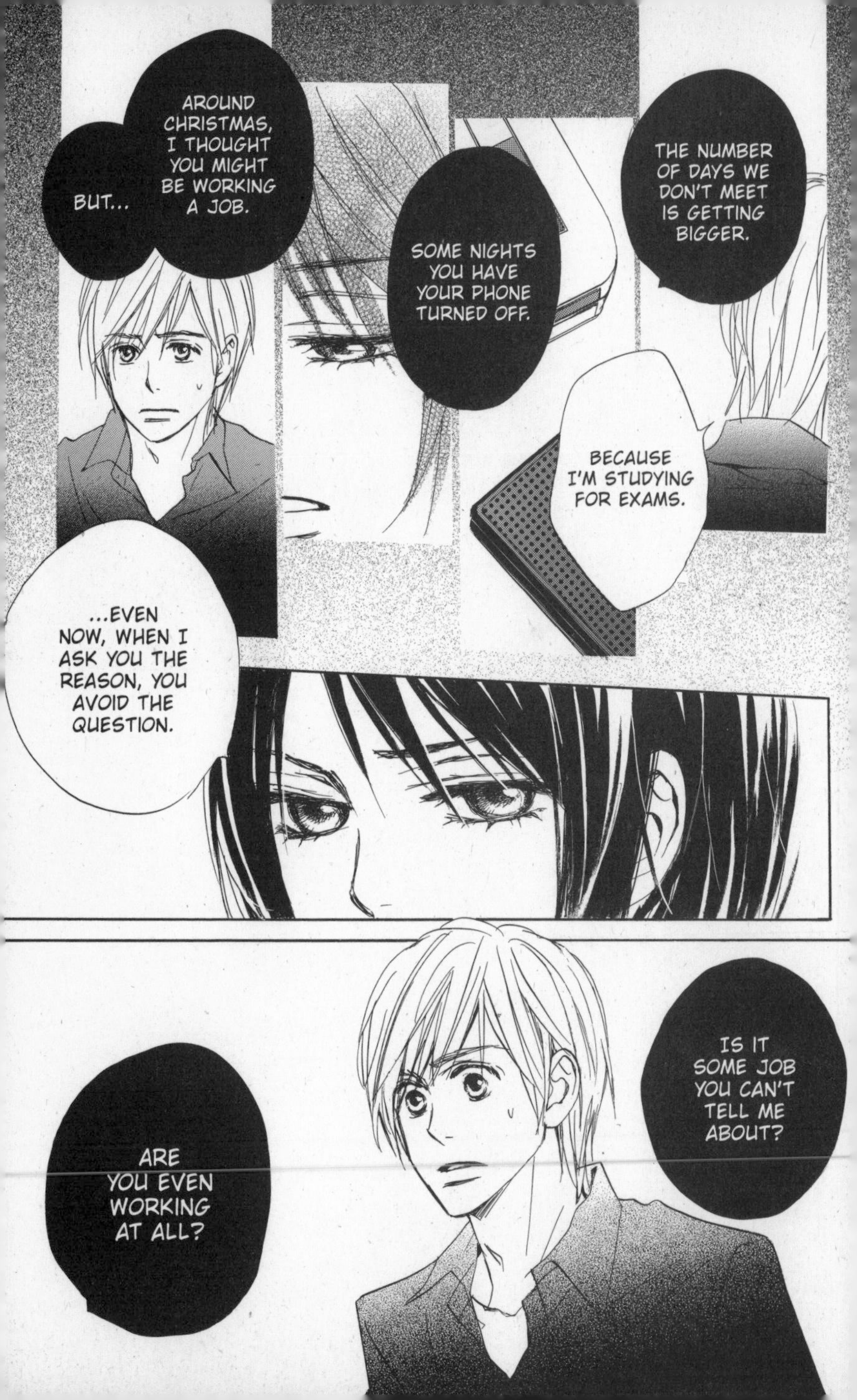
THE NUMBER OF DAYS WE DON'T MEET IS GETTING BIGGER.
BECAUSE I'M STUDYING FOR EXAMS.
SOME NIGHTS YOU HAVE YOUR PHONE TURNED OFF.
AROUND CHRISTMAS, I THOUGHT YOU MIGHT BE WORKING A JOB.
BUT...
...EVEN NOW, WHEN I ASK YOU THE REASON, YOU AVOID THE QUESTION.
IS IT SOME JOB YOU CAN'T TELL ME ABOUT?
ARE YOU EVEN WORKING AT ALL?

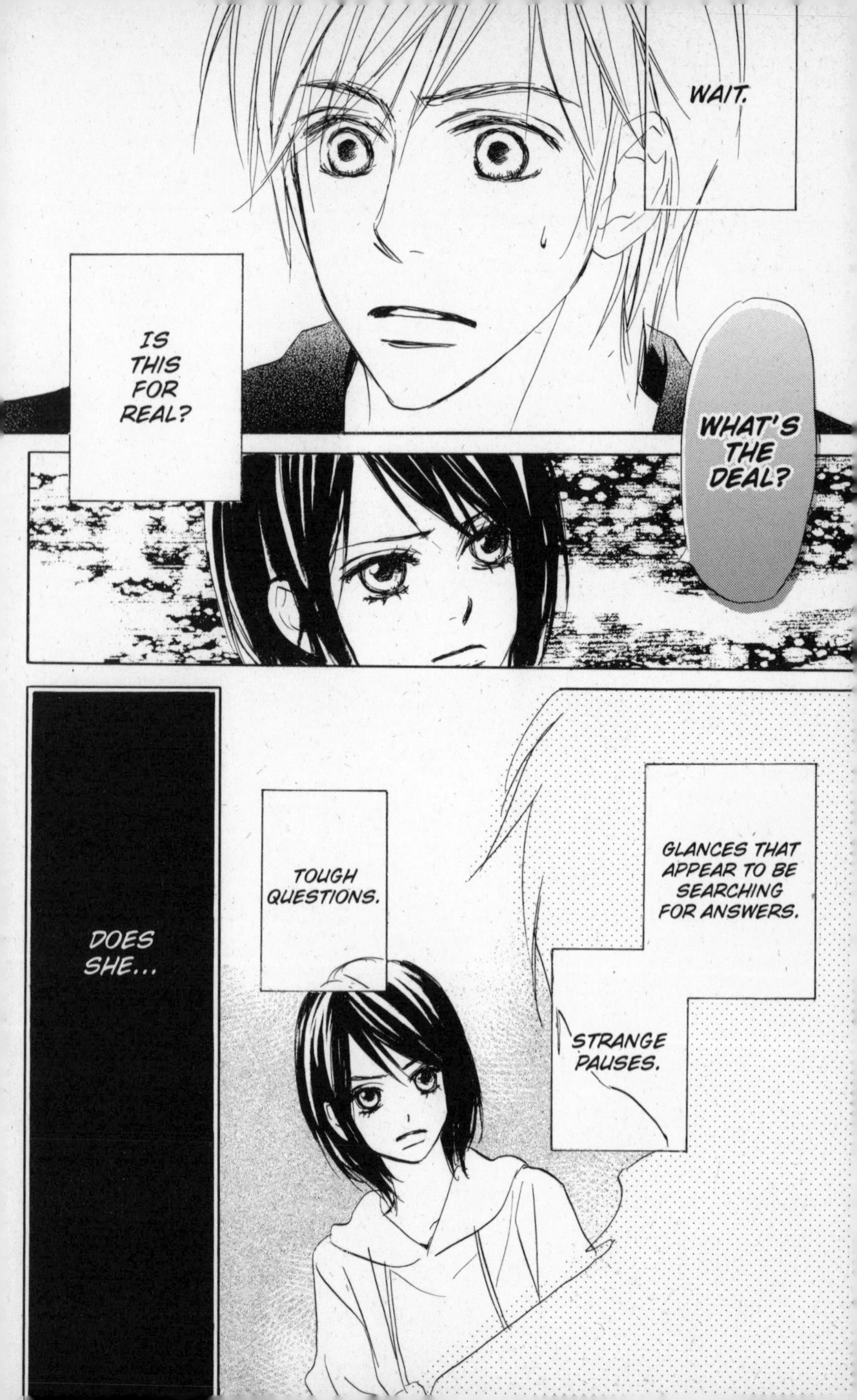
WAIT.
WHAT'S THE DEAL?
IS THIS FOR REAL?
GLANCES THAT APPEAR TO BE SEARCHING FOR ANSWERS.
TOUGH QUESTIONS.
STRANGE PAUSES.
DOES SHE...

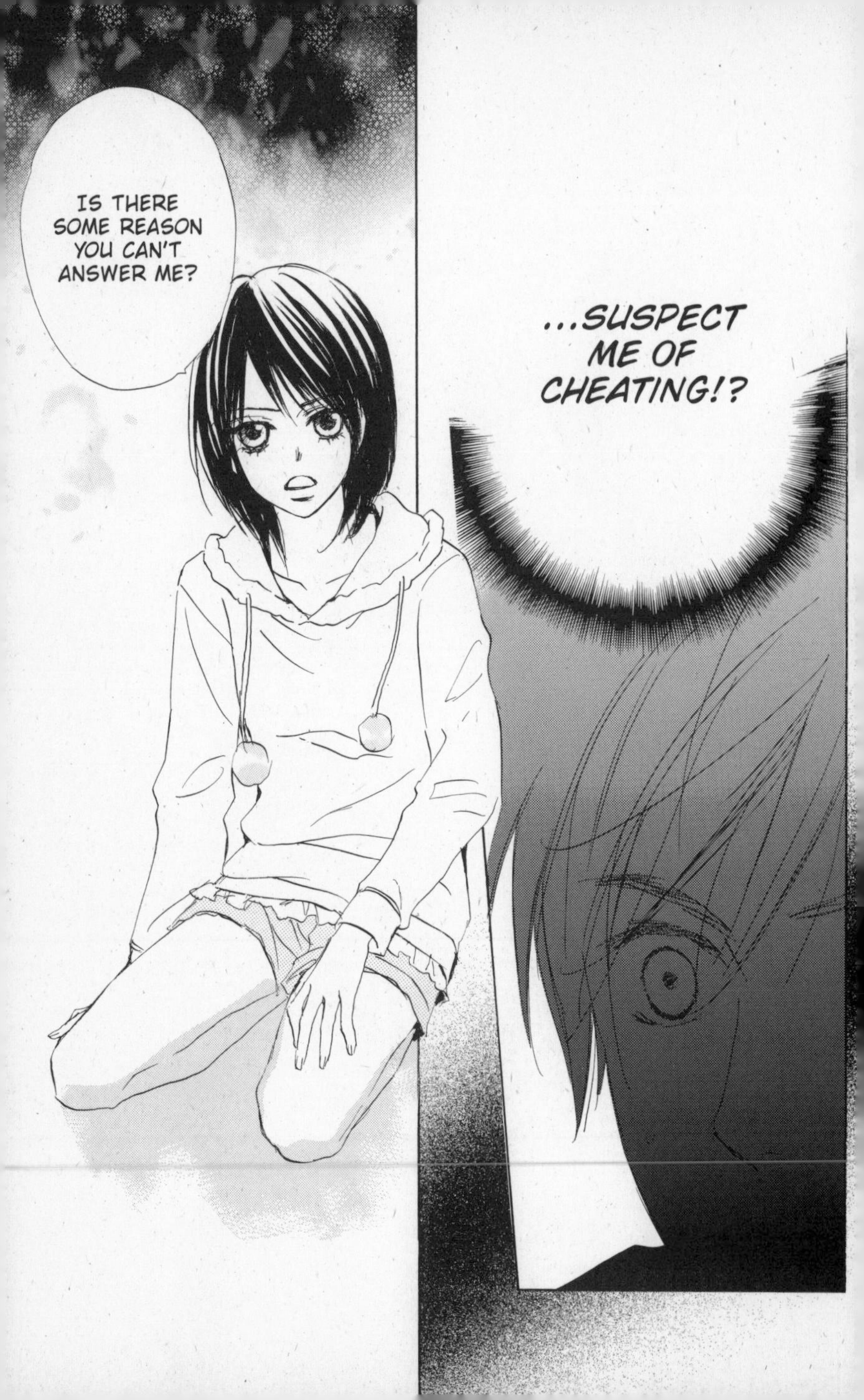
...SUSPECT ME OF CHEATING!?
IS THERE SOME REASON YOU CAN'T ANSWER ME?

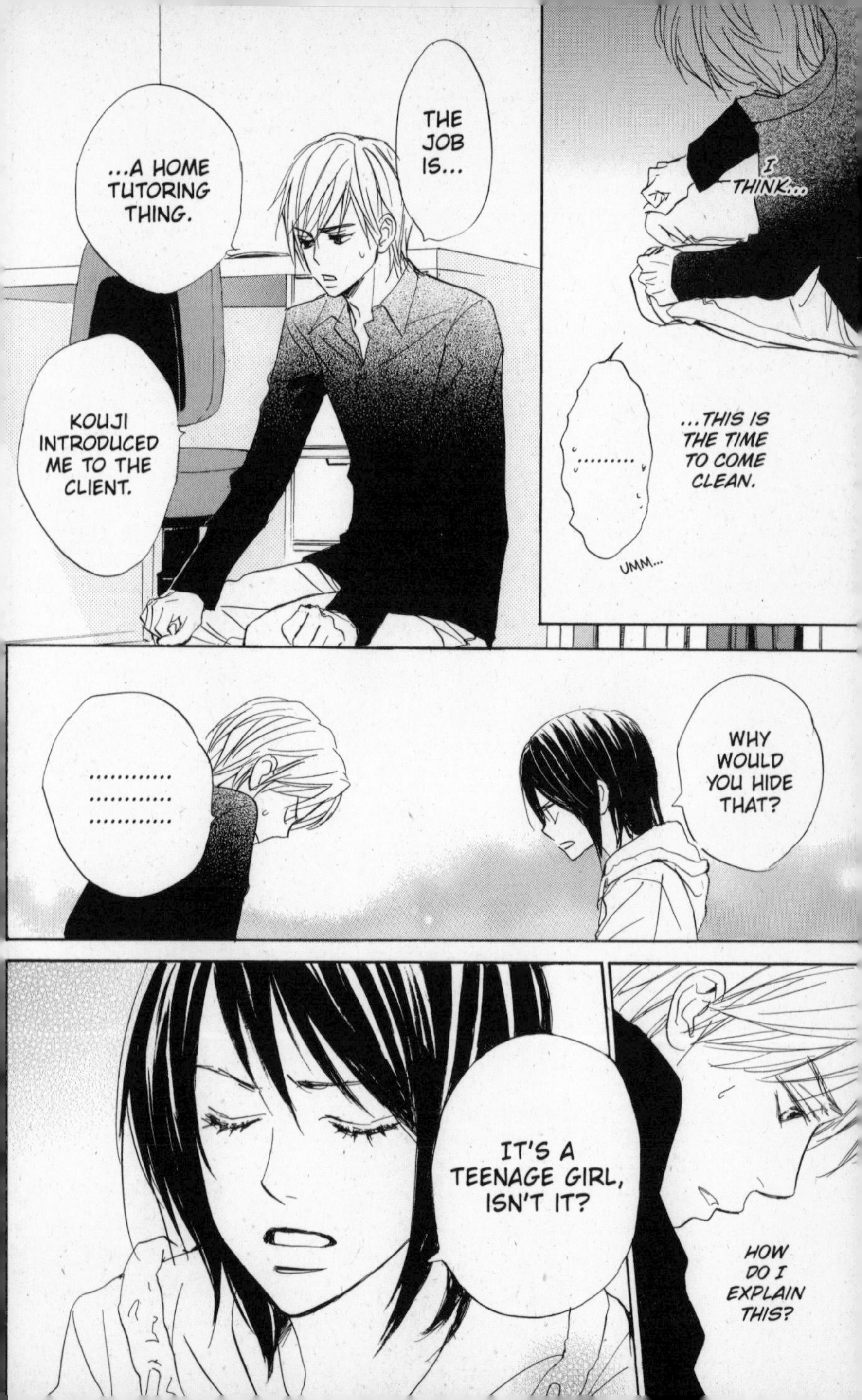
I THINK...
...THIS IS THE TIME TO COME CLEAN.
....
UMM...
THE JOB IS...
...A HOME TUTORING THING.
KOUJI INTRODUCED ME TO THE CLIENT.
WHY WOULD YOU HIDE THAT?
....
HOW DO I EXPLAIN THIS?
IT'S A TEENAGE GIRL, ISN'T IT?

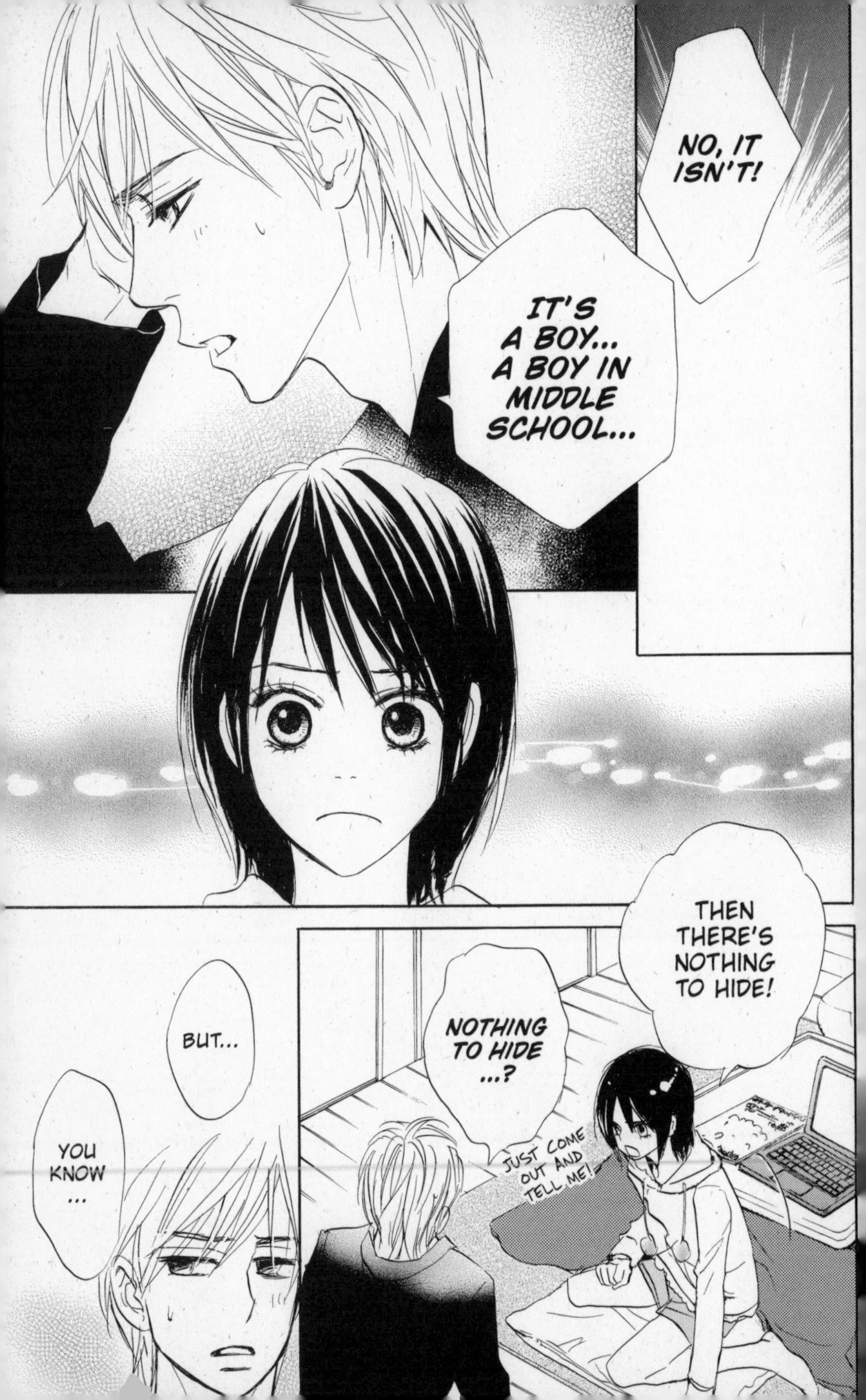
NO, IT ISN'T!
IT'S A BOY... A BOY IN MIDDLE SCHOOL...
THEN THERE'S NOTHING TO HIDE!
JUST COME OUT AND TELL ME!
NOTHING TO HIDE ...?
BUT...
YOU KNOW ...

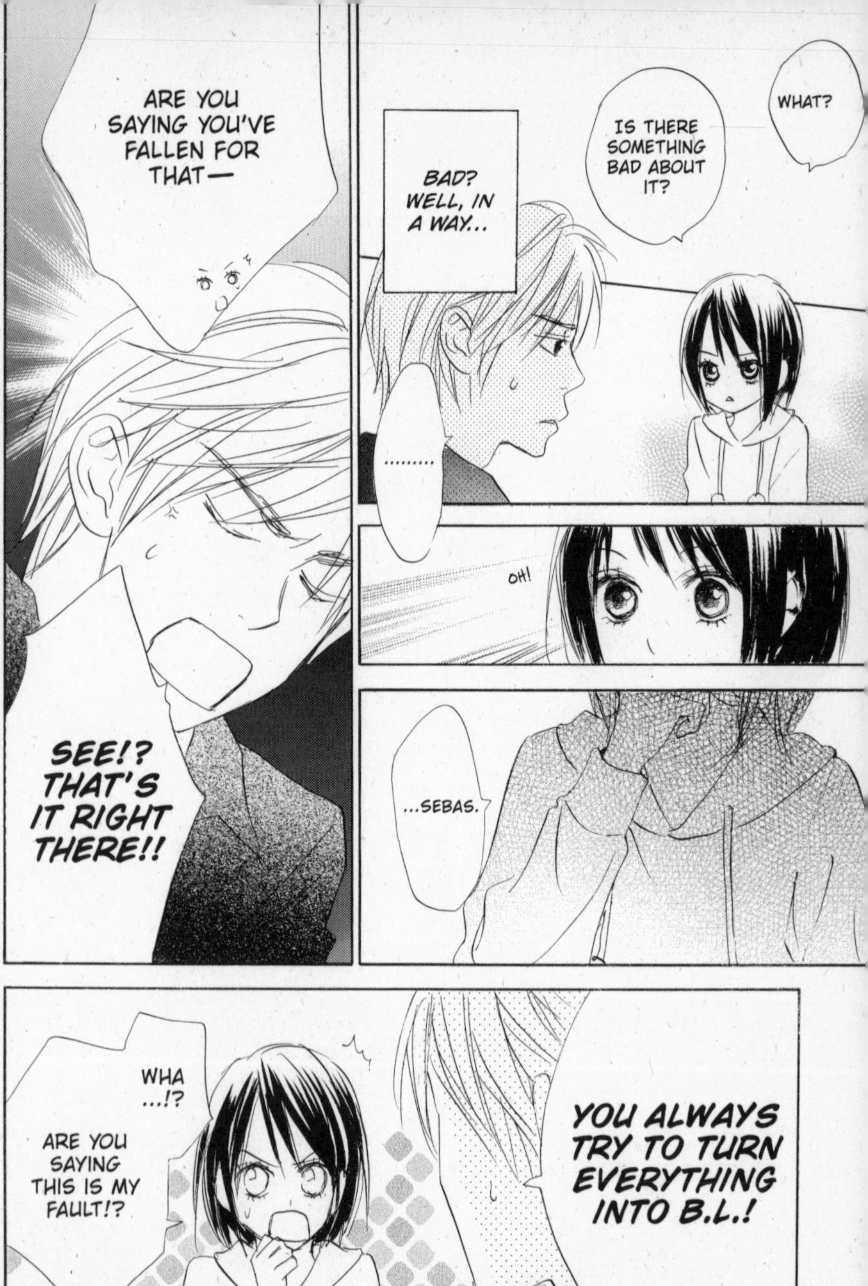
WHAT?
IS THERE SOMETHING BAD ABOUT IT?
BAD? WELL, IN A WAY...
....
OH!
...SEBAS.
ARE YOU SAYING YOU'VE FALLEN FOR THAT—
SEE!? THAT'S IT RIGHT THERE!!
YOU ALWAYS TRY TO TURN EVERYTHING INTO B.L.!
WHA ...!?
ARE YOU SAYING THIS IS MY FAULT!?

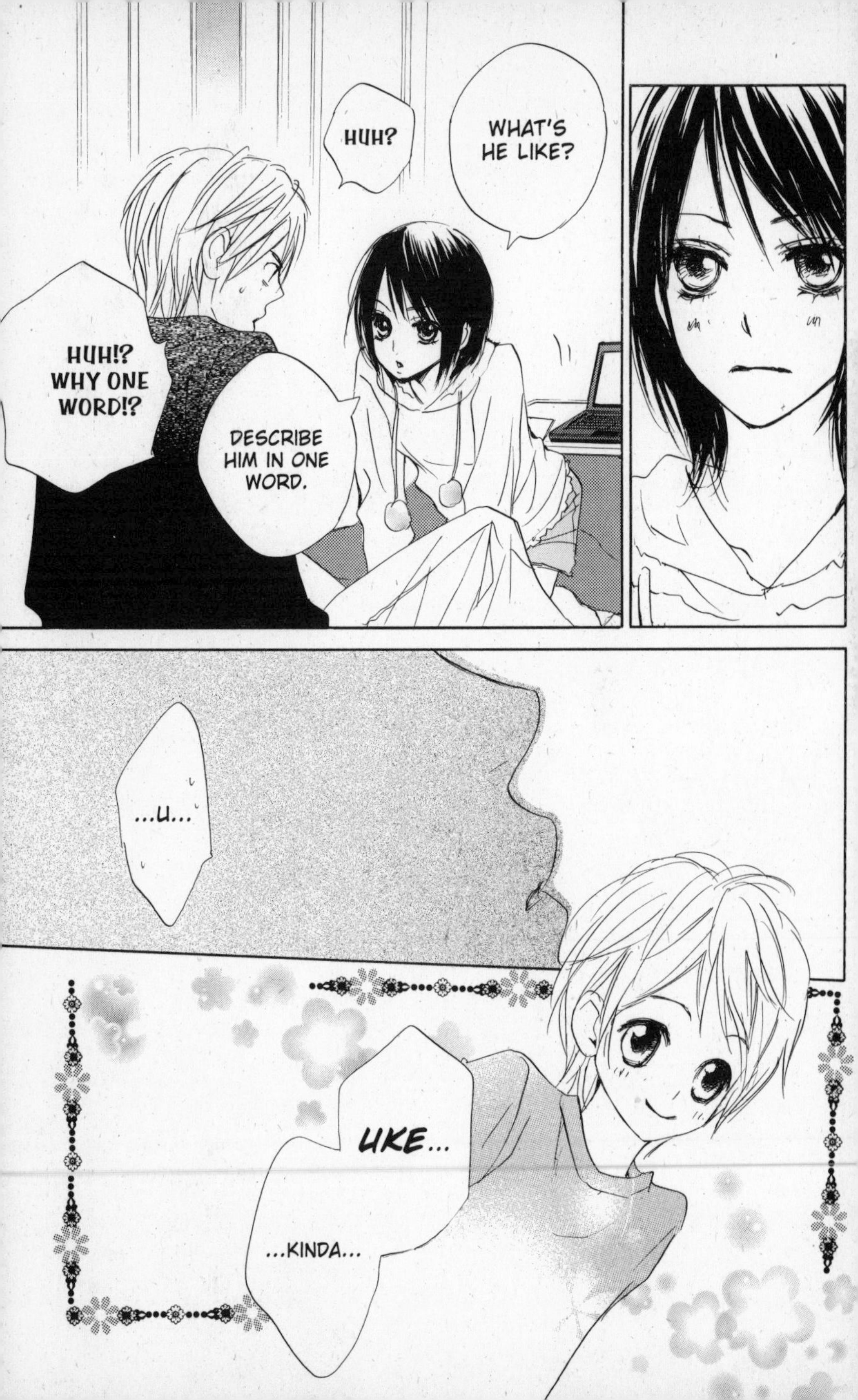
WHAT'S HE LIKE?
HUH?
DESCRIBE HIM IN ONE WORD.
HUH!? WHY ONE WORD!?
...U...
UKE...
...KINDA...

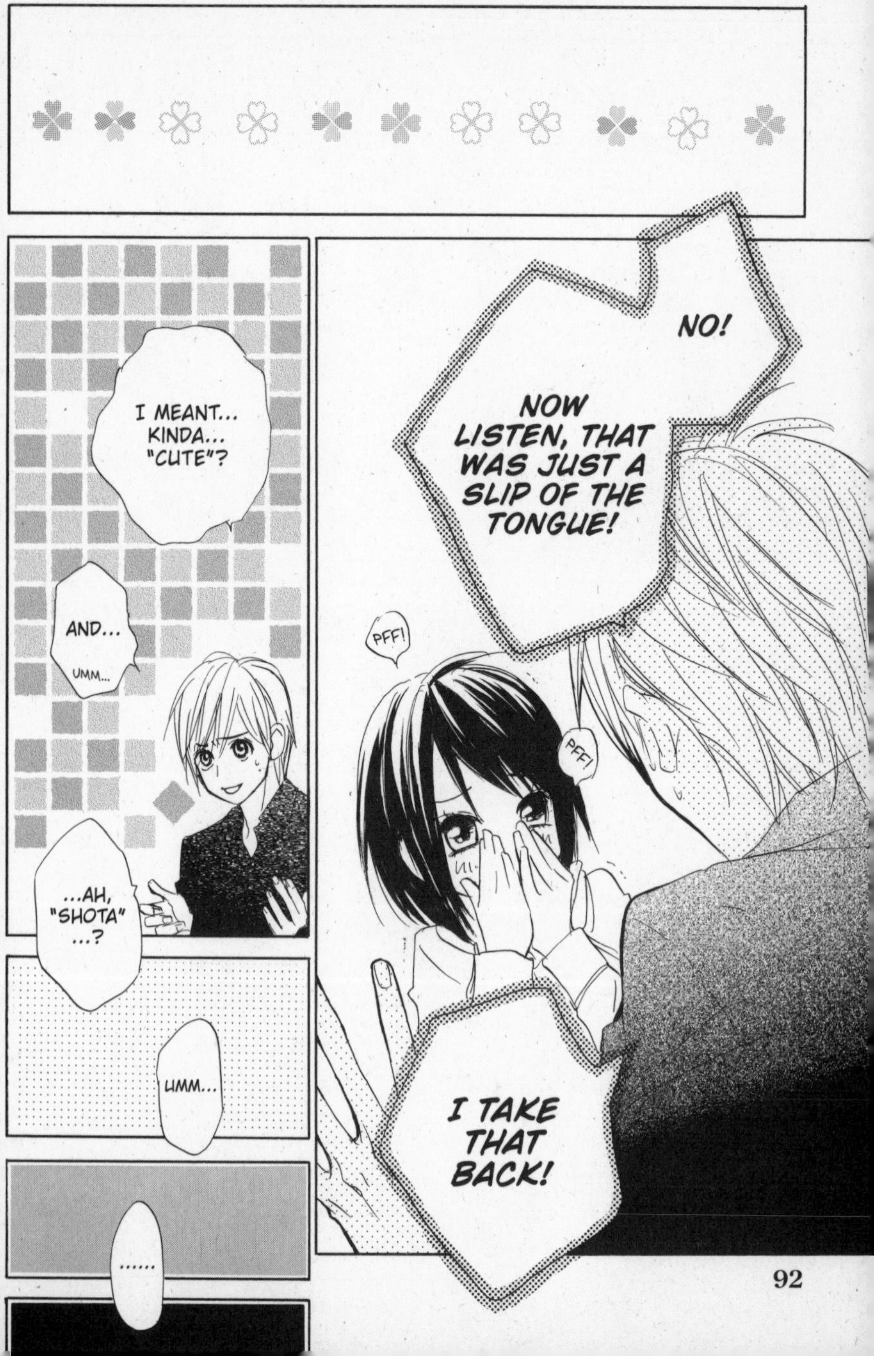
NO!
NOW LISTEN, THAT WAS JUST A SLIP OF THE TONGUE!
PFF!
PFF!
I TAKE THAT BACK!
I MEANT... KINDA... "CUTE"?
AND...
UMM...
...AH, "SHOTA" ...?
UMM...
......

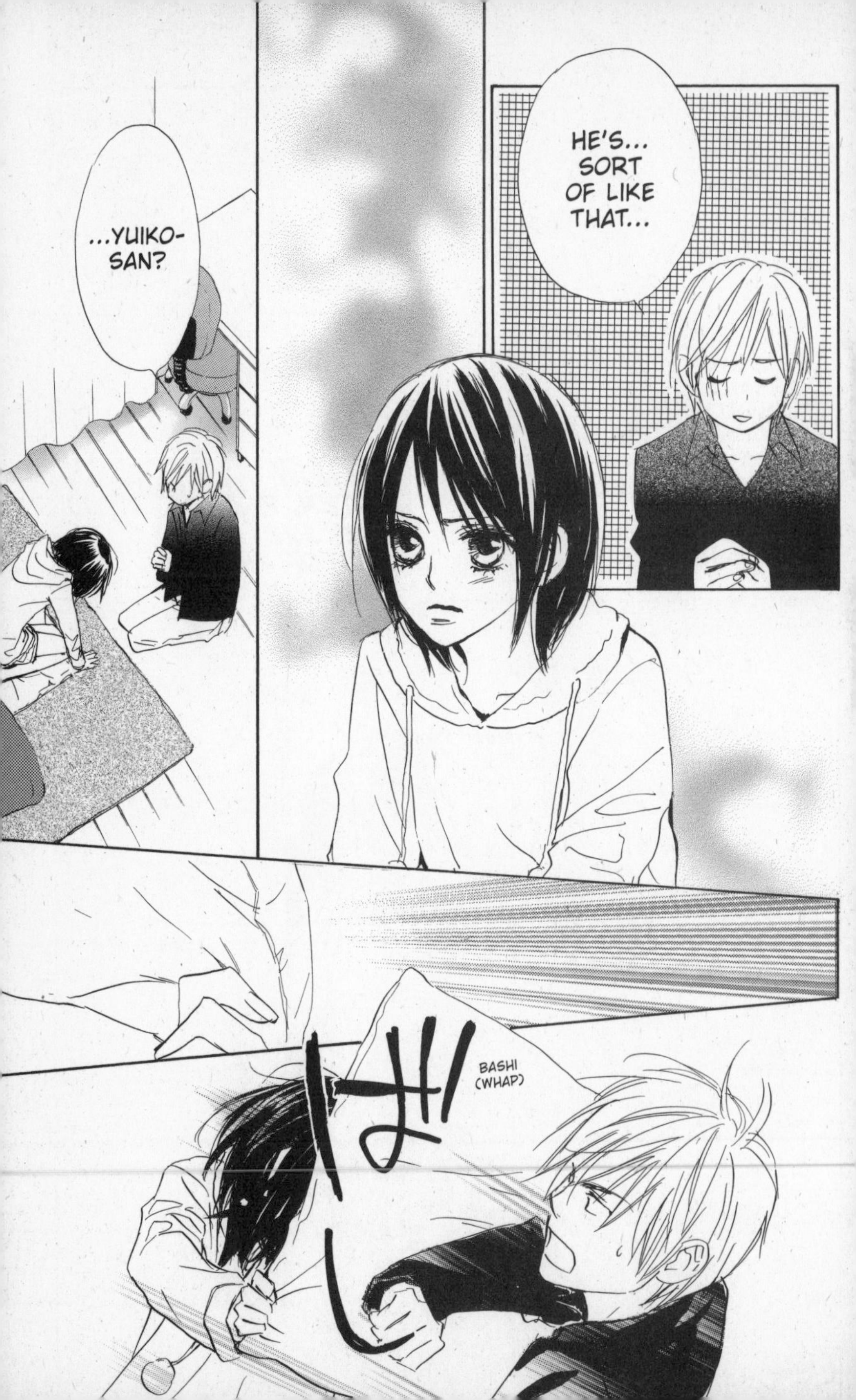
HE'S... SORT OF LIKE THAT...
...YUIKO-SAN?
BASHI (WHAP)

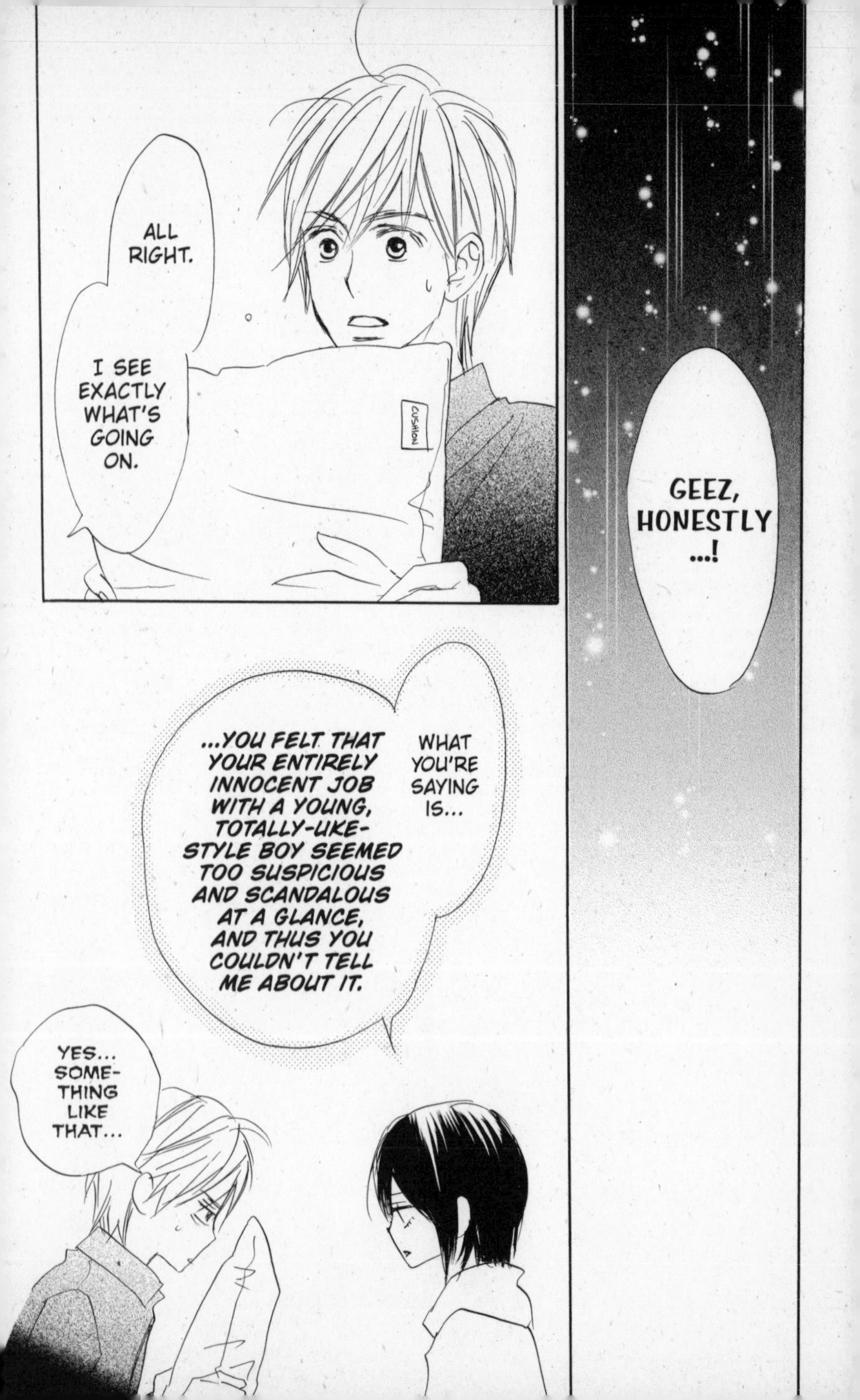
GEEZ, HONESTLY ...!
ALL RIGHT.
I SEE EXACTLY WHAT'S GOING ON.
CUSHION
WHAT YOU'RE SAYING IS...
...YOU FELT THAT YOUR ENTIRELY INNOCENT JOB WITH A YOUNG, TOTALLY-UKE-STYLE BOY SEEMED TOO SUSPICIOUS AND SCANDALOUS AT A GLANCE, AND THUS YOU COULDN'T TELL ME ABOUT IT.
YES... SOME-THING LIKE THAT...

...SO I TRIED NOT TO TELL YOU ABOUT IT.

...I DIDN'T WANT YOU TO HAVE SCANDALOUS FANTASIES ABOUT ME...

TO CORRECT YOUR SUMMATION SLIGHTLY...

OKAY. I SEE.

I'M NOT CHEATING ON YOU.

SORRY.

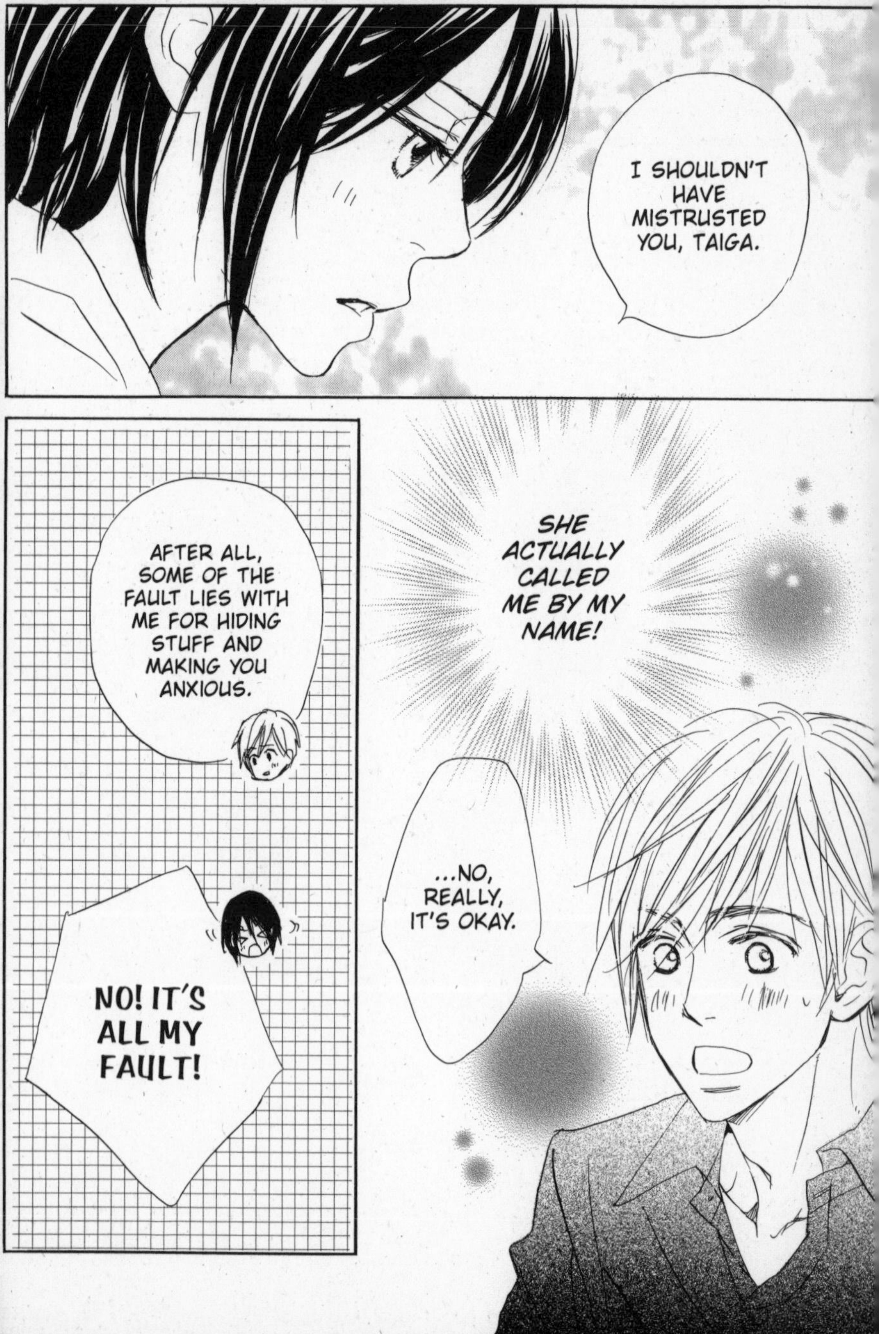
I SHOULDN'T HAVE MISTRUSTED YOU, TAIGA.
SHE ACTUALLY CALLED ME BY MY NAME!
...NO, REALLY, IT'S OKAY.
AFTER ALL, SOME OF THE FAULT LIES WITH ME FOR HIDING STUFF AND MAKING YOU ANXIOUS.
NO! IT'S ALL MY FAULT!

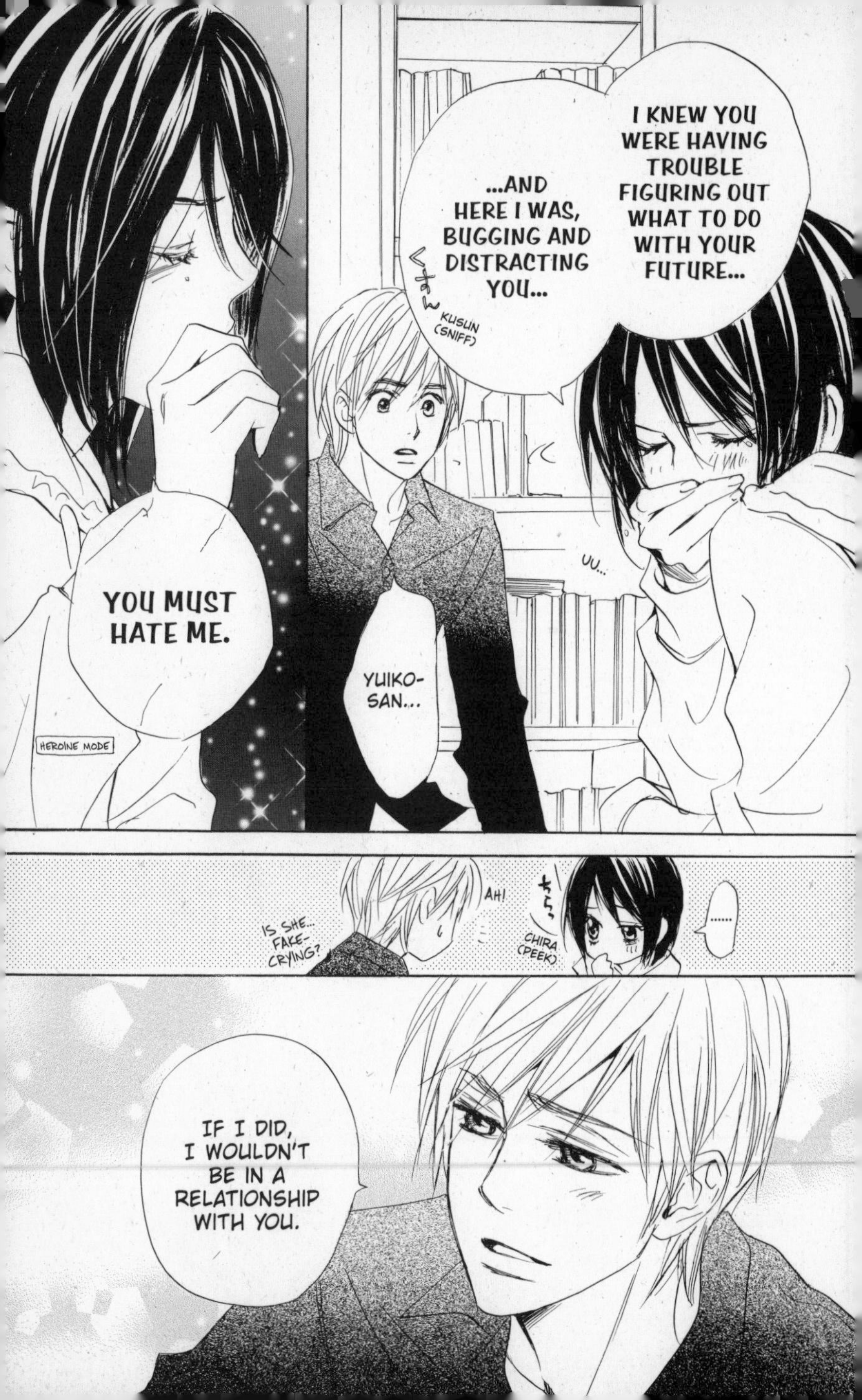
I KNEW YOU WERE HAVING TROUBLE FIGURING OUT WHAT TO DO WITH YOUR FUTURE...
...AND HERE I WAS, BUGGING AND DISTRACTING YOU...
KUSUN (SNIFF)
UU...
YUIKO-SAN...
YOU MUST HATE ME.
HEROINE MODE
......
CHIRA (PEEK)
AH!
IS SHE... FAKE-CRYING?
IF I DID, I WOULDN'T BE IN A RELATIONSHIP WITH YOU.

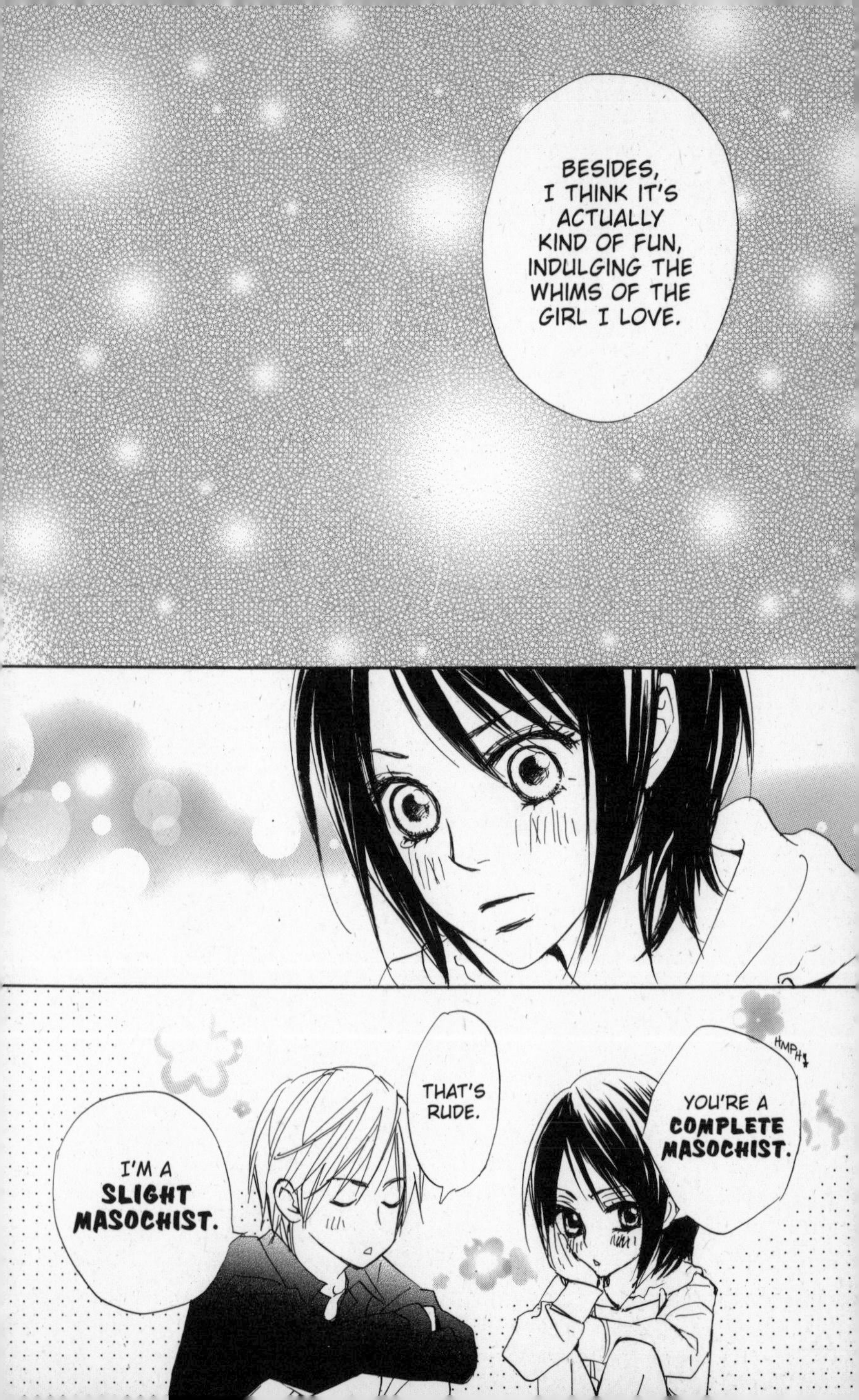
BESIDES, I THINK IT'S ACTUALLY KIND OF FUN, INDULGING THE WHIMS OF THE GIRL I LOVE.
HMPH!
YOU'RE A COMPLETE MASOCHIST.
THAT'S RUDE.
I'M A SLIGHT MASOCHIST.

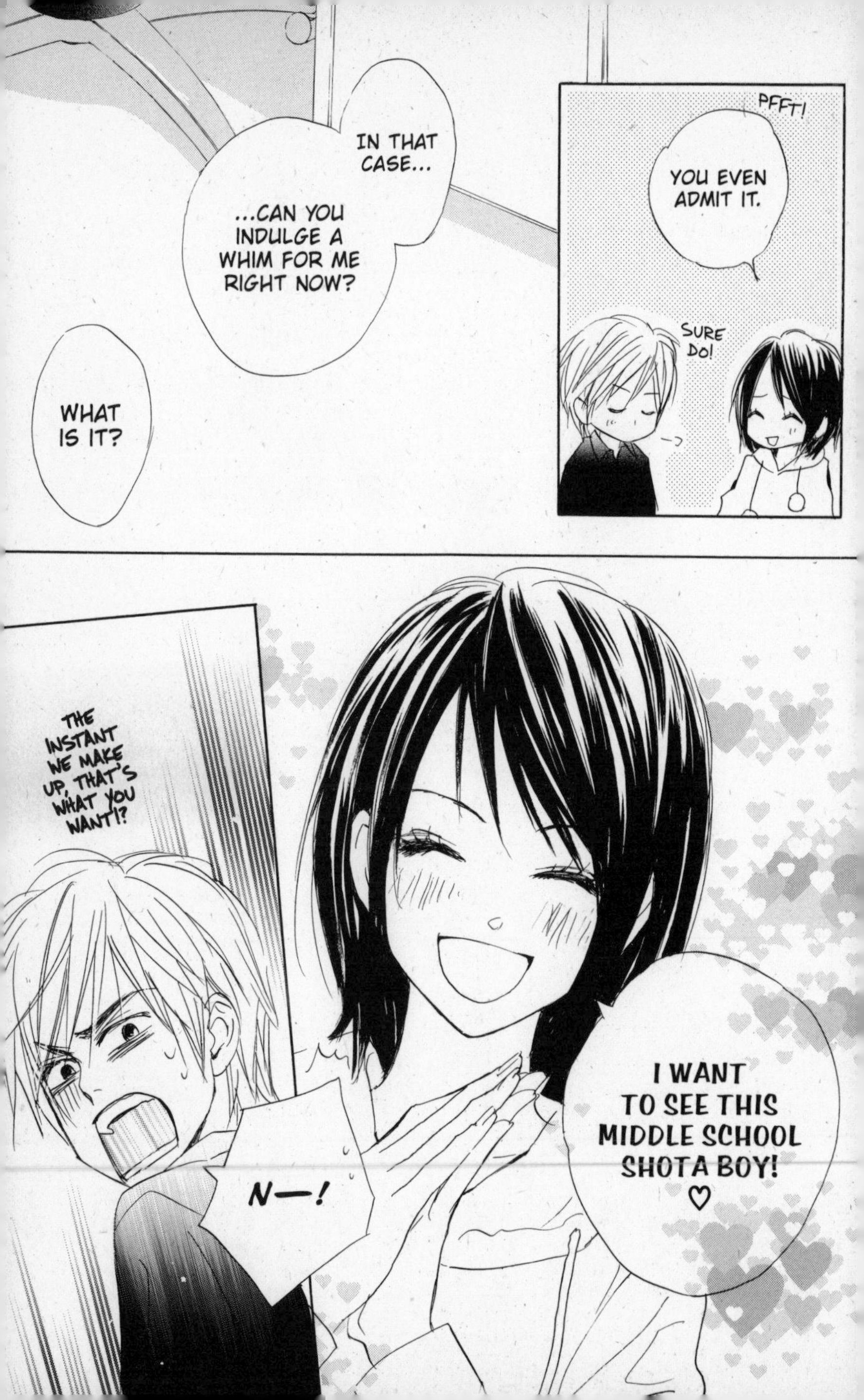
PFFT!
YOU EVEN ADMIT IT.
SURE DO!
IN THAT CASE...
...CAN YOU INDULGE A WHIM FOR ME RIGHT NOW?
WHAT IS IT?
I WANT TO SEE THIS MIDDLE SCHOOL SHOTA BOY! ♡
N—!
THE INSTANT WE MAKE UP, THAT'S WHAT YOU WANT!?

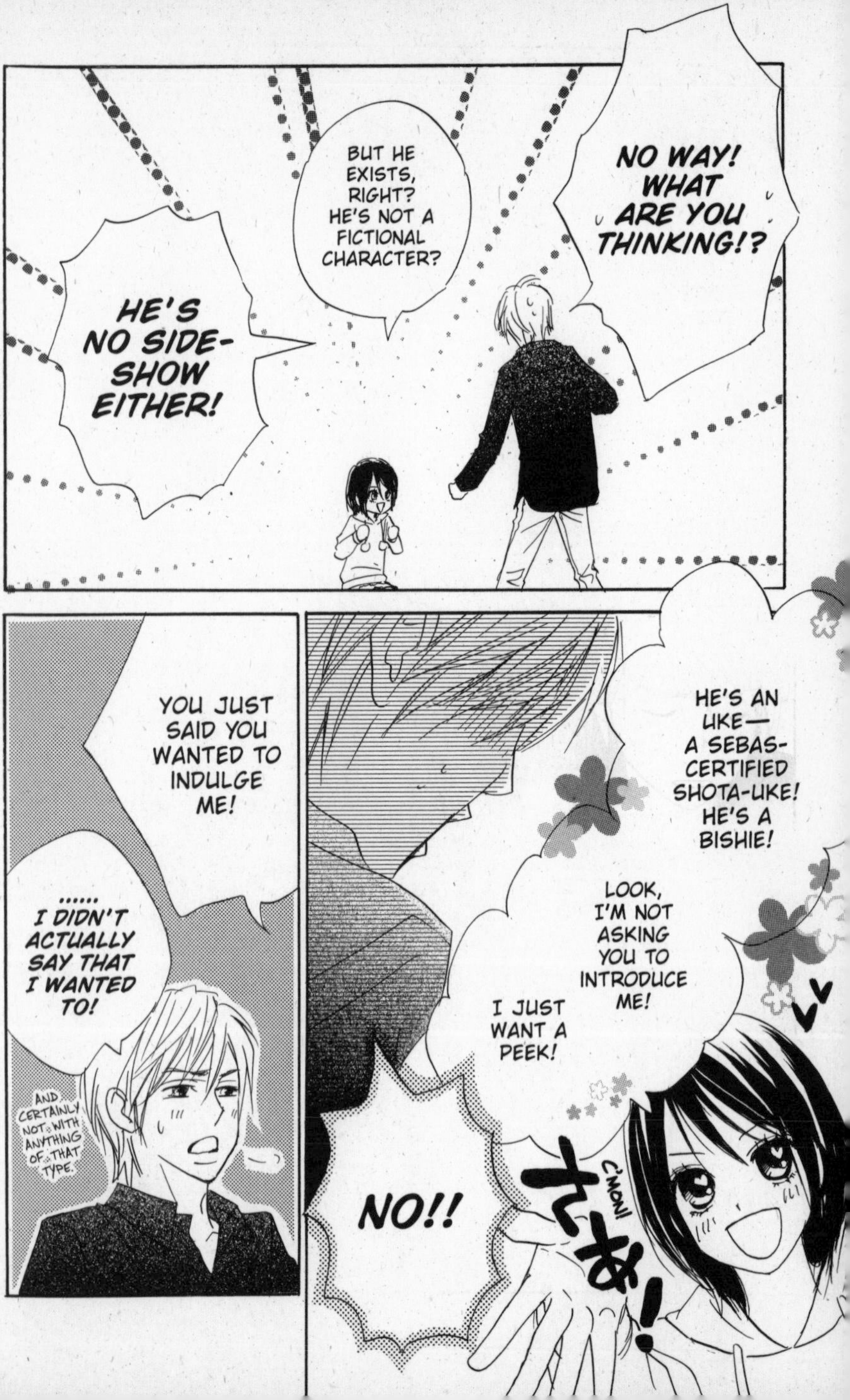

NO WAY! WHAT ARE YOU THINKING!?
BUT HE EXISTS, RIGHT? HE'S NOT A FICTIONAL CHARACTER?
HE'S NO SIDE-SHOW EITHER!
HE'S AN UKE— A SEBAS-CERTIFIED SHOTA-UKE! HE'S A BISHIE!
LOOK, I'M NOT ASKING YOU TO INTRODUCE ME!
I JUST WANT A PEEK!
さあ!
C'MON!
NO!!
YOU JUST SAID YOU WANTED TO INDULGE ME!
...... I DIDN'T ACTUALLY SAY THAT I WANTED TO!
AND CERTAINLY NOT WITH ANYTHING OF THAT TYPE.

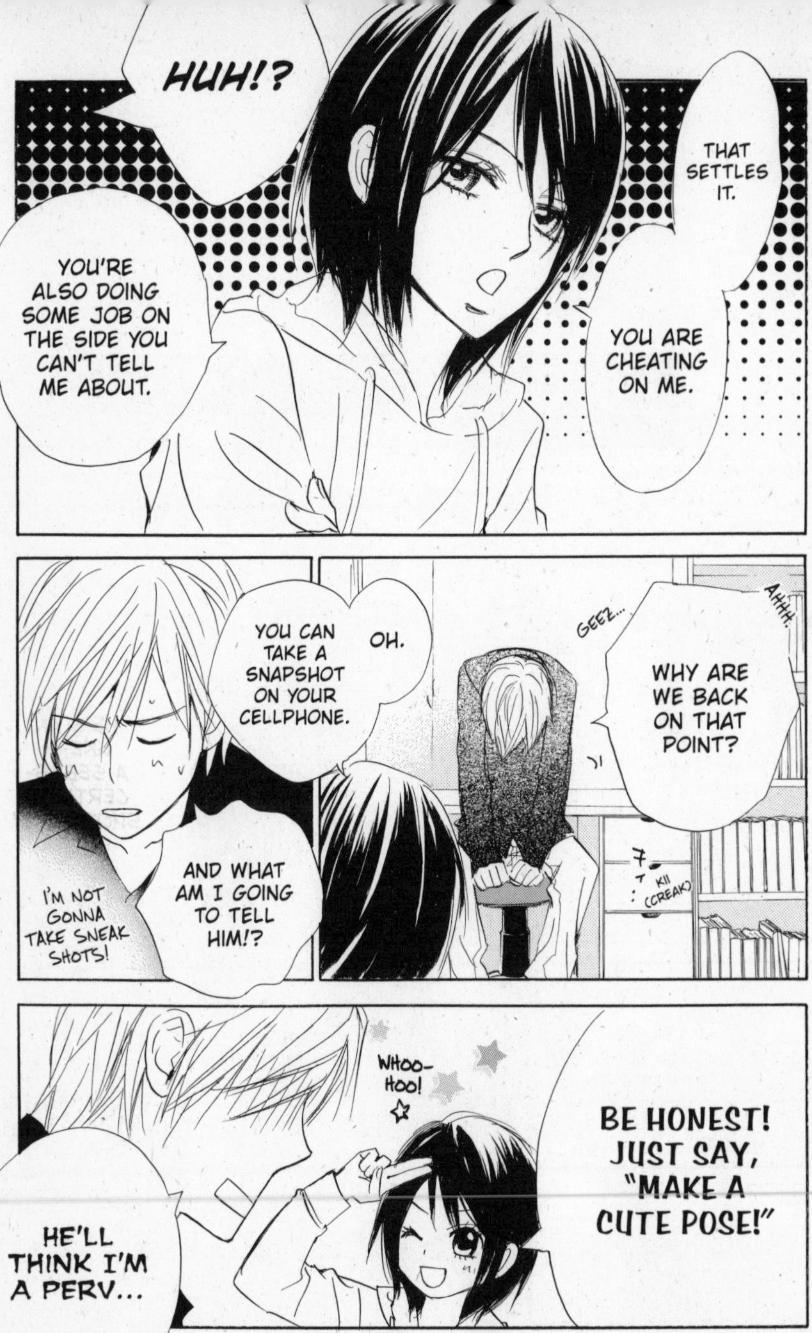
THAT SETTLES IT.
HUH!?
YOU ARE CHEATING ON ME.
YOU'RE ALSO DOING SOME JOB ON THE SIDE YOU CAN'T TELL ME ABOUT.
AHHH.
GEEZ...
WHY ARE WE BACK ON THAT POINT?
KII (CREAK)
OH.
YOU CAN TAKE A SNAPSHOT ON YOUR CELLPHONE.
AND WHAT AM I GOING TO TELL HIM!?
I'M NOT GONNA TAKE SNEAK SHOTS!
BE HONEST! JUST SAY, "MAKE A CUTE POSE!"
WHOO-HOO!
HE'LL THINK I'M A PERV...

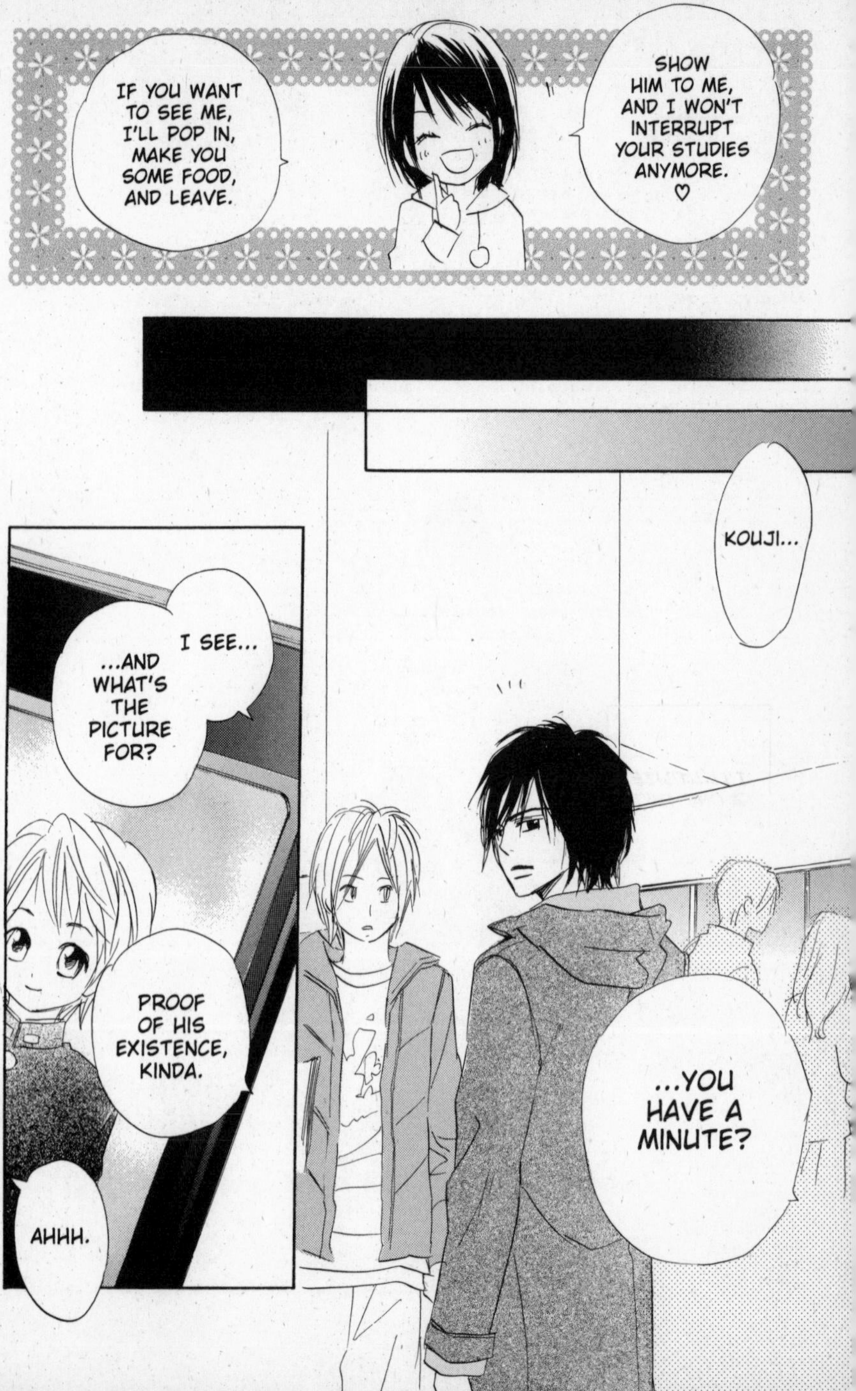
SHOW HIM TO ME, AND I WON'T INTERRUPT YOUR STUDIES ANYMORE. ♡
IF YOU WANT TO SEE ME, I'LL POP IN, MAKE YOU SOME FOOD, AND LEAVE.
I SEE...
...AND WHAT'S THE PICTURE FOR?
PROOF OF HIS EXISTENCE, KINDA.
AHHH.
KOUJI...
...YOU HAVE A MINUTE?

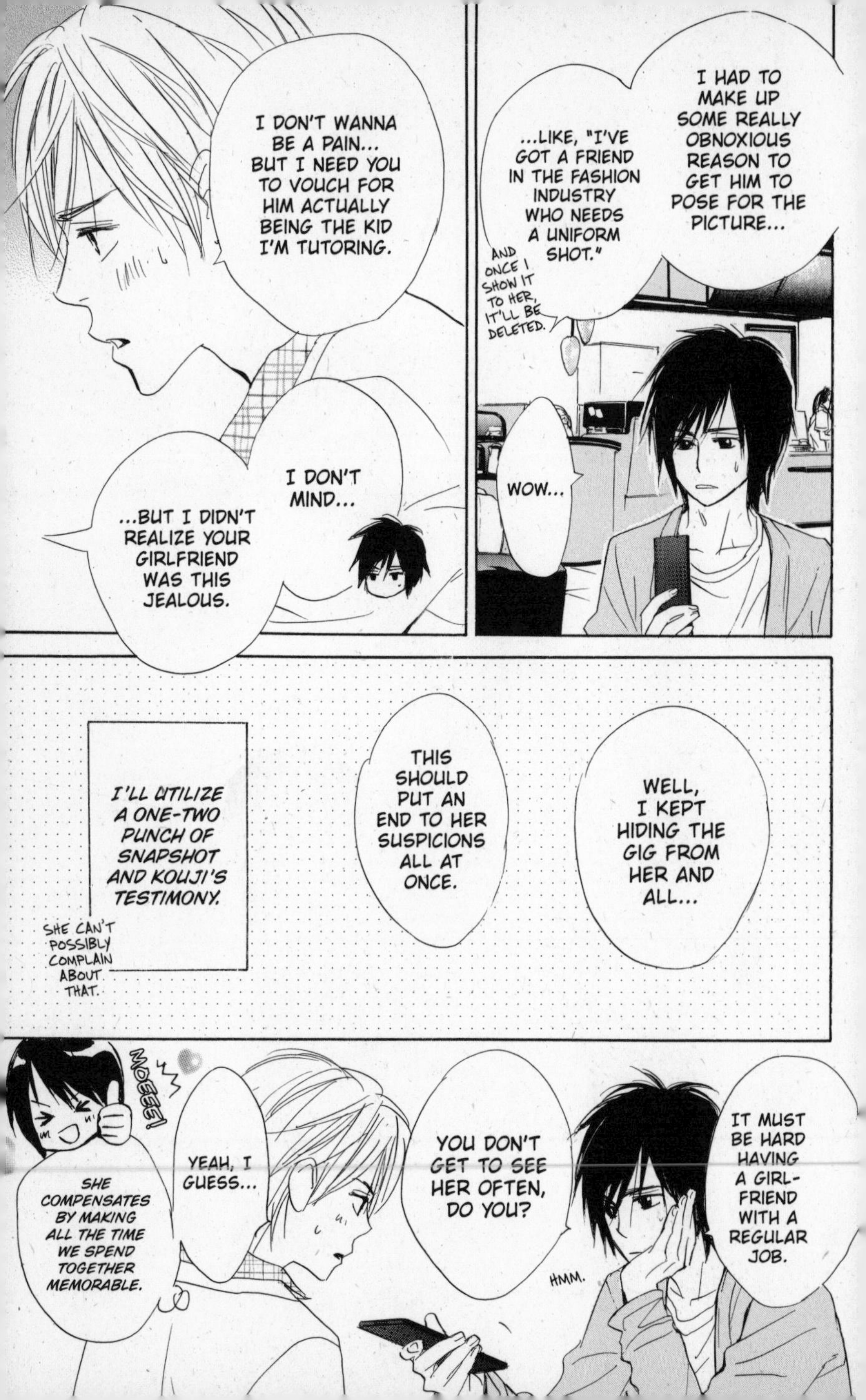
I HAD TO MAKE UP SOME REALLY OBNOXIOUS REASON TO GET HIM TO POSE FOR THE PICTURE...
...LIKE, "I'VE GOT A FRIEND IN THE FASHION INDUSTRY WHO NEEDS A UNIFORM SHOT."
AND ONCE I SHOW IT TO HER, IT'LL BE DELETED.
WOW...
I DON'T WANNA BE A PAIN... BUT I NEED YOU TO VOUCH FOR HIM ACTUALLY BEING THE KID I'M TUTORING.
I DON'T MIND...
...BUT I DIDN'T REALIZE YOUR GIRLFRIEND WAS THIS JEALOUS.
WELL, I KEPT HIDING THE GIG FROM HER AND ALL...
THIS SHOULD PUT AN END TO HER SUSPICIONS ALL AT ONCE.
I'LL UTILIZE A ONE-TWO PUNCH OF SNAPSHOT AND KOUJI'S TESTIMONY.
SHE CAN'T POSSIBLY COMPLAIN ABOUT THAT.
IT MUST BE HARD HAVING A GIRL-FRIEND WITH A REGULAR JOB.
HMM.
YOU DON'T GET TO SEE HER OFTEN, DO YOU?
YEAH, I GUESS...
MOEEE!
SHE COMPENSATES BY MAKING ALL THE TIME WE SPEND TOGETHER MEMORABLE.

SURE ENOUGH, THAT'S A BOY.

WELL, THERE IT IS.

WOW, IN A UNIFORM AND ALL!

SEE?

NO, IT'S COOL. YOU UNDERSTAND NOW, AND THAT'S WHAT MATTERS.

I'M SORRY, TAIGA.

I JUST COULDN'T FIND IT IN MY HEART TO UNDERSTAND AT THE TIME.

ACTING LIKE A NORMAL O.L.

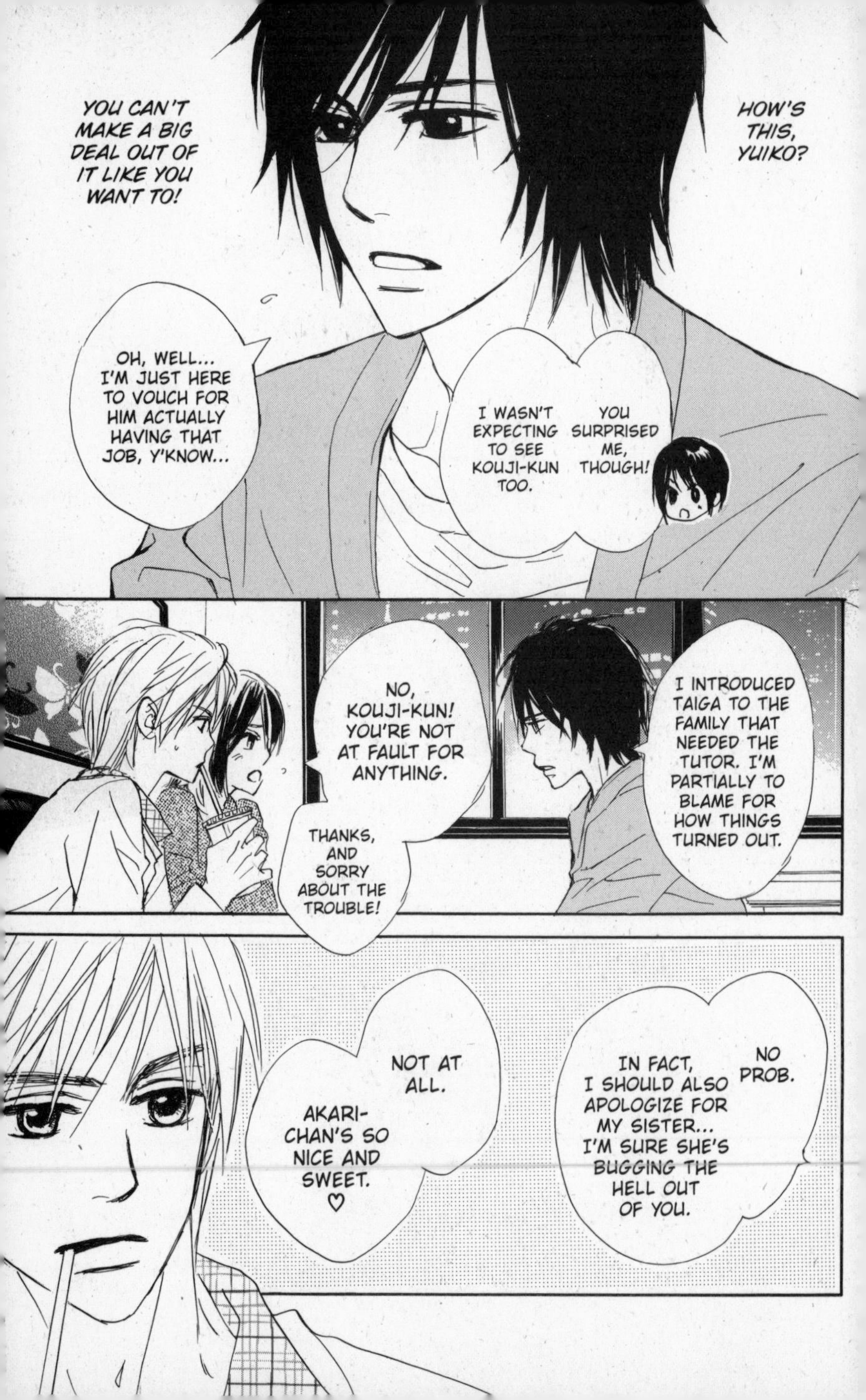
HOW'S THIS, YUIKO?
YOU CAN'T MAKE A BIG DEAL OUT OF IT LIKE YOU WANT TO!
YOU SURPRISED ME, THOUGH! I WASN'T EXPECTING TO SEE KOUJI-KUN TOO.
OH, WELL... I'M JUST HERE TO VOUCH FOR HIM ACTUALLY HAVING THAT JOB, Y'KNOW...
I INTRODUCED TAIGA TO THE FAMILY THAT NEEDED THE TUTOR. I'M PARTIALLY TO BLAME FOR HOW THINGS TURNED OUT.
NO, KOUJI-KUN! YOU'RE NOT AT FAULT FOR ANYTHING.
THANKS, AND SORRY ABOUT THE TROUBLE!
NO PROB. IN FACT, I SHOULD ALSO APOLOGIZE FOR MY SISTER... I'M SURE SHE'S BUGGING THE HELL OUT OF YOU.
NOT AT ALL. AKARI-CHAN'S SO NICE AND SWEET. ♡

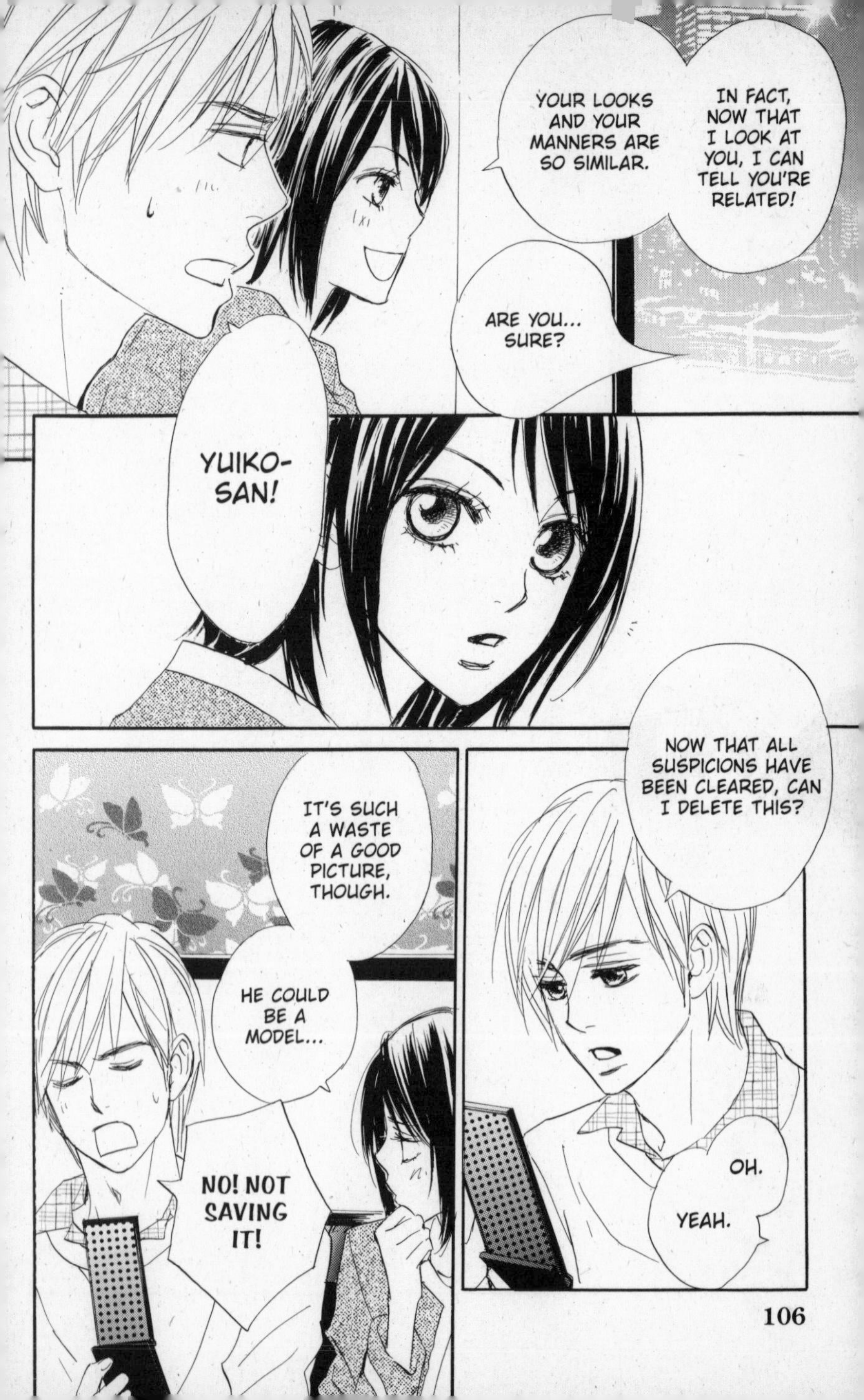
IN FACT, NOW THAT I LOOK AT YOU, I CAN TELL YOU'RE RELATED!
YOUR LOOKS AND YOUR MANNERS ARE SO SIMILAR.
ARE YOU... SURE?
YUIKO-SAN!
NOW THAT ALL SUSPICIONS HAVE BEEN CLEARED, CAN I DELETE THIS?
OH.
YEAH.
IT'S SUCH A WASTE OF A GOOD PICTURE, THOUGH.
HE COULD BE A MODEL...
NO! NOT SAVING IT!

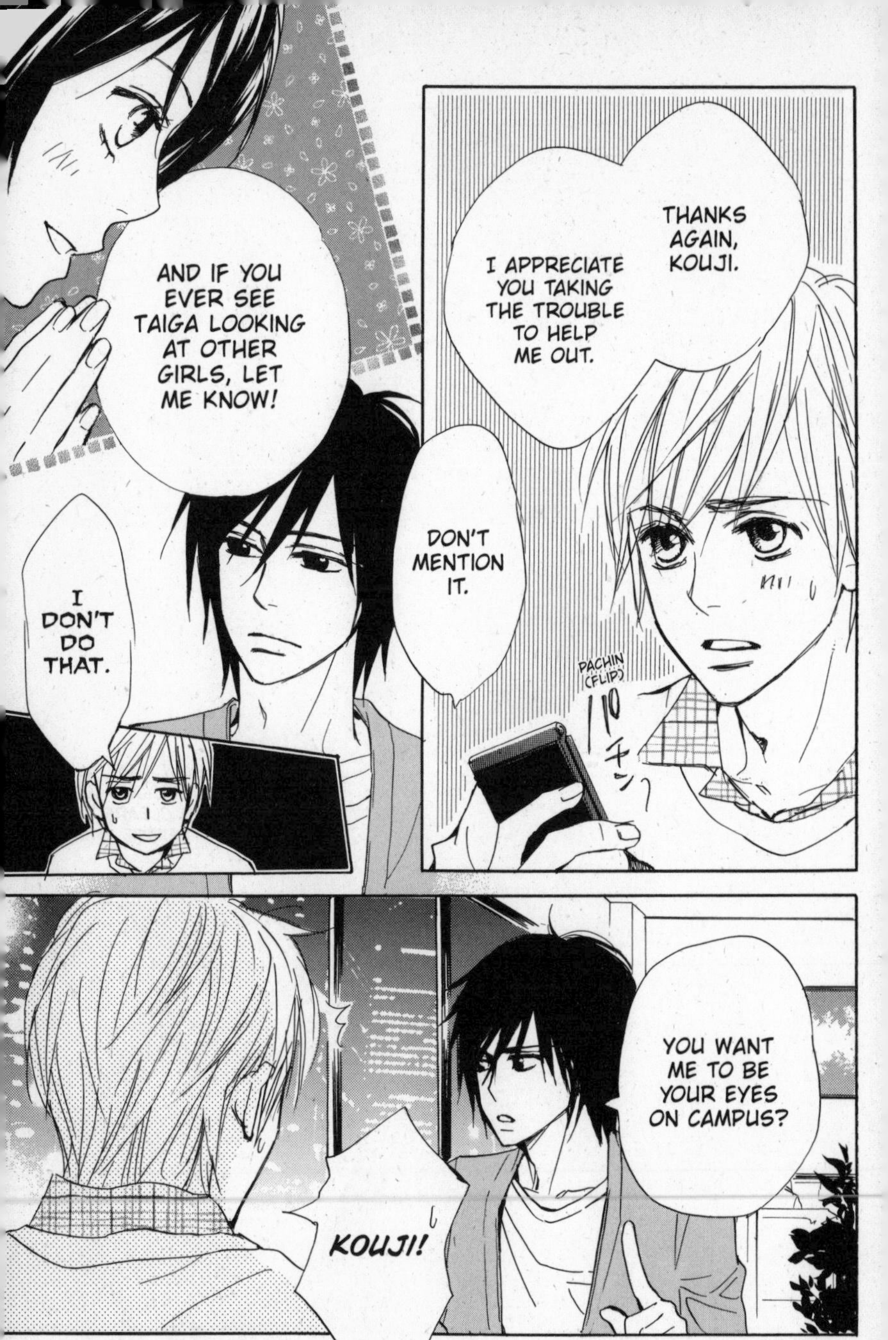
THANKS AGAIN, KOUJI.
I APPRECIATE YOU TAKING THE TROUBLE TO HELP ME OUT.
DON'T MENTION IT.
PACHIN (FLIP)
AND IF YOU EVER SEE TAIGA LOOKING AT OTHER GIRLS, LET ME KNOW!
I DON'T DO THAT.
YOU WANT ME TO BE YOUR EYES ON CAMPUS?
KOUJI!

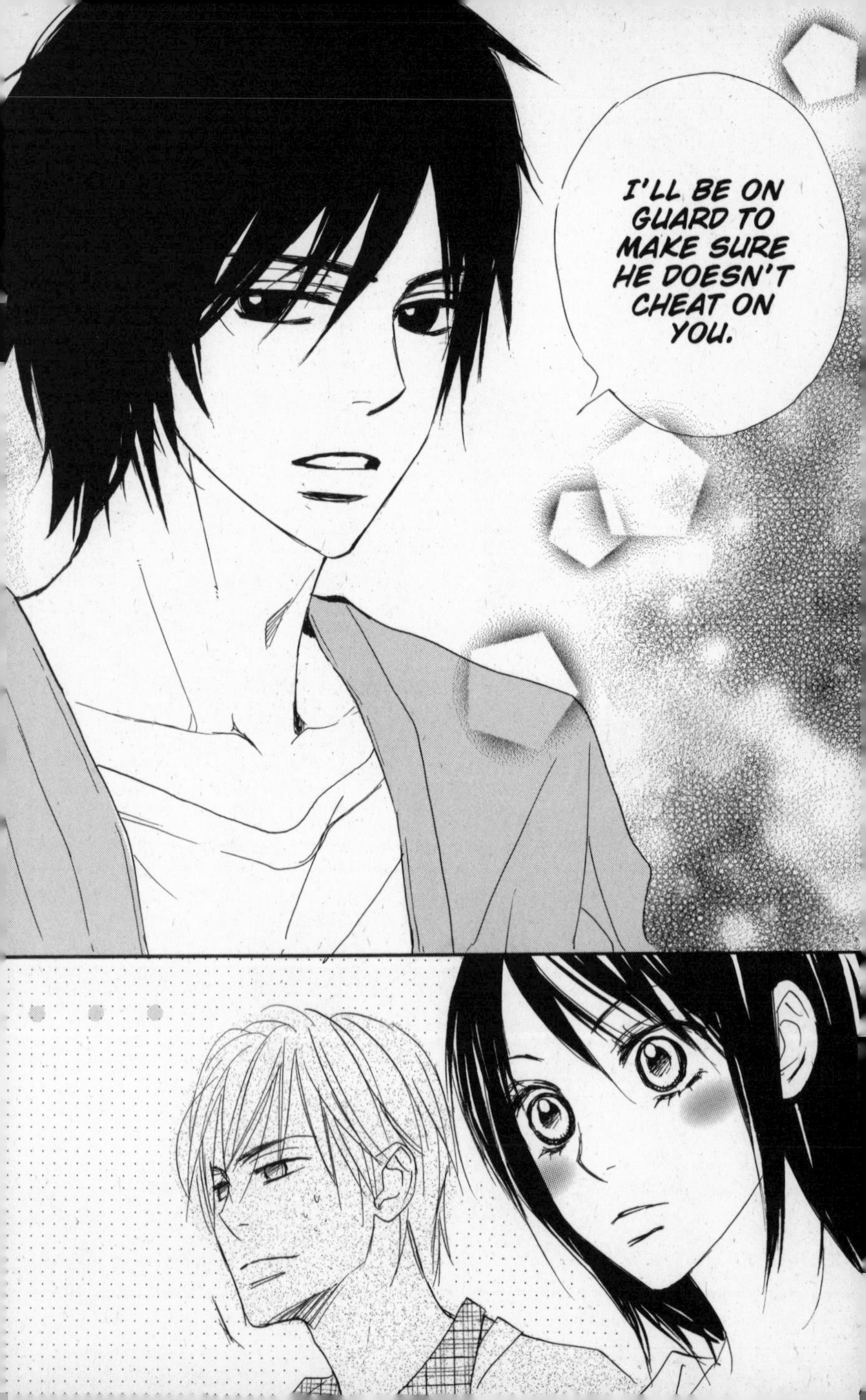
I'LL BE ON GUARD TO MAKE SURE HE DOESN'T CHEAT ON YOU.

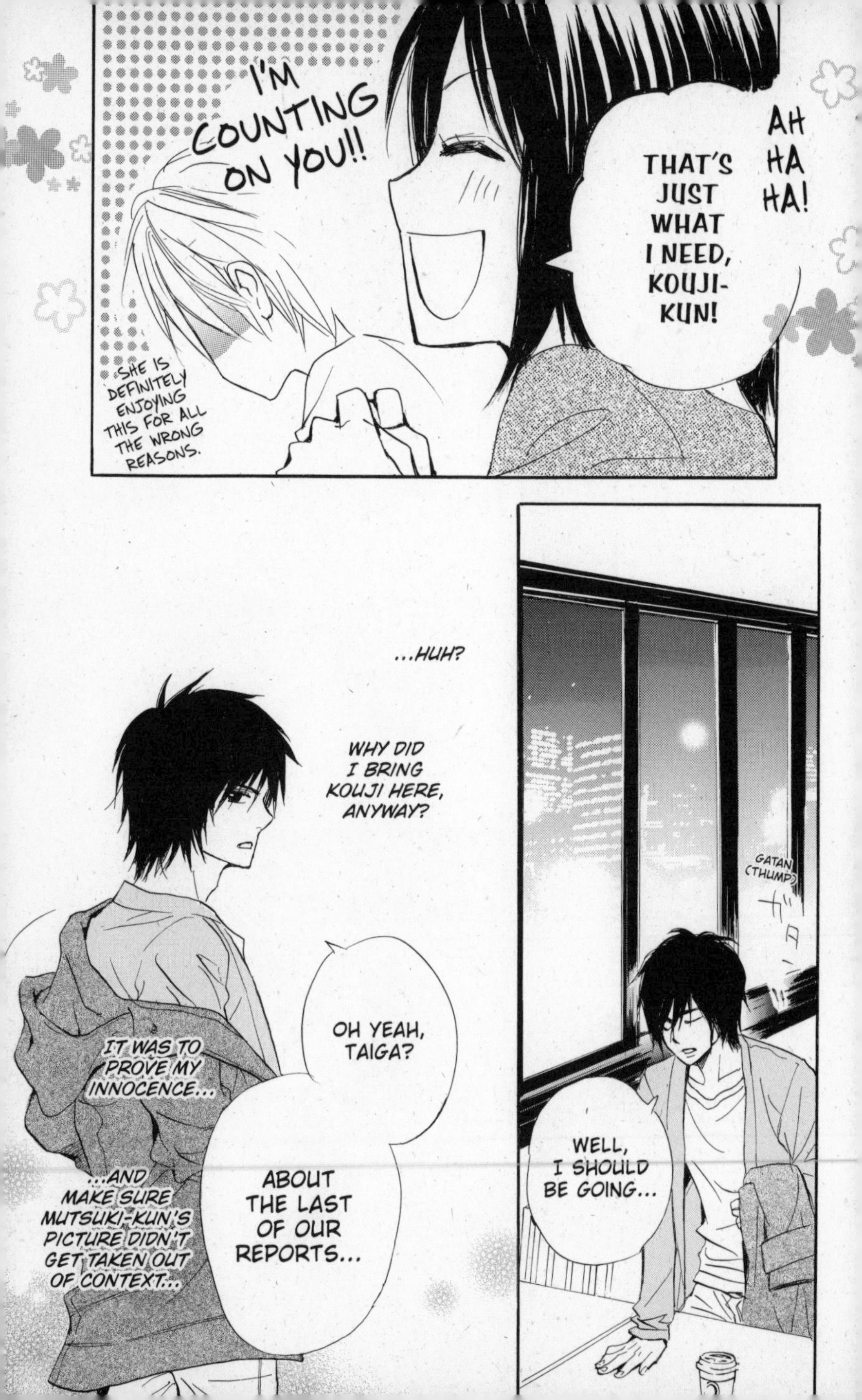
AH HA HA!
THAT'S JUST WHAT I NEED, KOUJI-KUN!
I'M COUNTING ON YOU!!
SHE IS DEFINITELY ENJOYING THIS FOR ALL THE WRONG REASONS.
GATAN (THUMP)
WELL, I SHOULD BE GOING...
...HUH?
WHY DID I BRING KOUJI HERE, ANYWAY?
OH YEAH, TAIGA?
ABOUT THE LAST OF OUR REPORTS...
IT WAS TO PROVE MY INNOCENCE...
...AND MAKE SURE MUTSUKI-KUN'S PICTURE DIDN'T GET TAKEN OUT OF CONTEXT...

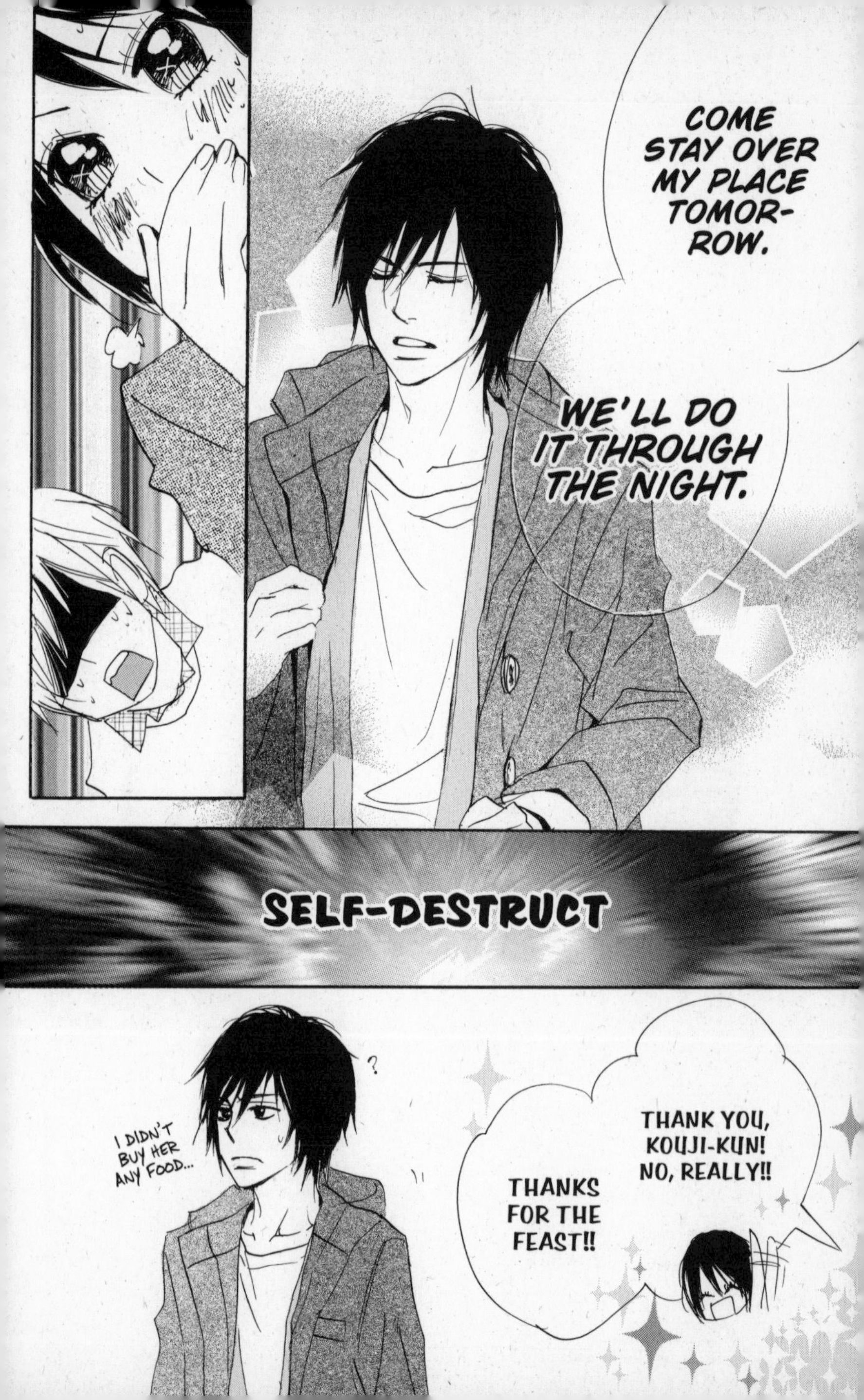
COME STAY OVER MY PLACE TOMOR-ROW.
WE'LL DO IT THROUGH THE NIGHT.
SELF-DESTRUCT
THANK YOU, KOUJI-KUN! NO, REALLY!!
THANKS FOR THE FEAST!!
?
I DIDN'T BUY HER ANY FOOD...

FUJOSHI NEWS

vol.12

SURPRISE! INTERVIEW WITH THE FUJOSHI NEXT DOOR ④

SURPRISE! INTERVIEW WITH THE FUJOSHI NEXT DOOR ④

COSPLAY LOVER ♥

♥FUJOSHI No.004♥ COSPLAY LOVER

TOKYO, Y.K.-SAN

AGE: 21
OCCUPATION: NURSE
MONTHLY HOBBY COSTS: ¥50,000
MOE FETISH: BLACK HAIR AND KIMONO

[TYPICAL ACTIVITIES]
CREATING COSPLAY OUTFITS FROM SCRATCH; MAKING MY OWN COSTUMES AND TAKING PICTURES WEARING THEM IN ABANDONED BUILDINGS OR SNOWY MOUNTAINS; HAVING EXHIBITS

[TYPICAL EVENTS]
PHOTOGRAPHY MEETINGS, DOJINSHI EVENTS WHERE COSPLAYING IS WELCOME

[SPECIAL POWER]
MAKING WEAPONS (I CREATE THEM BY POURING SILICONE INTO PLASTER CASTS.)

[RECENT TROUBLES]
I'M ABOUT TO COSPLAY A CHARACTER WHO EXPOSES THE BELLY, AND SO I BOUGHT AN EXERCISE MACHINE TO SLIM DOWN AND TONE UP. BUT WHEN I USE IT AT NIGHT, MY FAMILY YELLS AT ME FOR MAKING TOO MUCH NOISE.

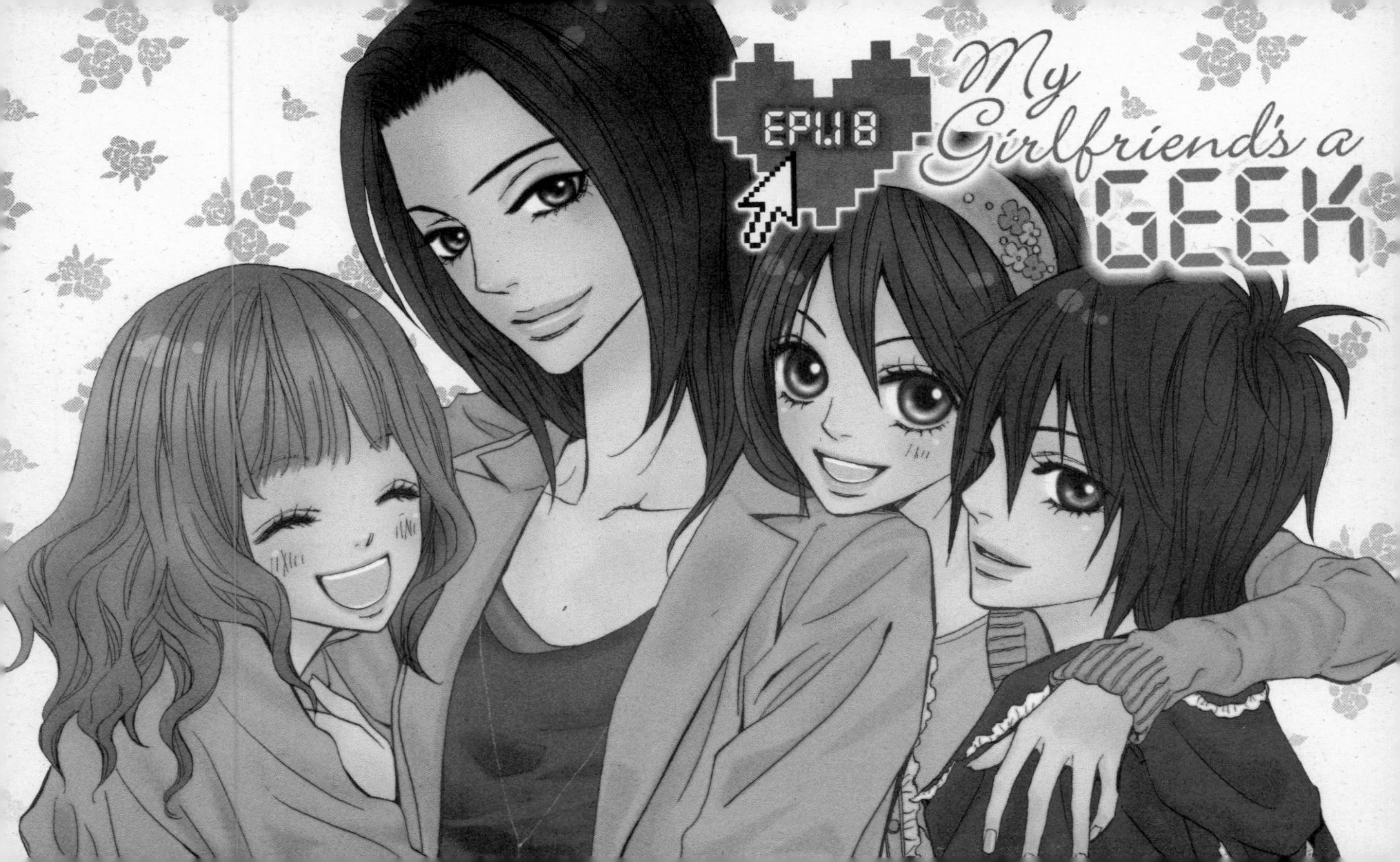
EPI.I 8
My Girlfriend's a GEEK

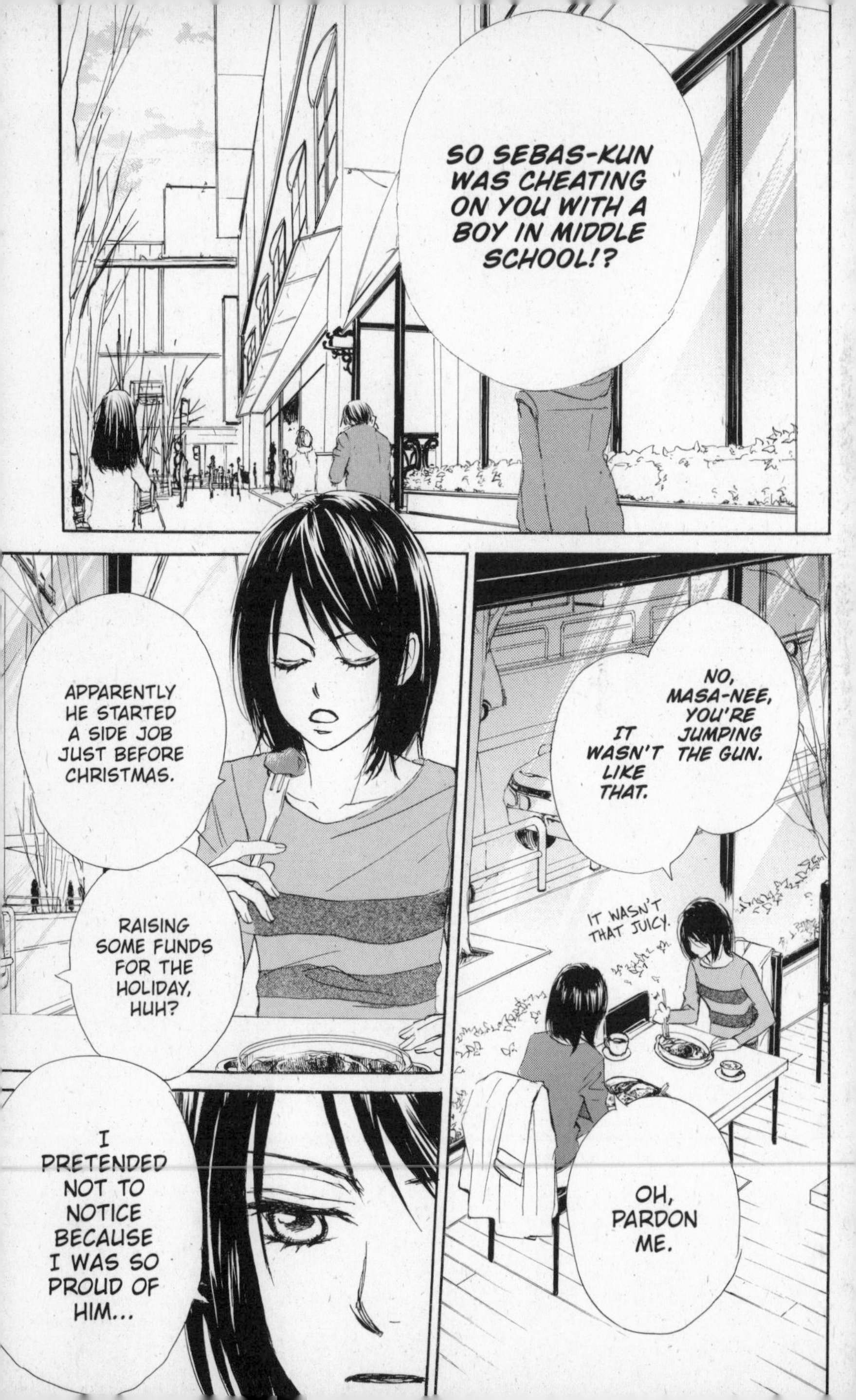
SO SEBAS-KUN WAS CHEATING ON YOU WITH A BOY IN MIDDLE SCHOOL!?
NO, MASA-NEE, YOU'RE JUMPING THE GUN.
IT WASN'T LIKE THAT.
IT WASN'T THAT JUICY.
OH, PARDON ME.
APPARENTLY HE STARTED A SIDE JOB JUST BEFORE CHRISTMAS.
RAISING SOME FUNDS FOR THE HOLIDAY, HUH?
I PRETENDED NOT TO NOTICE BECAUSE I WAS SO PROUD OF HIM...

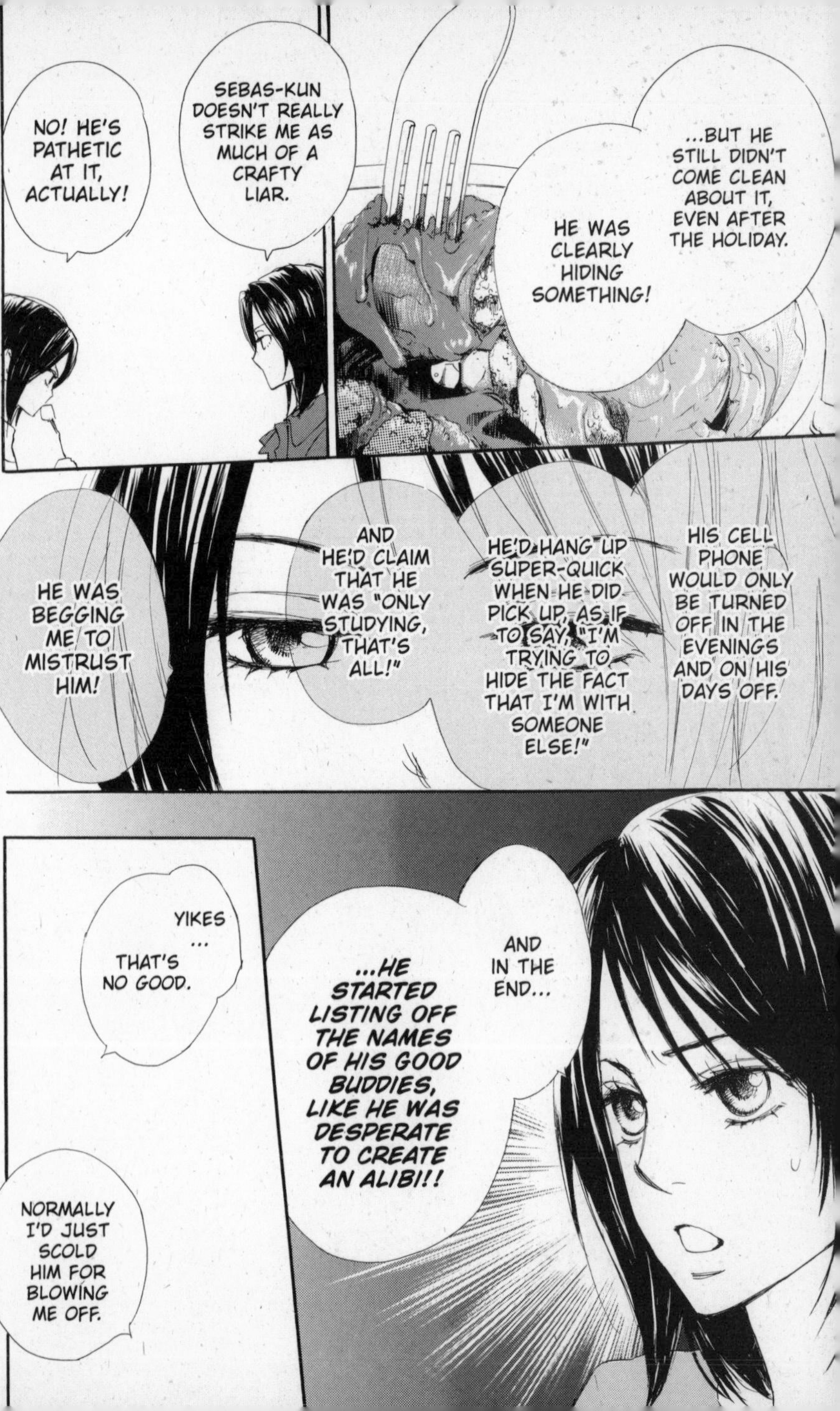
...BUT HE STILL DIDN'T COME CLEAN ABOUT IT, EVEN AFTER THE HOLIDAY.
HE WAS CLEARLY HIDING SOMETHING!
SEBAS-KUN DOESN'T REALLY STRIKE ME AS MUCH OF A CRAFTY LIAR.
NO! HE'S PATHETIC AT IT, ACTUALLY!
HIS CELL PHONE WOULD ONLY BE TURNED OFF IN THE EVENINGS AND ON HIS DAYS OFF.
HE'D HANG UP SUPER-QUICK WHEN HE DID PICK UP, AS IF TO SAY, "I'M TRYING TO HIDE THE FACT THAT I'M WITH SOMEONE ELSE!"
AND HE'D CLAIM THAT HE WAS "ONLY STUDYING, THAT'S ALL!"
HE WAS BEGGING ME TO MISTRUST HIM!
AND IN THE END...
...HE STARTED LISTING OFF THE NAMES OF HIS GOOD BUDDIES, LIKE HE WAS DESPERATE TO CREATE AN ALIBI!!
YIKES... THAT'S NO GOOD.
NORMALLY I'D JUST SCOLD HIM FOR BLOWING ME OFF.

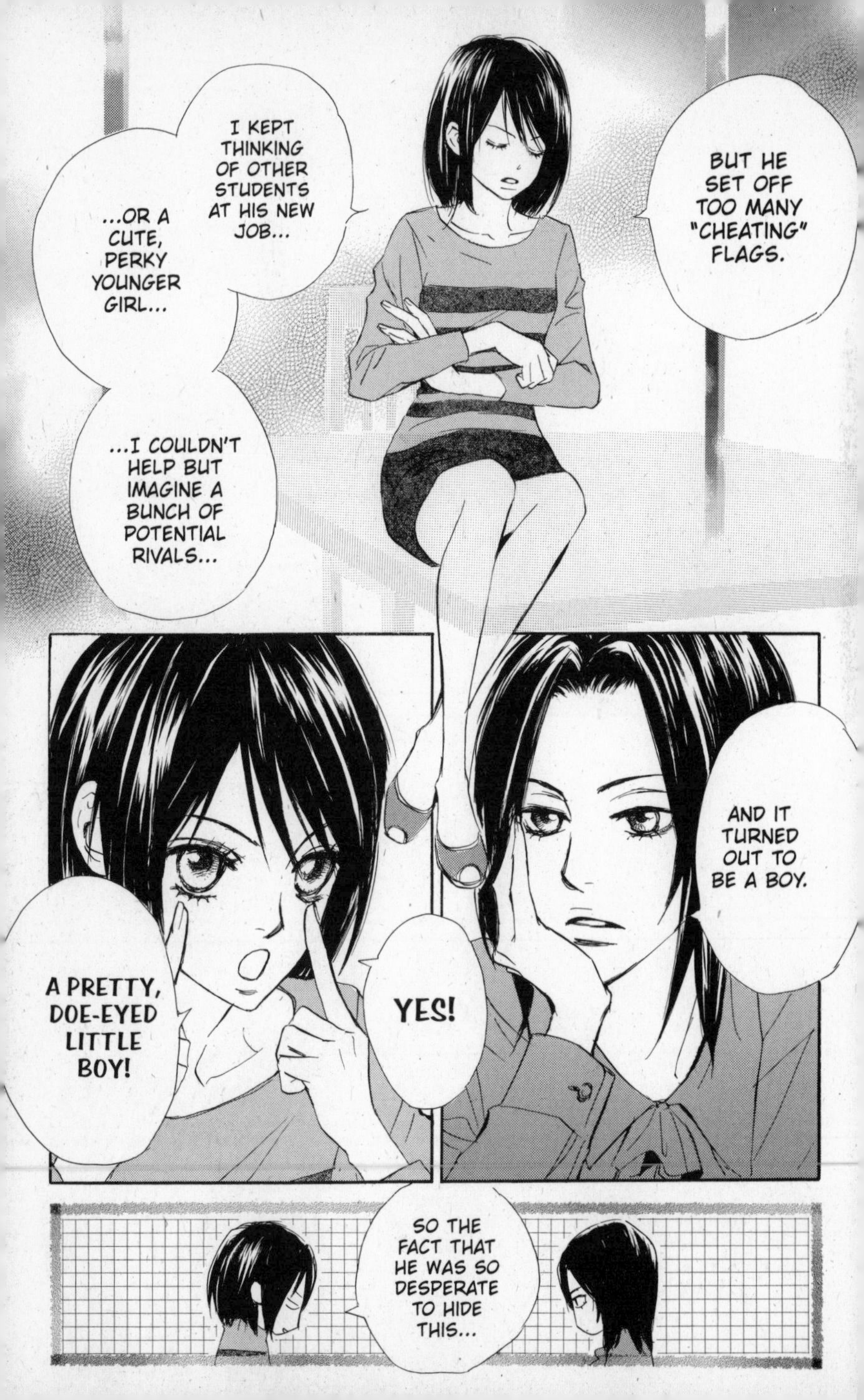
BUT HE SET OFF TOO MANY "CHEATING" FLAGS.
I KEPT THINKING OF OTHER STUDENTS AT HIS NEW JOB...
...OR A CUTE, PERKY YOUNGER GIRL...
...I COULDN'T HELP BUT IMAGINE A BUNCH OF POTENTIAL RIVALS...
AND IT TURNED OUT TO BE A BOY.
A PRETTY, DOE-EYED LITTLE BOY!
YES!
SO THE FACT THAT HE WAS SO DESPERATE TO HIDE THIS...

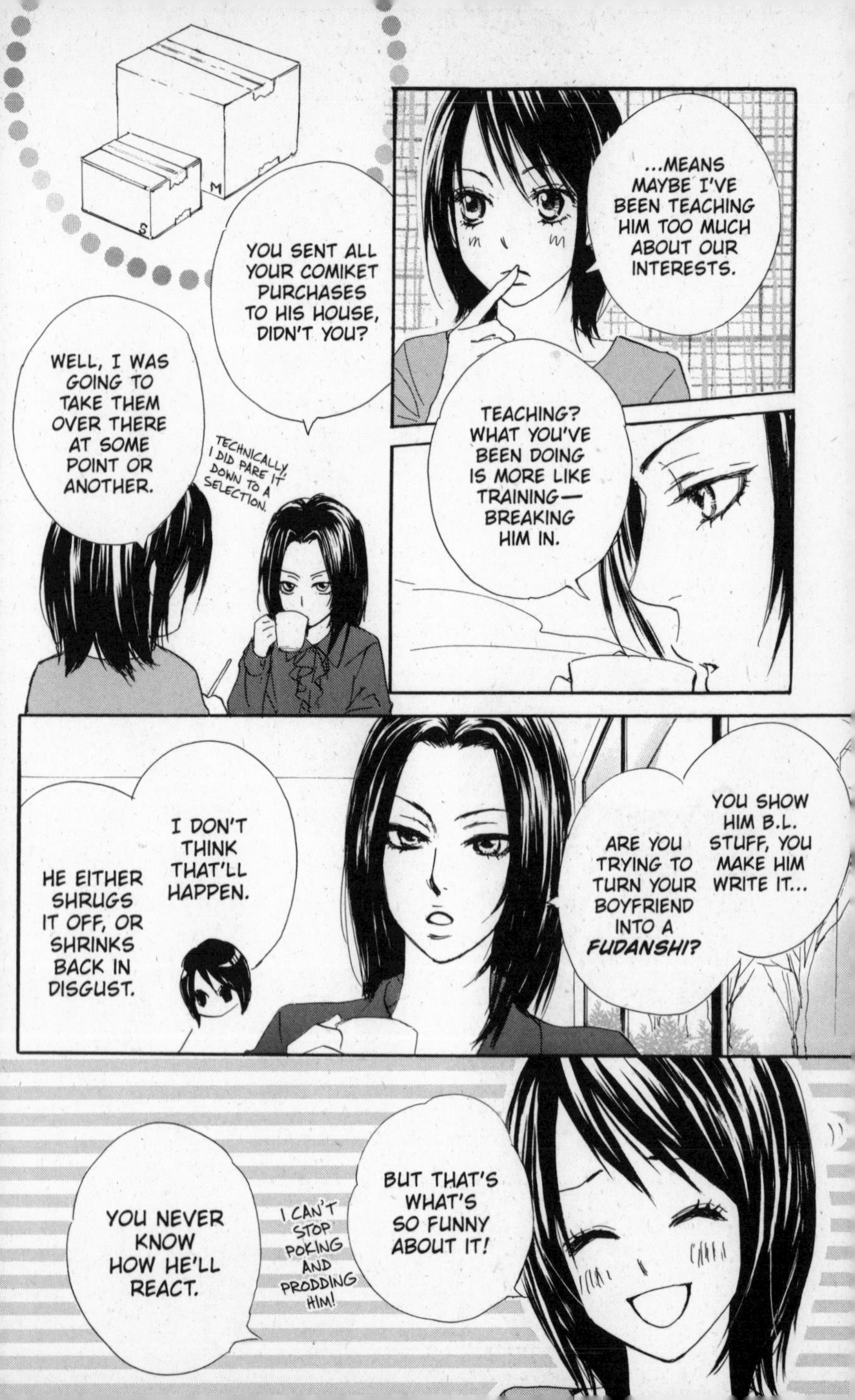
...MEANS MAYBE I'VE BEEN TEACHING HIM TOO MUCH ABOUT OUR INTERESTS.
TEACHING? WHAT YOU'VE BEEN DOING IS MORE LIKE TRAINING—BREAKING HIM IN.
YOU SENT ALL YOUR COMIKET PURCHASES TO HIS HOUSE, DIDN'T YOU?
WELL, I WAS GOING TO TAKE THEM OVER THERE AT SOME POINT OR ANOTHER.
TECHNICALLY, I DID PARE IT DOWN TO A SELECTION.
YOU SHOW HIM B.L. STUFF, YOU MAKE HIM WRITE IT...
ARE YOU TRYING TO TURN YOUR BOYFRIEND INTO A *FUDANSHI?*
I DON'T THINK THAT'LL HAPPEN.
HE EITHER SHRUGS IT OFF, OR SHRINKS BACK IN DISGUST.
BUT THAT'S WHAT'S SO FUNNY ABOUT IT!
I CAN'T STOP POKING AND PRODDING HIM!
YOU NEVER KNOW HOW HE'LL REACT.

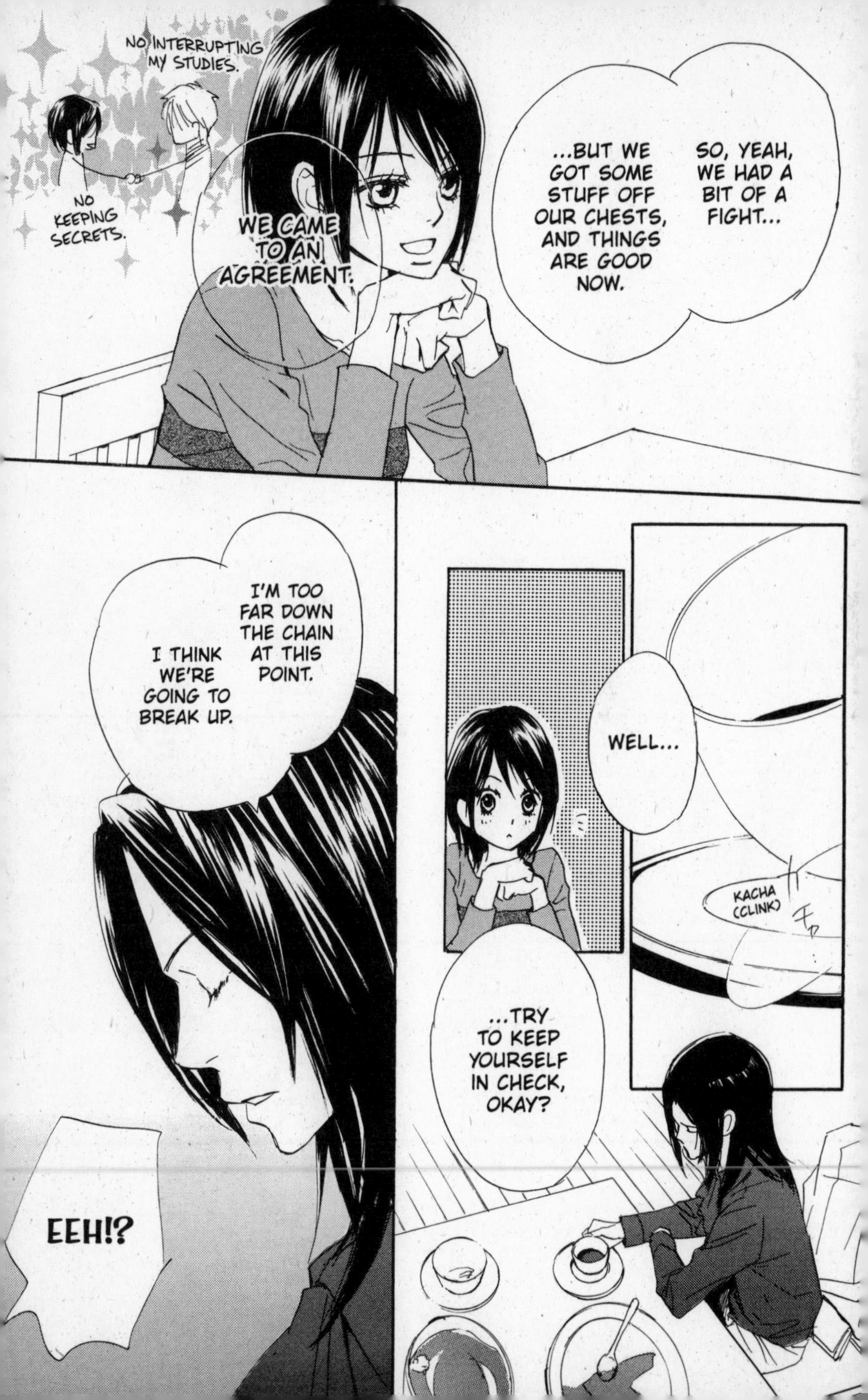
SO, YEAH, WE HAD A BIT OF A FIGHT...
...BUT WE GOT SOME STUFF OFF OUR CHESTS, AND THINGS ARE GOOD NOW.
WE CAME TO AN AGREEMENT.
NO INTERRUPTING MY STUDIES.
NO KEEPING SECRETS.
WELL...
KACHA (CLINK)
...TRY TO KEEP YOURSELF IN CHECK, OKAY?
I'M TOO FAR DOWN THE CHAIN AT THIS POINT.
I THINK WE'RE GOING TO BREAK UP.
EEH!?

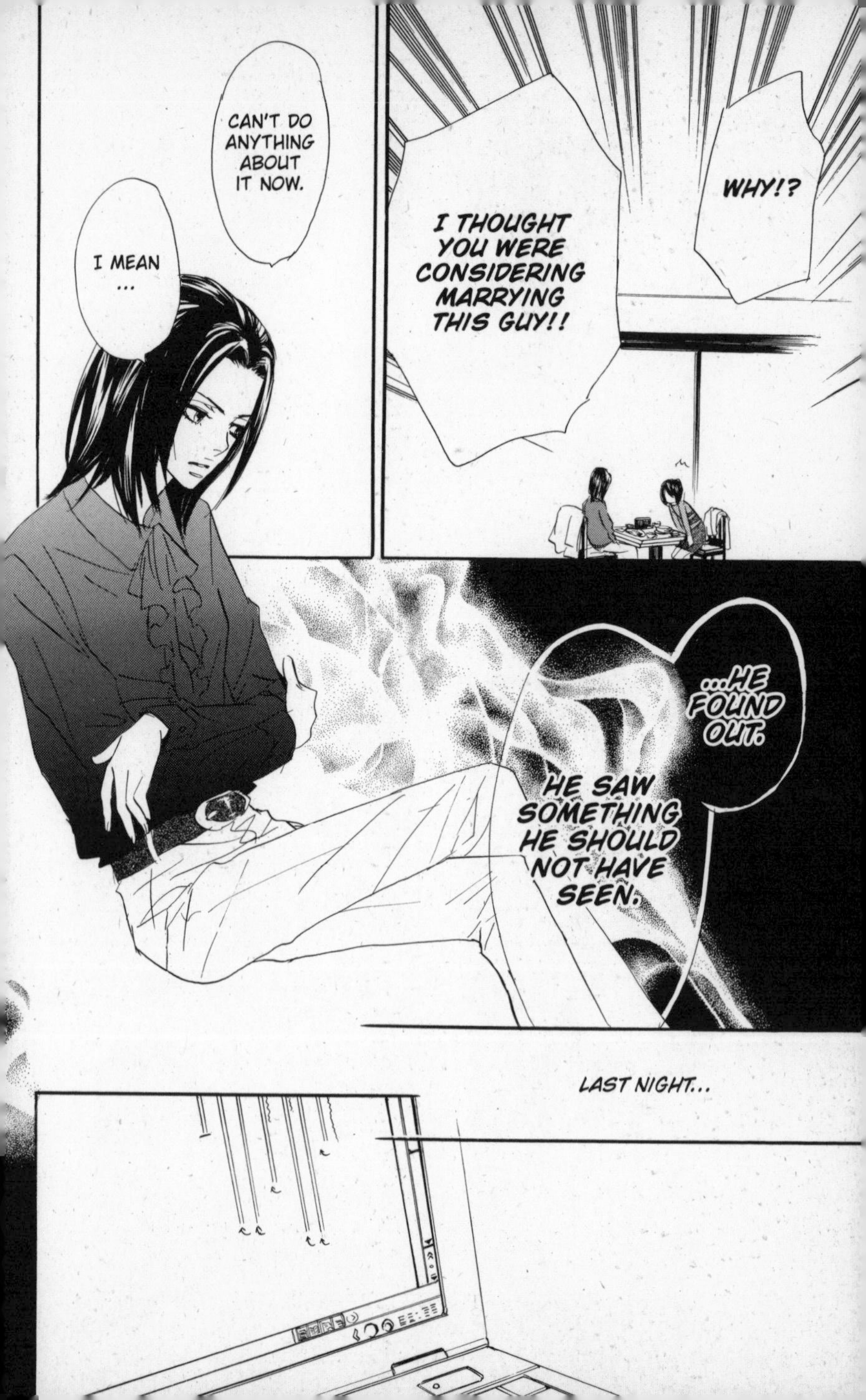
WHY!?
I THOUGHT YOU WERE CONSIDERING MARRYING THIS GUY!!
CAN'T DO ANYTHING ABOUT IT NOW.
I MEAN ...
...HE FOUND OUT.
HE SAW SOMETHING HE SHOULD NOT HAVE SEEN.
LAST NIGHT...

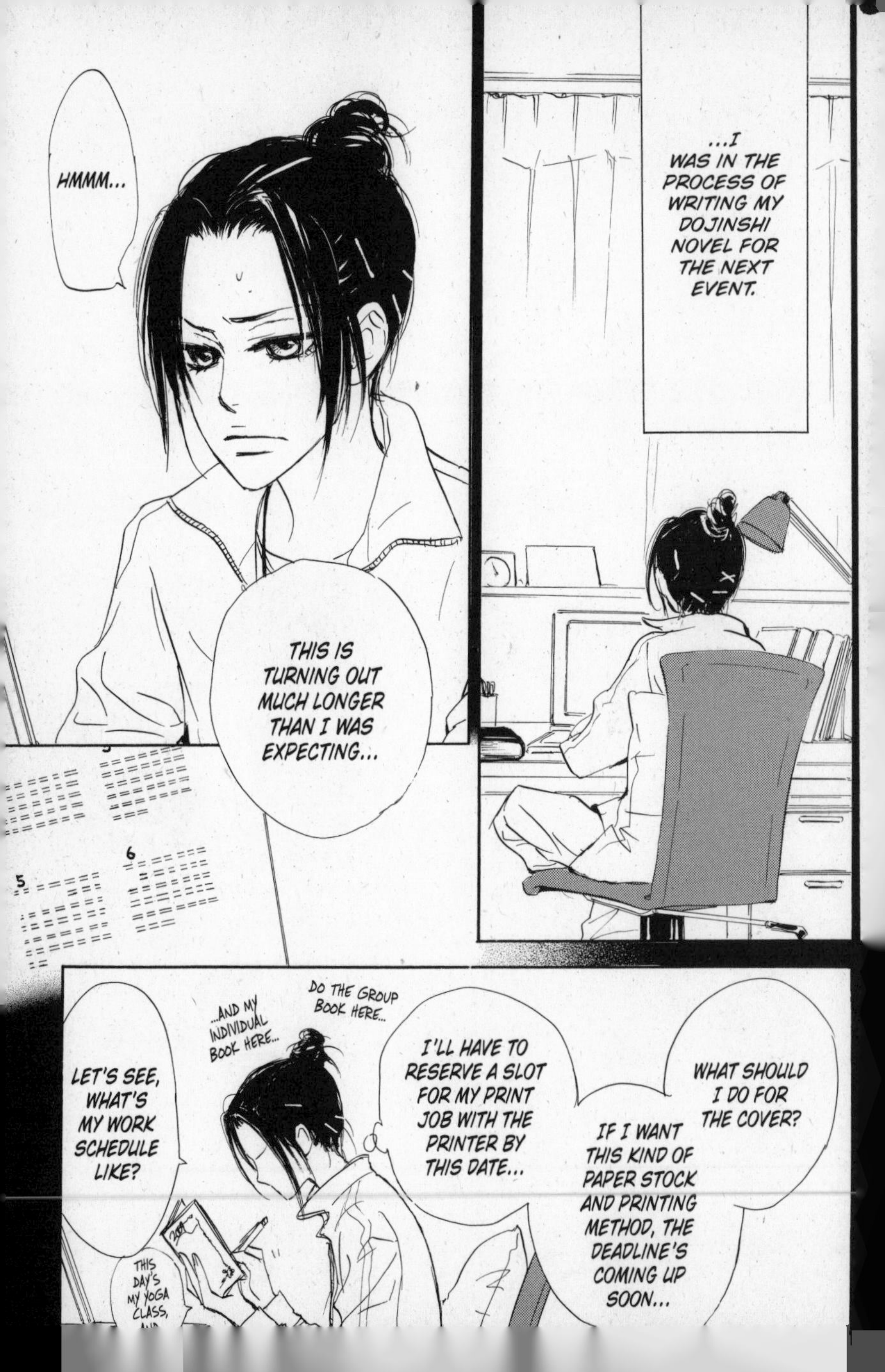
...I WAS IN THE PROCESS OF WRITING MY DOJINSHI NOVEL FOR THE NEXT EVENT.
HMMM...
THIS IS TURNING OUT MUCH LONGER THAN I WAS EXPECTING...
WHAT SHOULD I DO FOR THE COVER?
IF I WANT THIS KIND OF PAPER STOCK AND PRINTING METHOD, THE DEADLINE'S COMING UP SOON...
I'LL HAVE TO RESERVE A SLOT FOR MY PRINT JOB WITH THE PRINTER BY THIS DATE...
DO THE GROUP BOOK HERE...
...AND MY INDIVIDUAL BOOK HERE...
LET'S SEE, WHAT'S MY WORK SCHEDULE LIKE?
THIS DAY'S MY YOGA CLASS,

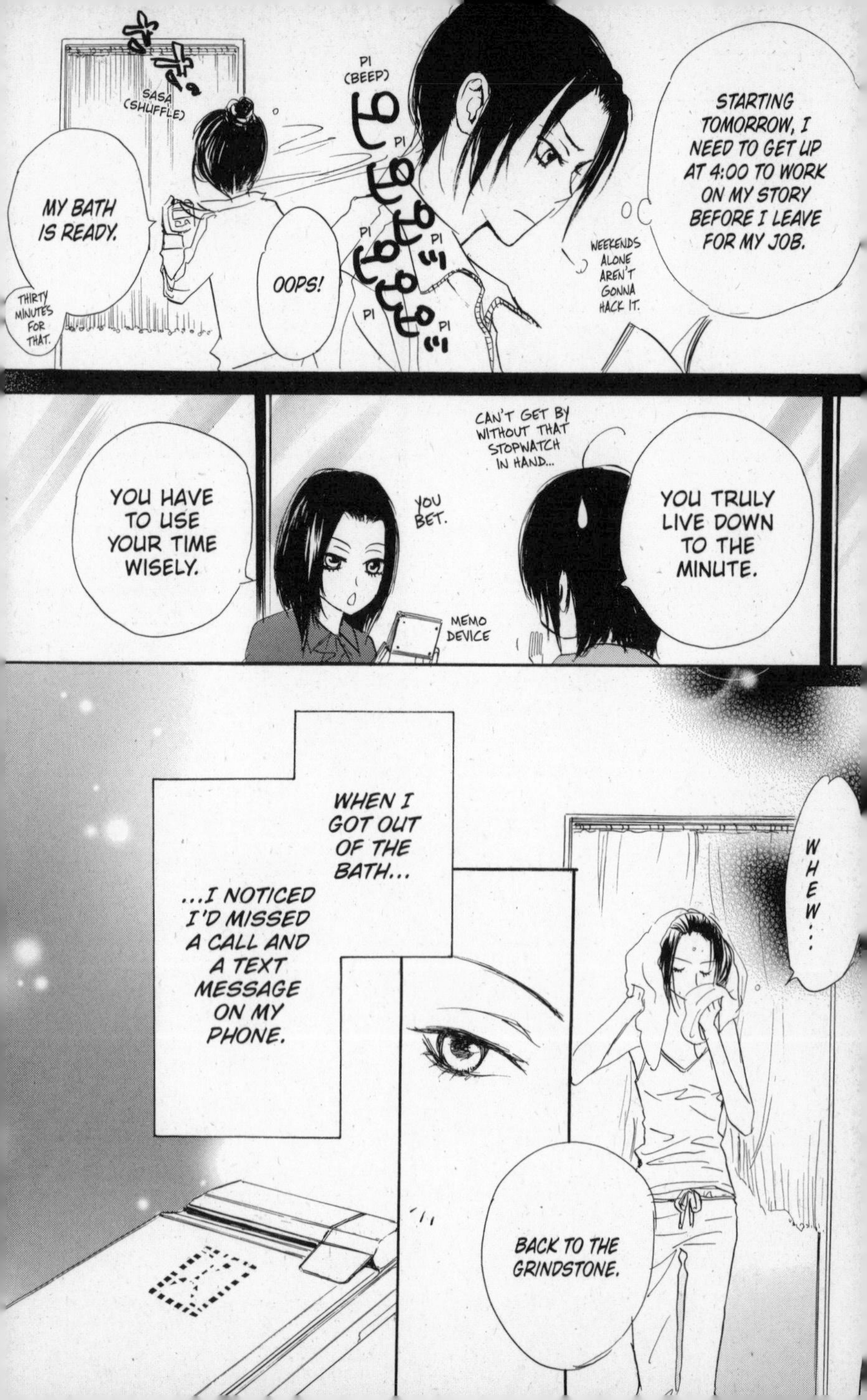
STARTING TOMORROW, I NEED TO GET UP AT 4:00 TO WORK ON MY STORY BEFORE I LEAVE FOR MY JOB.
WEEKENDS ALONE AREN'T GONNA HACK IT.
PI (BEEP)
PI
PI
PI
PI
PI
OOPS!
SASA (SHUFFLE)
MY BATH IS READY.
THIRTY MINUTES FOR THAT.
YOU TRULY LIVE DOWN TO THE MINUTE.
CAN'T GET BY WITHOUT THAT STOPWATCH IN HAND...
YOU BET.
MEMO DEVICE
YOU HAVE TO USE YOUR TIME WISELY.
WHEW...
WHEN I GOT OUT OF THE BATH...
...I NOTICED I'D MISSED A CALL AND A TEXT MESSAGE ON MY PHONE.
BACK TO THE GRINDSTONE.

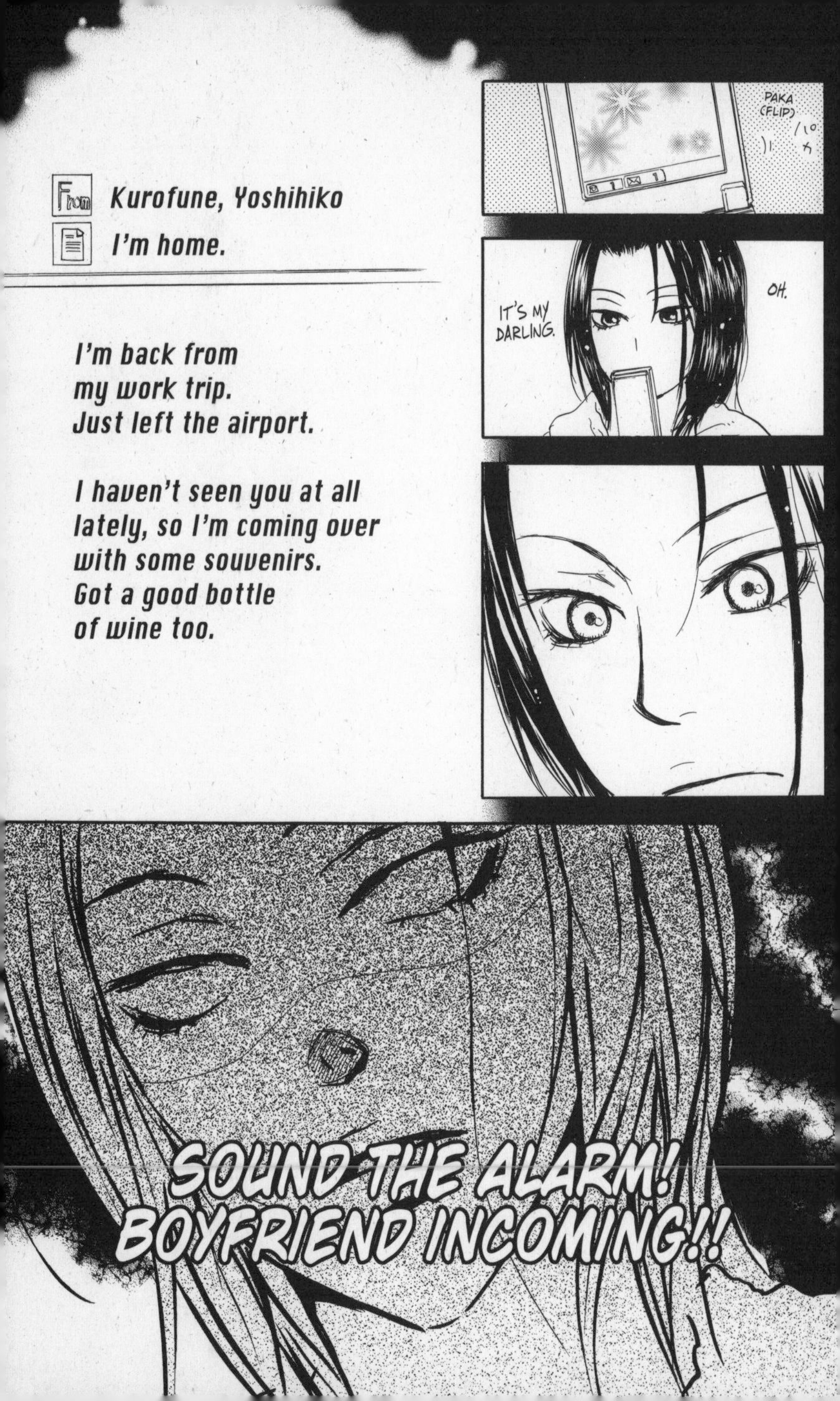
PAKA (FLIP)
OH.
IT'S MY DARLING.
From Kurofune, Yoshihiko
I'm home.
I'm back from my work trip. Just left the airport.
I haven't seen you at all lately, so I'm coming over with some souvenirs. Got a good bottle of wine too.
SOUND THE ALARM! BOYFRIEND INCOMING!!

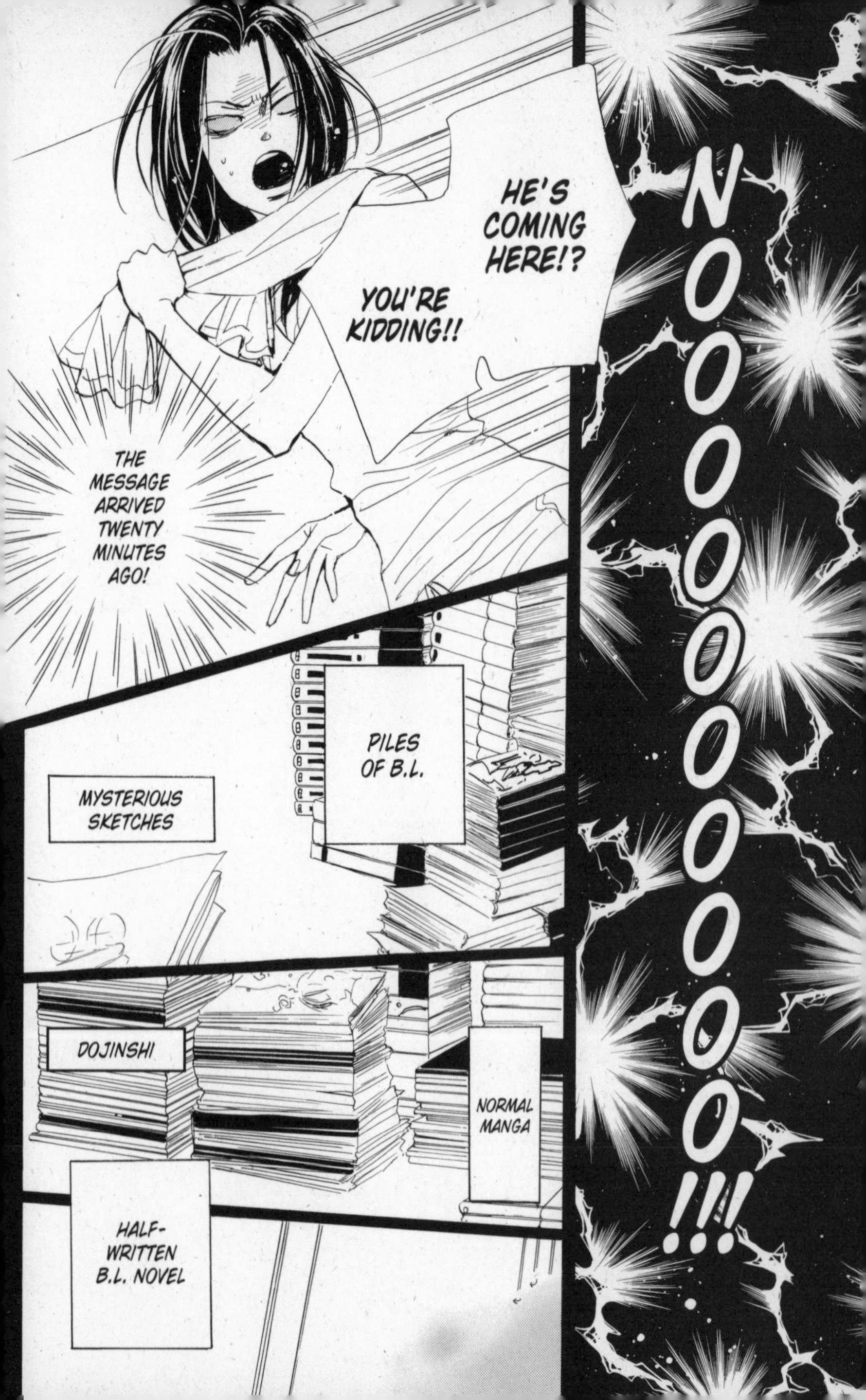
NOOOOOOOOOOOO!!!
HE'S COMING HERE!?
YOU'RE KIDDING!!
THE MESSAGE ARRIVED TWENTY MINUTES AGO!
PILES OF B.L.
MYSTERIOUS SKETCHES
NORMAL MANGA
DOJINSHI
HALF-WRITTEN B.L. NOVEL

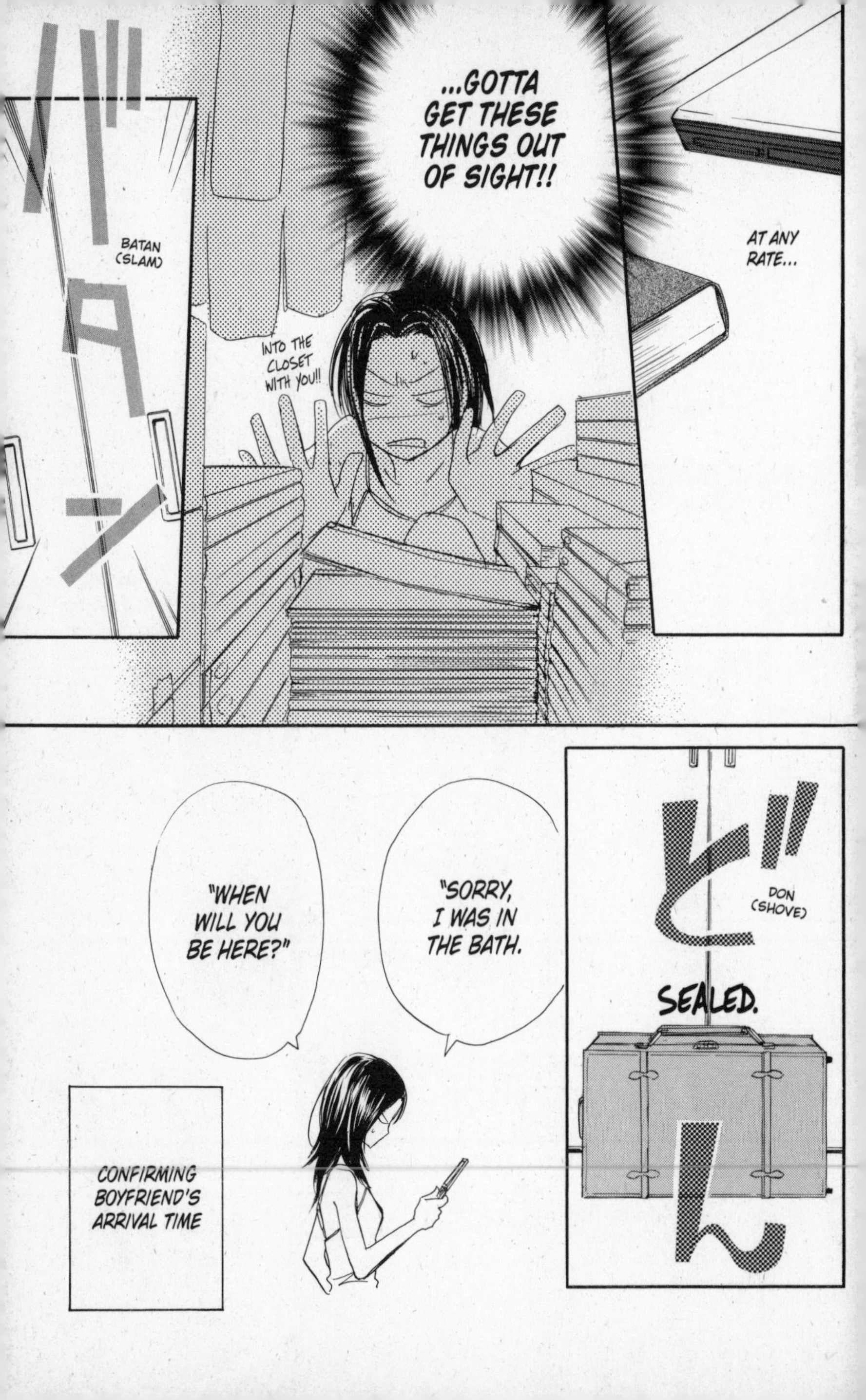
AT ANY RATE...
...GOTTA GET THESE THINGS OUT OF SIGHT!!
INTO THE CLOSET WITH YOU!!
BATAN (SLAM)
DON (SHOVE)
SEALED.
"SORRY, I WAS IN THE BATH.
"WHEN WILL YOU BE HERE?"
CONFIRMING BOYFRIEND'S ARRIVAL TIME

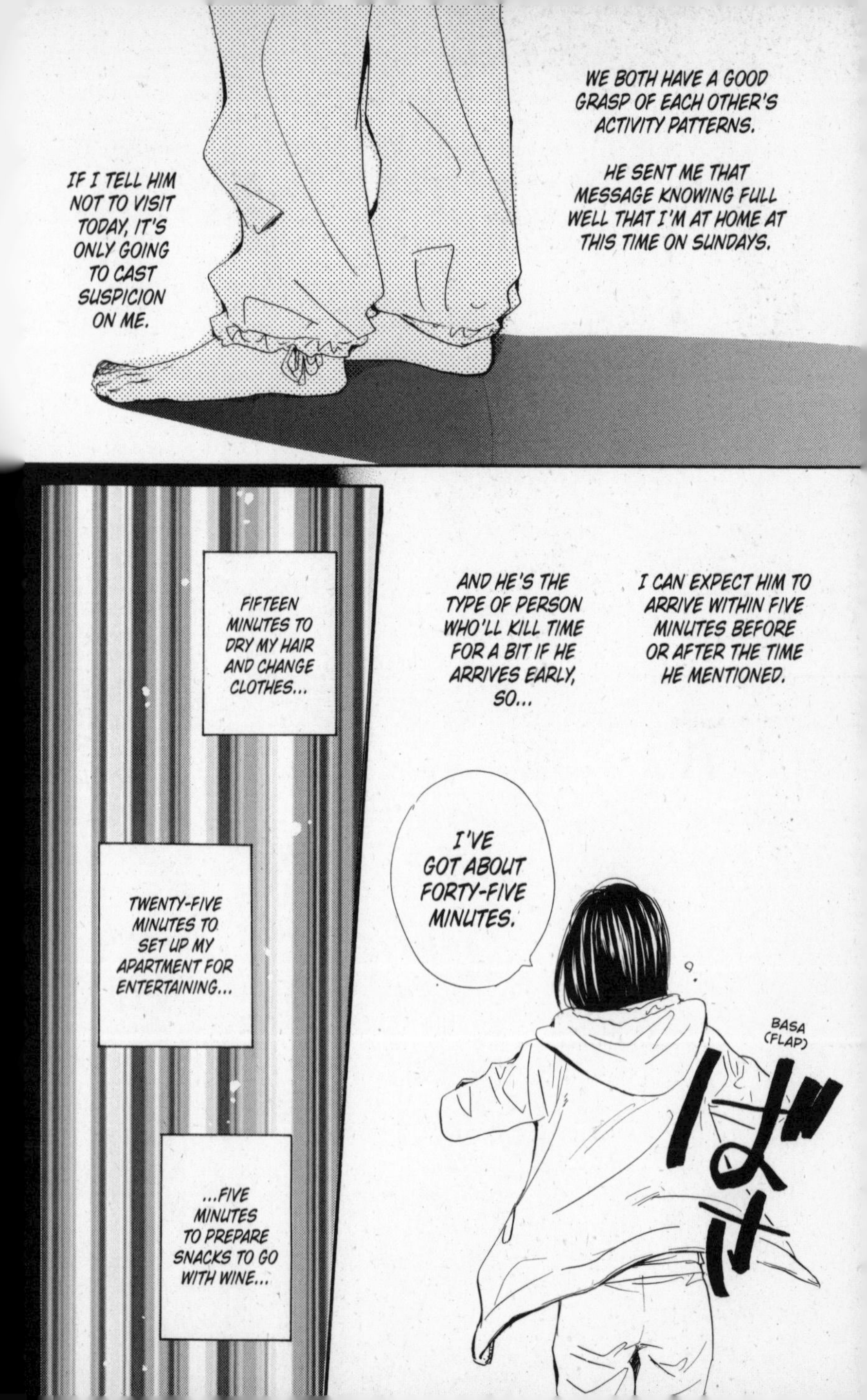
WE BOTH HAVE A GOOD GRASP OF EACH OTHER'S ACTIVITY PATTERNS.
HE SENT ME THAT MESSAGE KNOWING FULL WELL THAT I'M AT HOME AT THIS TIME ON SUNDAYS.
IF I TELL HIM NOT TO VISIT TODAY, IT'S ONLY GOING TO CAST SUSPICION ON ME.
I CAN EXPECT HIM TO ARRIVE WITHIN FIVE MINUTES BEFORE OR AFTER THE TIME HE MENTIONED.
AND HE'S THE TYPE OF PERSON WHO'LL KILL TIME FOR A BIT IF HE ARRIVES EARLY, SO...
I'VE GOT ABOUT FORTY-FIVE MINUTES.
ばさ
BASA (FLAP)
FIFTEEN MINUTES TO DRY MY HAIR AND CHANGE CLOTHES...
TWENTY-FIVE MINUTES TO SET UP MY APARTMENT FOR ENTERTAINING...
...FIVE MINUTES TO PREPARE SNACKS TO GO WITH WINE...

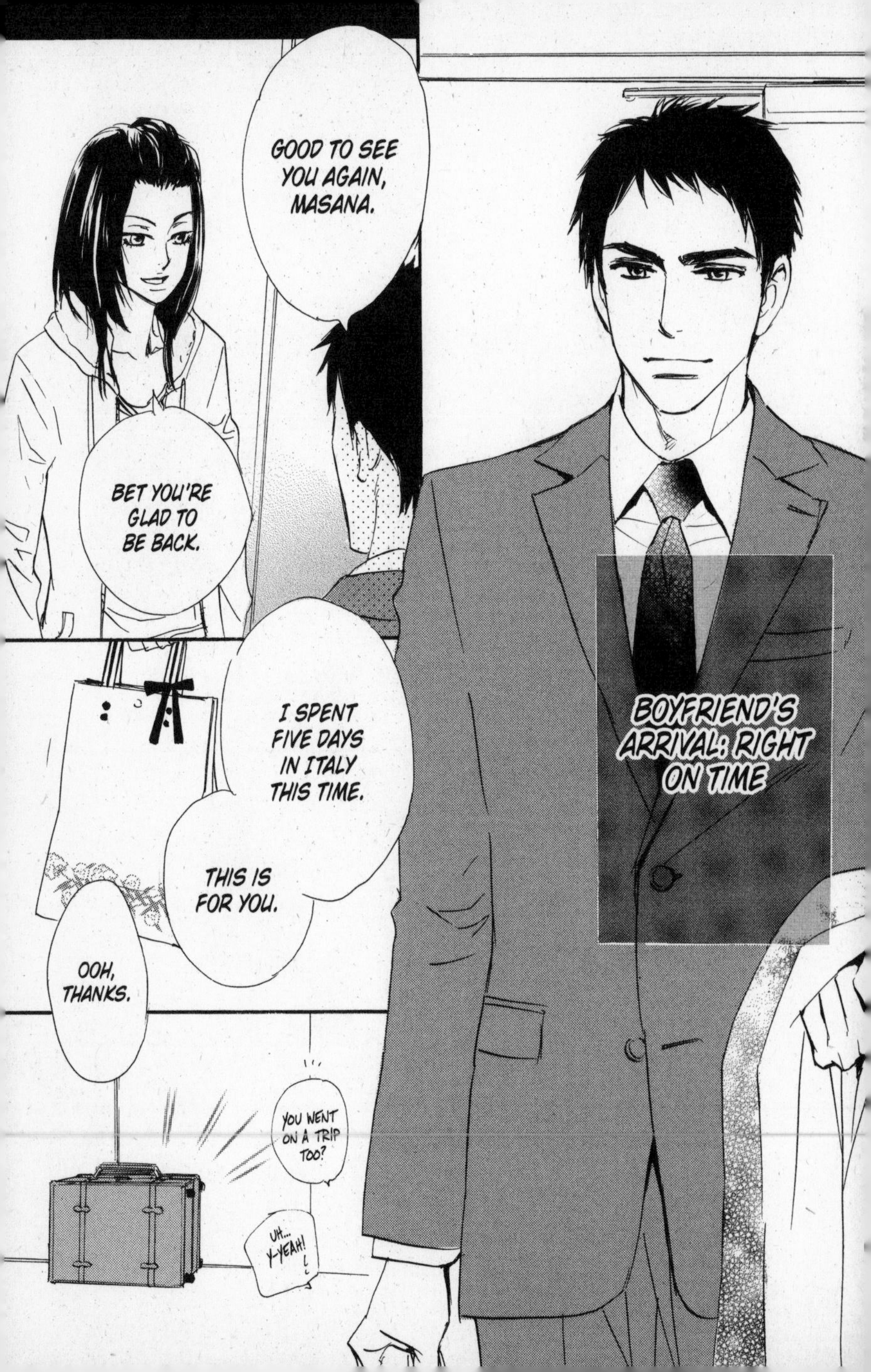
BOYFRIEND'S ARRIVAL: RIGHT ON TIME
GOOD TO SEE YOU AGAIN, MASANA.
BET YOU'RE GLAD TO BE BACK.
I SPENT FIVE DAYS IN ITALY THIS TIME.
THIS IS FOR YOU.
OOH, THANKS.
YOU WENT ON A TRIP TOO?
UH... Y-YEAH!

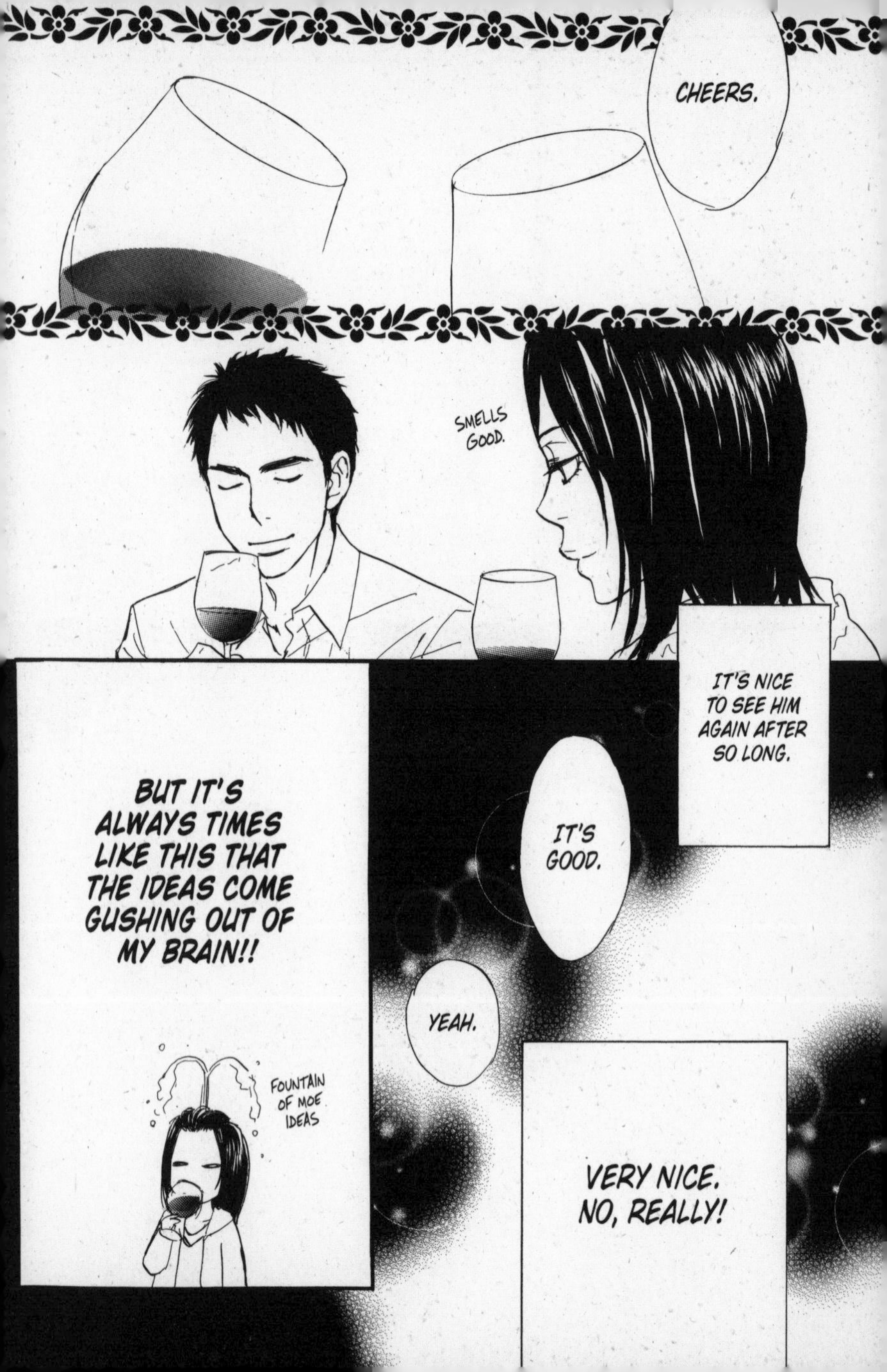
CHEERS.
SMELLS GOOD.
IT'S NICE TO SEE HIM AGAIN AFTER SO LONG.
IT'S GOOD.
YEAH.
VERY NICE. NO, REALLY!
BUT IT'S ALWAYS TIMES LIKE THIS THAT THE IDEAS COME GUSHING OUT OF MY BRAIN!!
FOUNTAIN OF MOE IDEAS

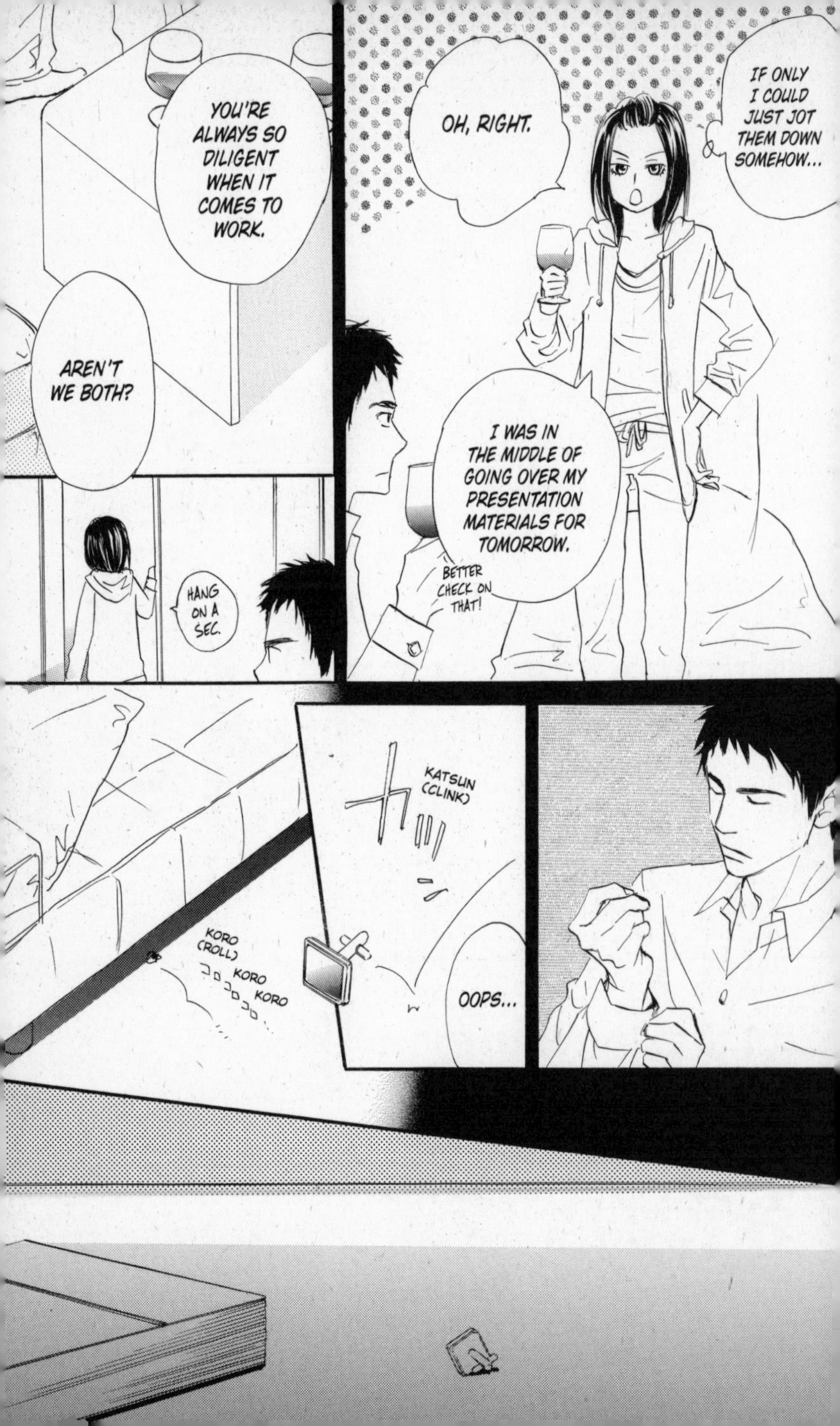
IF ONLY I COULD JUST JOT THEM DOWN SOMEHOW...
OH, RIGHT.
I WAS IN THE MIDDLE OF GOING OVER MY PRESENTATION MATERIALS FOR TOMORROW.
BETTER CHECK ON THAT!
YOU'RE ALWAYS SO DILIGENT WHEN IT COMES TO WORK.
AREN'T WE BOTH?
HANG ON A SEC.
KATSUN (CLINK)
OOPS...
KORO (ROLL)
KORO KORO

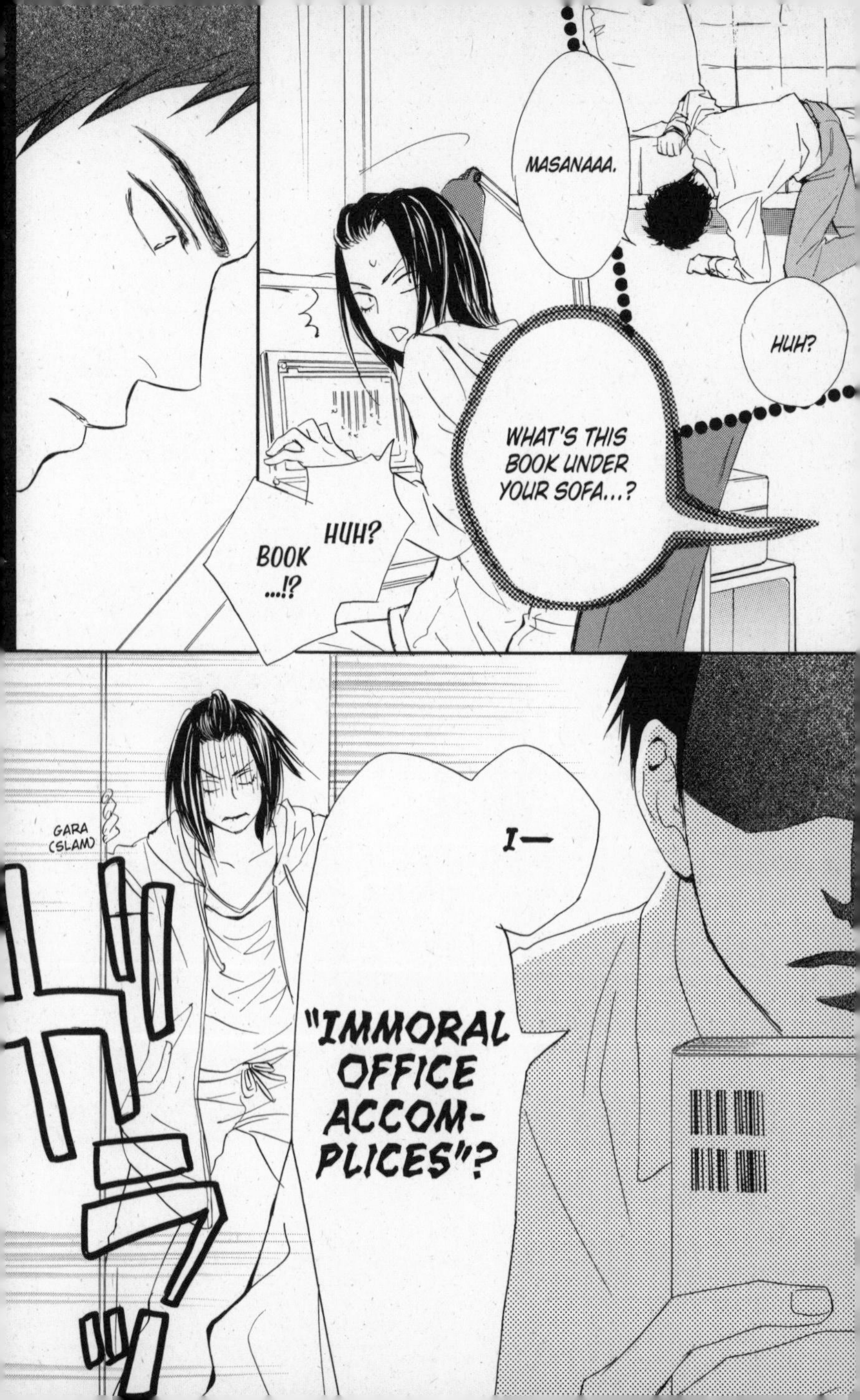
MASANAAA.
HUH?
WHAT'S THIS BOOK UNDER YOUR SOFA...?
HUH?
BOOK ...!?
I—
"IMMORAL OFFICE ACCOM-PLICES"?
GARA (SLAM)

A FATAL MISTAKE!

LYING UNDER THE SOFA WAS A B.L. PAPERBACK NOVEL WITH THE DUST JACKET REMOVED SO THAT I COULD CUT OUT THE MAIL-IN UPC.

PLUS...

...IT WAS A SALARYMAN-THEMED FIVESOME WITH A MIDDLE-AGED UKE AND A VERY OBVIOUS COVER ILLUSTRATION.

*X-RATED HARD-CORE B.L. IMAGES NOT REPRODUCED

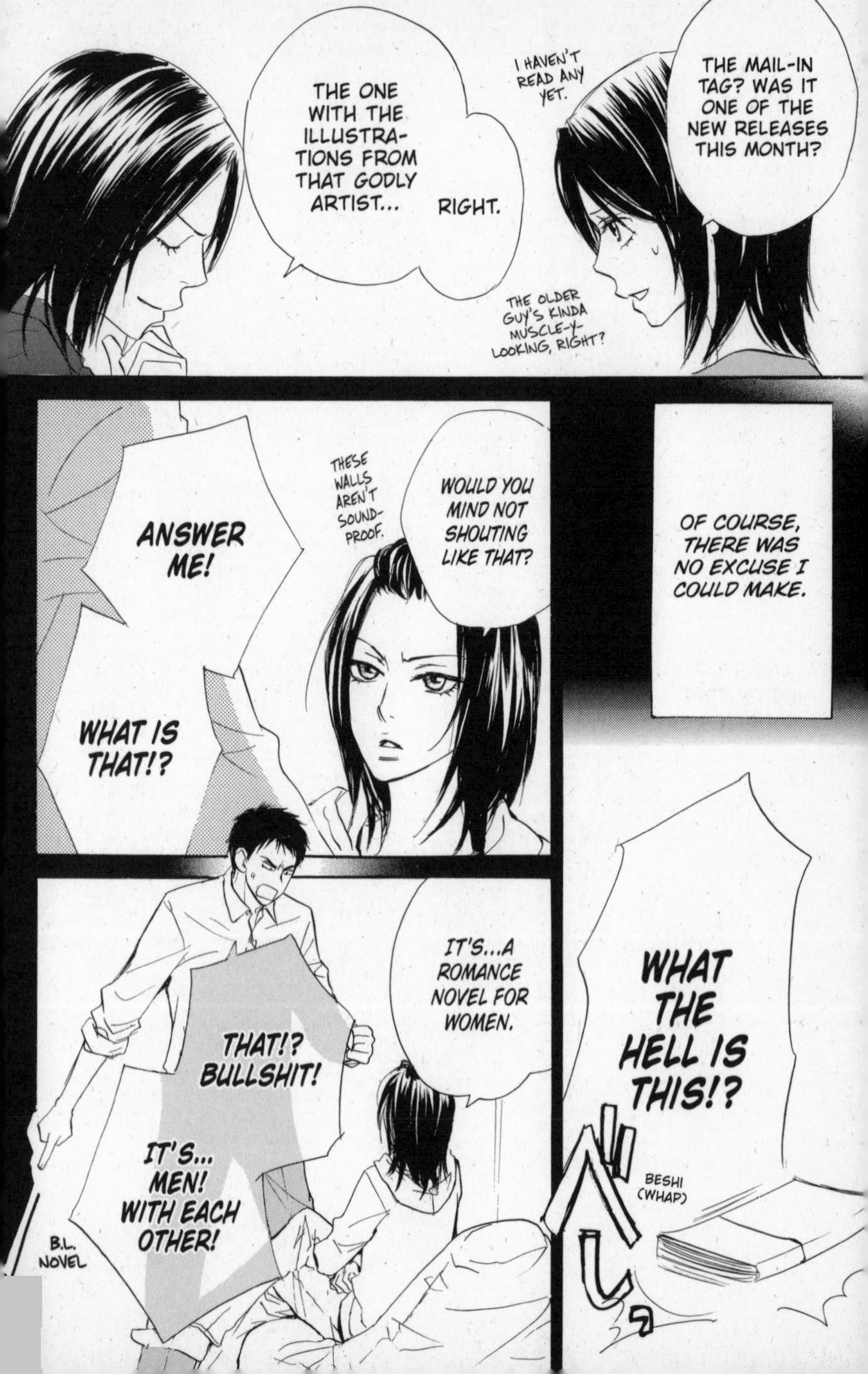
THE MAIL-IN TAG? WAS IT ONE OF THE NEW RELEASES THIS MONTH?
I HAVEN'T READ ANY YET.
THE ONE WITH THE ILLUSTRATIONS FROM THAT GODLY ARTIST...
THE OLDER GUY'S KINDA MUSCLE-Y-LOOKING, RIGHT?
RIGHT.
OF COURSE, THERE WAS NO EXCUSE I COULD MAKE.
WOULD YOU MIND NOT SHOUTING LIKE THAT?
THESE WALLS AREN'T SOUND-PROOF.
ANSWER ME!
WHAT IS THAT!?
WHAT THE HELL IS THIS!?
BESHI (WHAP)
IT'S...A ROMANCE NOVEL FOR WOMEN.
THAT!? BULLSHIT!
IT'S... MEN! WITH EACH OTHER!
B.L. NOVEL

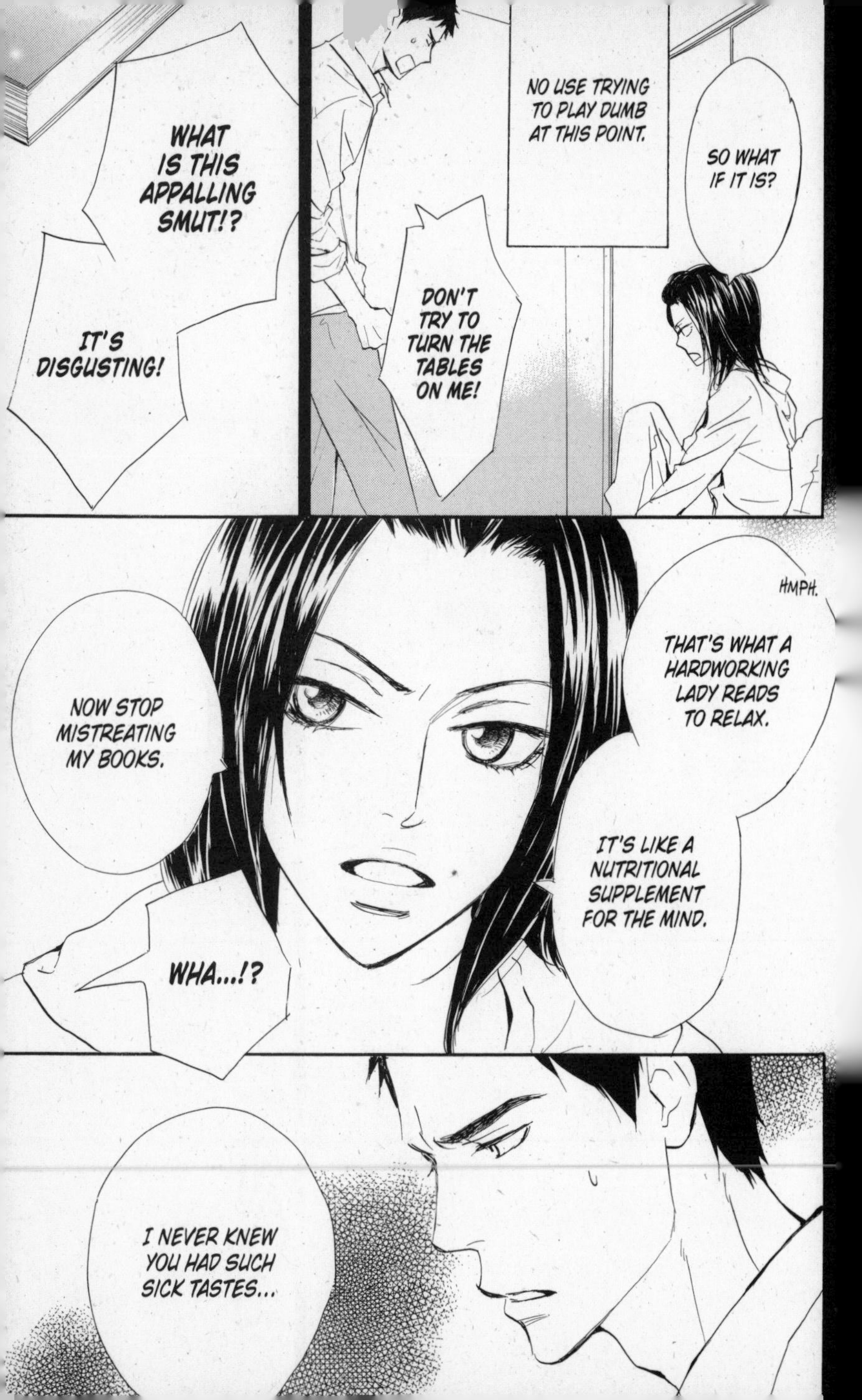
NO USE TRYING TO PLAY DUMB AT THIS POINT.
SO WHAT IF IT IS?
DON'T TRY TO TURN THE TABLES ON ME!
WHAT IS THIS APPALLING SMUT!?
IT'S DISGUSTING!
HMPH.
THAT'S WHAT A HARDWORKING LADY READS TO RELAX.
IT'S LIKE A NUTRITIONAL SUPPLEMENT FOR THE MIND.
NOW STOP MISTREATING MY BOOKS.
WHA...!?
I NEVER KNEW YOU HAD SUCH SICK TASTES...

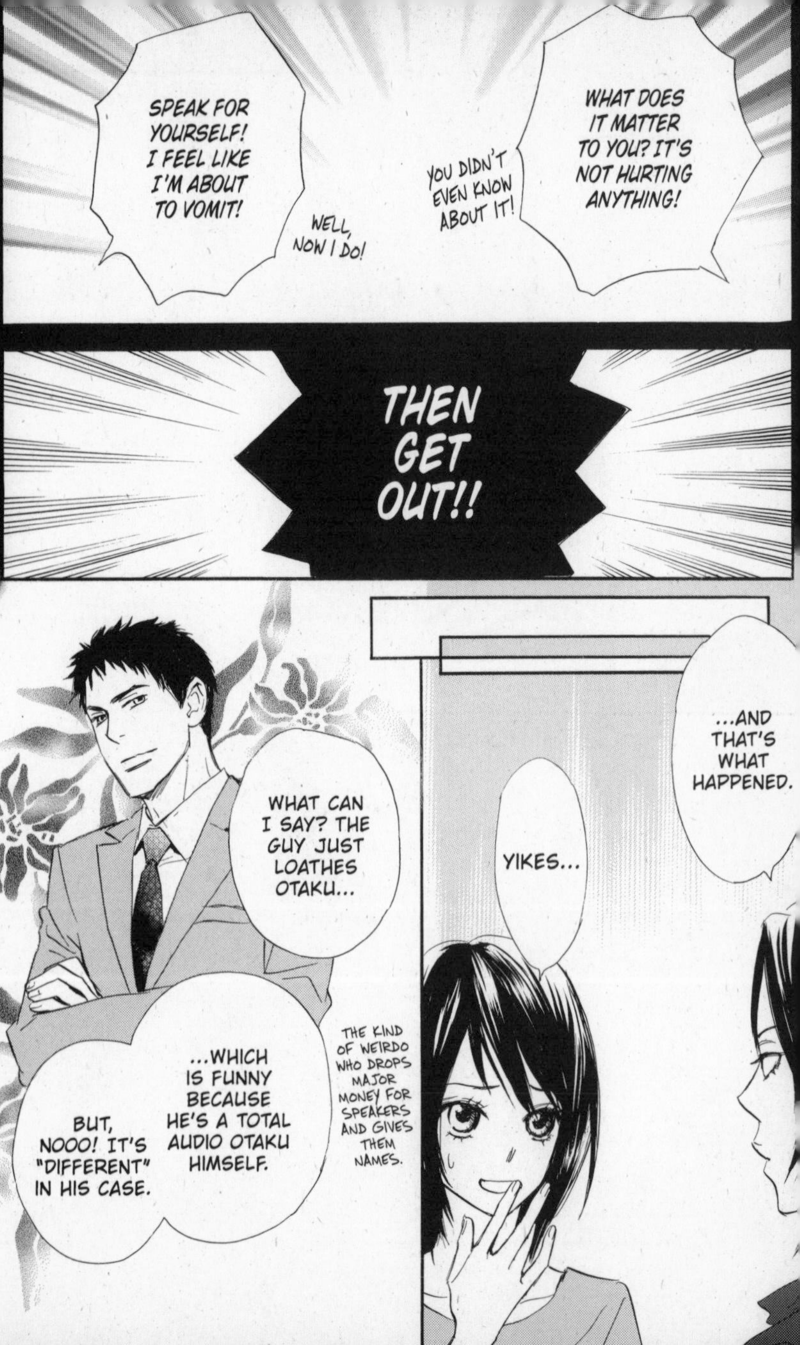
WHAT DOES IT MATTER TO YOU? IT'S NOT HURTING ANYTHING!
SPEAK FOR YOURSELF! I FEEL LIKE I'M ABOUT TO VOMIT!
YOU DIDN'T EVEN KNOW ABOUT IT!
WELL, NOW I DO!
THEN GET OUT!!
...AND THAT'S WHAT HAPPENED.
YIKES...
WHAT CAN I SAY? THE GUY JUST LOATHES OTAKU...
...WHICH IS FUNNY BECAUSE HE'S A TOTAL AUDIO OTAKU HIMSELF.
THE KIND OF WEIRDO WHO DROPS MAJOR MONEY FOR SPEAKERS AND GIVES THEM NAMES.
BUT, NOOO! IT'S "DIFFERENT" IN HIS CASE.

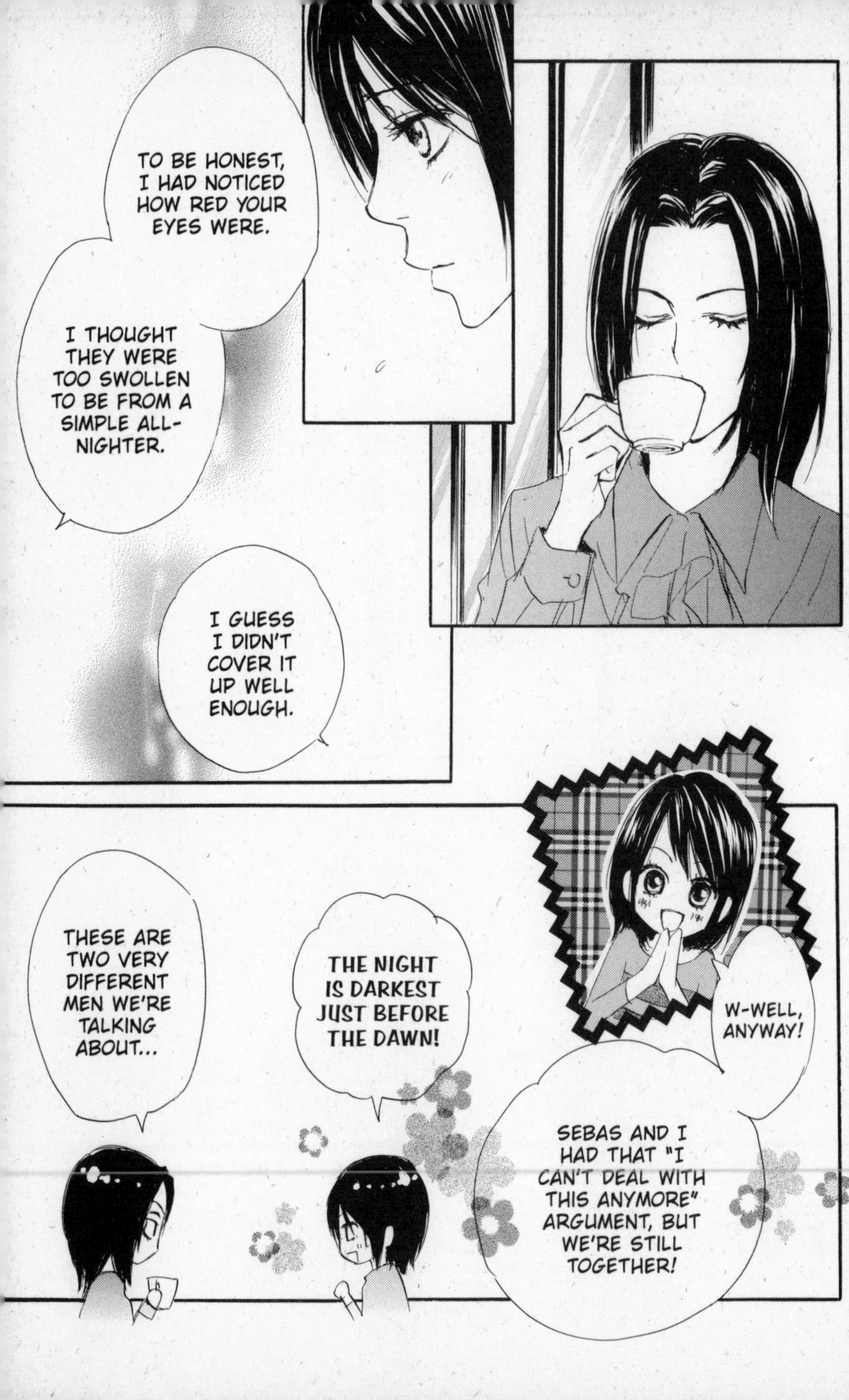
TO BE HONEST, I HAD NOTICED HOW RED YOUR EYES WERE.
I THOUGHT THEY WERE TOO SWOLLEN TO BE FROM A SIMPLE ALL-NIGHTER.
I GUESS I DIDN'T COVER IT UP WELL ENOUGH.
W-WELL, ANYWAY!
SEBAS AND I HAD THAT "I CAN'T DEAL WITH THIS ANYMORE" ARGUMENT, BUT WE'RE STILL TOGETHER!
THE NIGHT IS DARKEST JUST BEFORE THE DAWN!
THESE ARE TWO VERY DIFFERENT MEN WE'RE TALKING ABOUT...

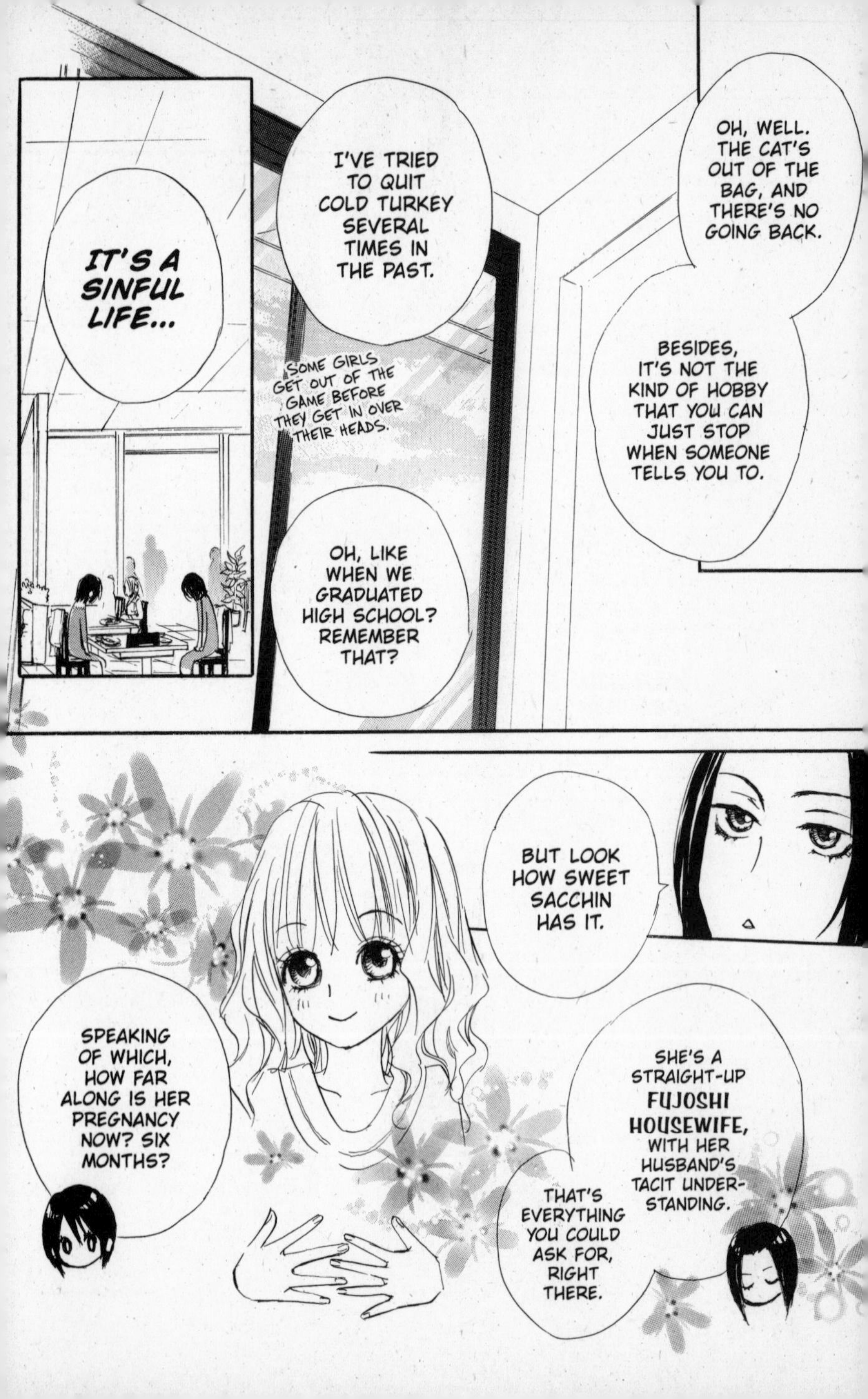
OH, WELL. THE CAT'S OUT OF THE BAG, AND THERE'S NO GOING BACK.
BESIDES, IT'S NOT THE KIND OF HOBBY THAT YOU CAN JUST STOP WHEN SOMEONE TELLS YOU TO.
I'VE TRIED TO QUIT COLD TURKEY SEVERAL TIMES IN THE PAST.
SOME GIRLS GET OUT OF THE GAME BEFORE THEY GET IN OVER THEIR HEADS.
OH, LIKE WHEN WE GRADUATED HIGH SCHOOL? REMEMBER THAT?
IT'S A SINFUL LIFE...
BUT LOOK HOW SWEET SACCHIN HAS IT.
SHE'S A STRAIGHT-UP **FUJOSHI HOUSEWIFE,** WITH HER HUSBAND'S TACIT UNDER-STANDING.
THAT'S EVERYTHING YOU COULD ASK FOR, RIGHT THERE.
SPEAKING OF WHICH, HOW FAR ALONG IS HER PREGNANCY NOW? SIX MONTHS?

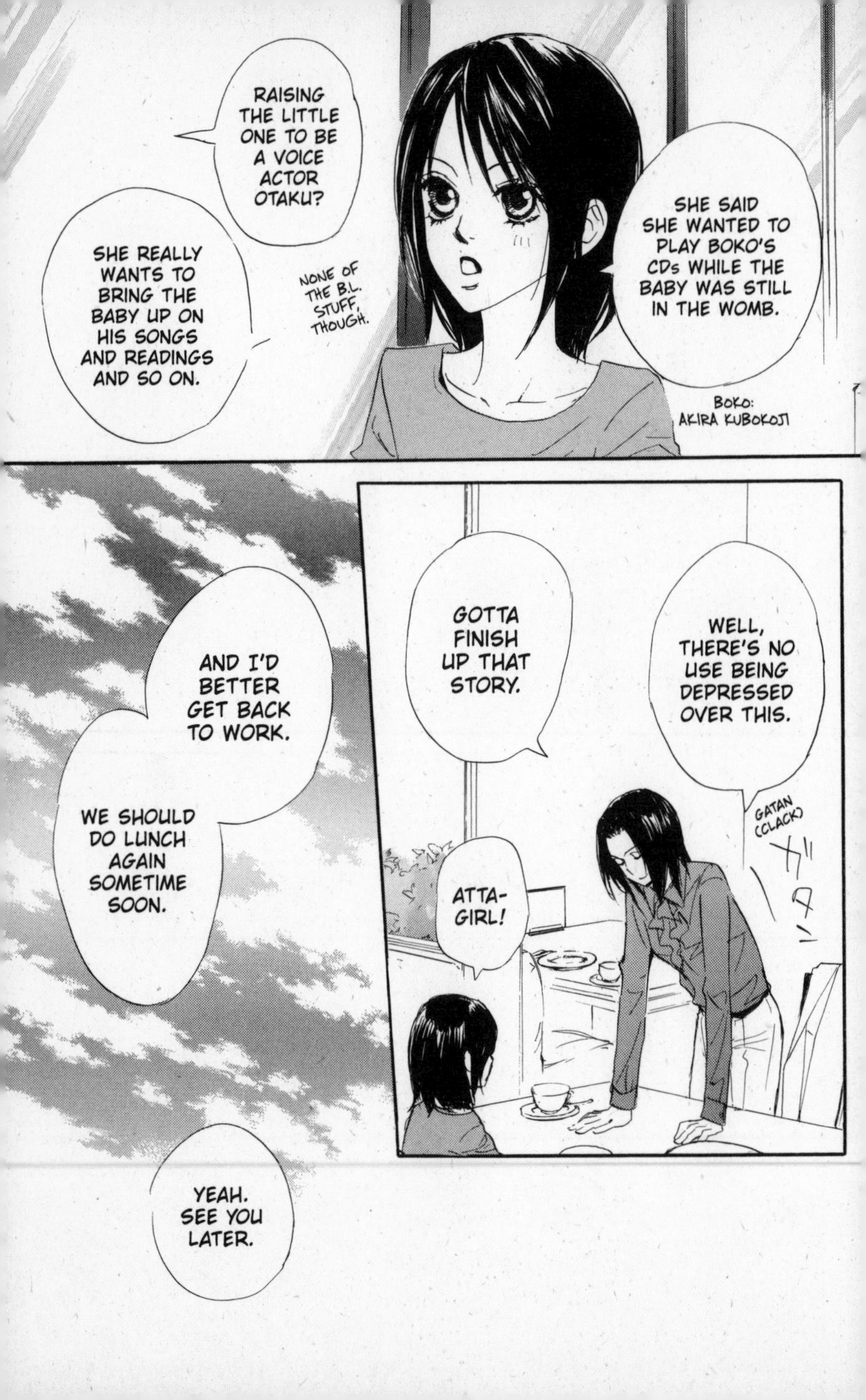
SHE SAID SHE WANTED TO PLAY BOKO'S CDs WHILE THE BABY WAS STILL IN THE WOMB.
BOKO: AKIRA KUBOKOJI
RAISING THE LITTLE ONE TO BE A VOICE ACTOR OTAKU?
NONE OF THE B.L. STUFF, THOUGH.
SHE REALLY WANTS TO BRING THE BABY UP ON HIS SONGS AND READINGS AND SO ON.
WELL, THERE'S NO USE BEING DEPRESSED OVER THIS.
GATAN (CLACK)
GOTTA FINISH UP THAT STORY.
ATTA-GIRL!
AND I'D BETTER GET BACK TO WORK.
WE SHOULD DO LUNCH AGAIN SOMETIME SOON.
YEAH. SEE YOU LATER.

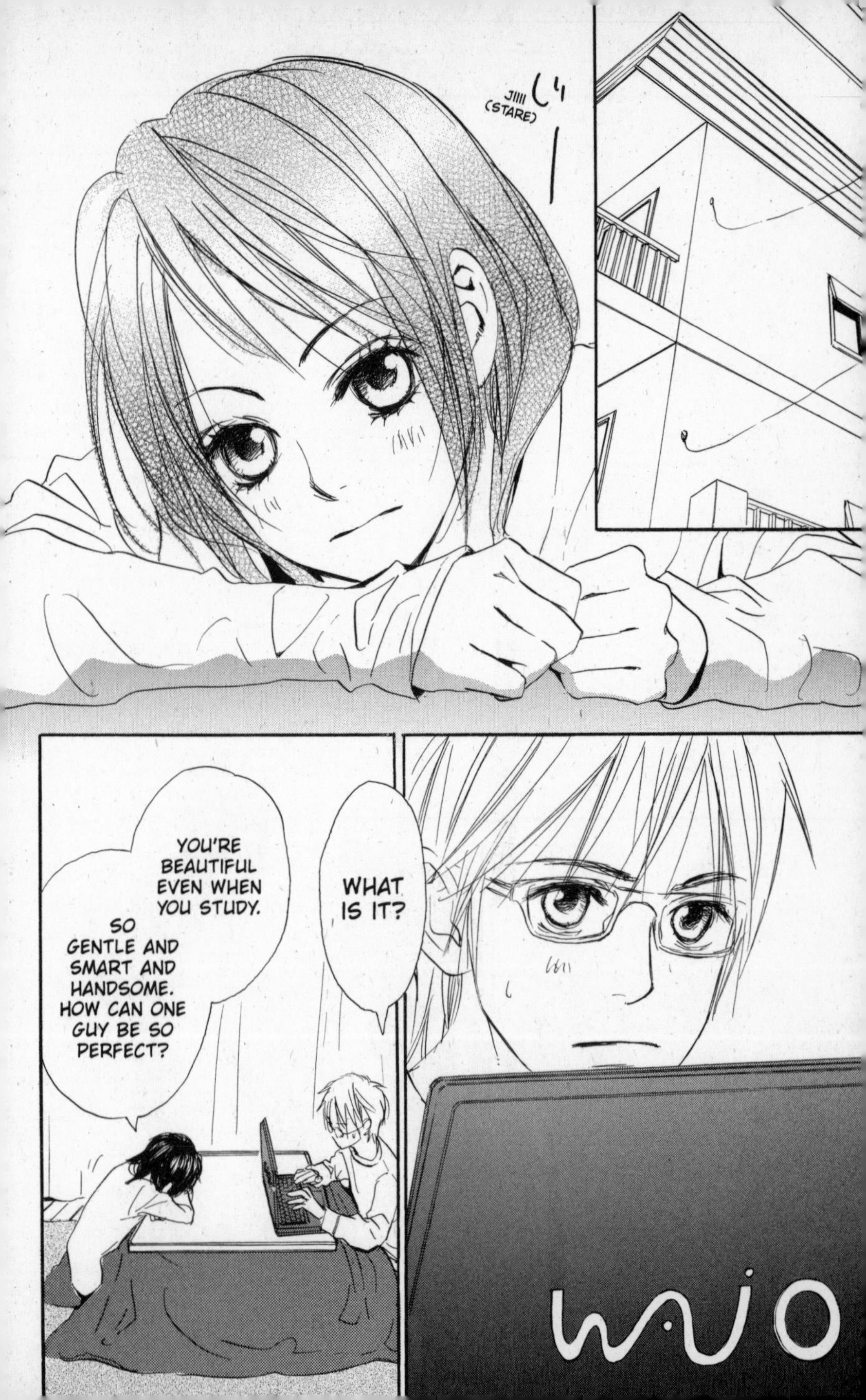

JIIII (STARE)
WHAT IS IT?
YOU'RE BEAUTIFUL EVEN WHEN YOU STUDY.
SO GENTLE AND SMART AND HANDSOME. HOW CAN ONE GUY BE SO PERFECT?

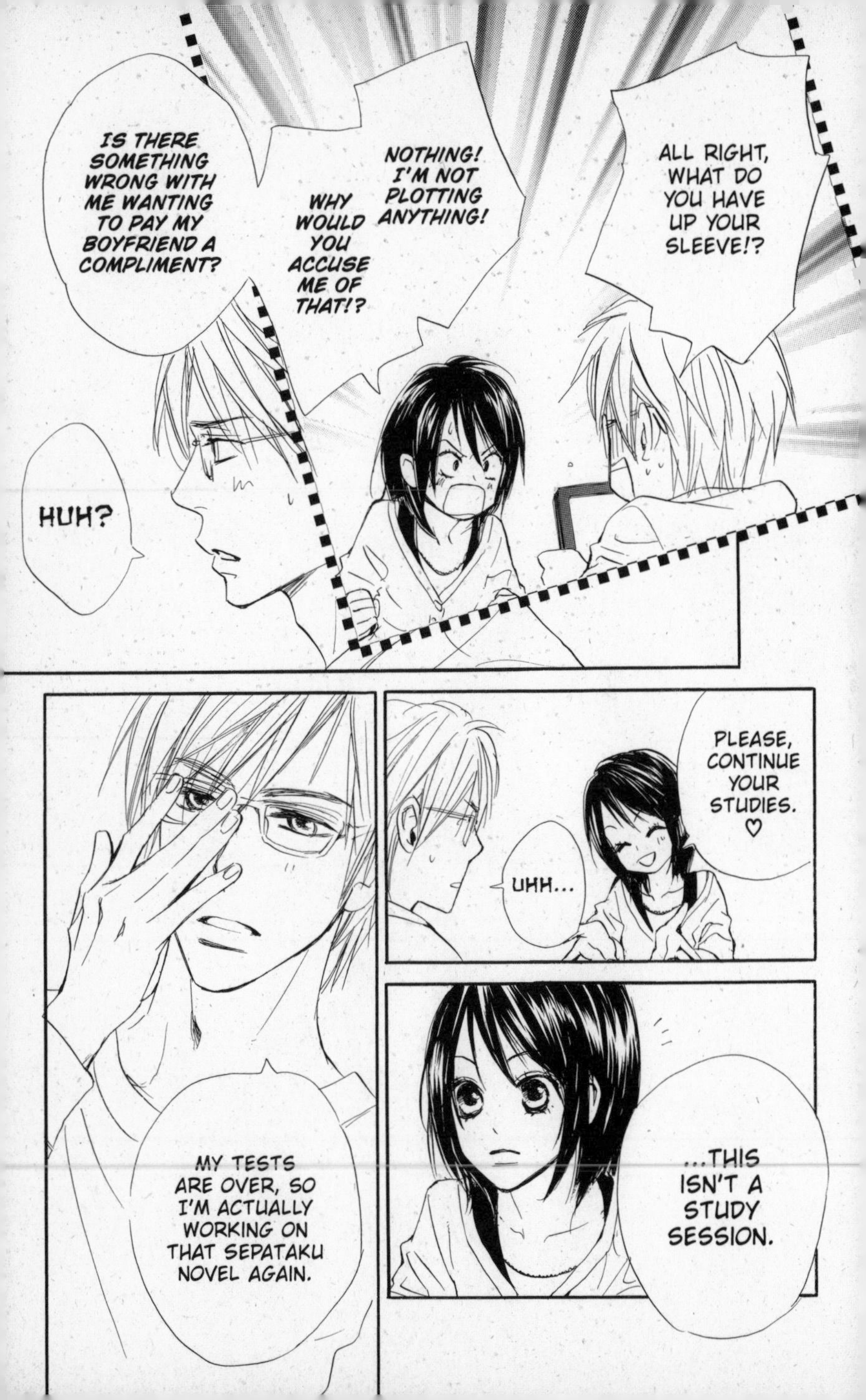
ALL RIGHT, WHAT DO YOU HAVE UP YOUR SLEEVE!?
NOTHING! I'M NOT PLOTTING ANYTHING!
WHY WOULD YOU ACCUSE ME OF THAT!?
IS THERE SOMETHING WRONG WITH ME WANTING TO PAY MY BOYFRIEND A COMPLIMENT?
HUH?
PLEASE, CONTINUE YOUR STUDIES. ♡
UHH...
...THIS ISN'T A STUDY SESSION.
MY TESTS ARE OVER, SO I'M ACTUALLY WORKING ON THAT SEPATAKU NOVEL AGAIN.

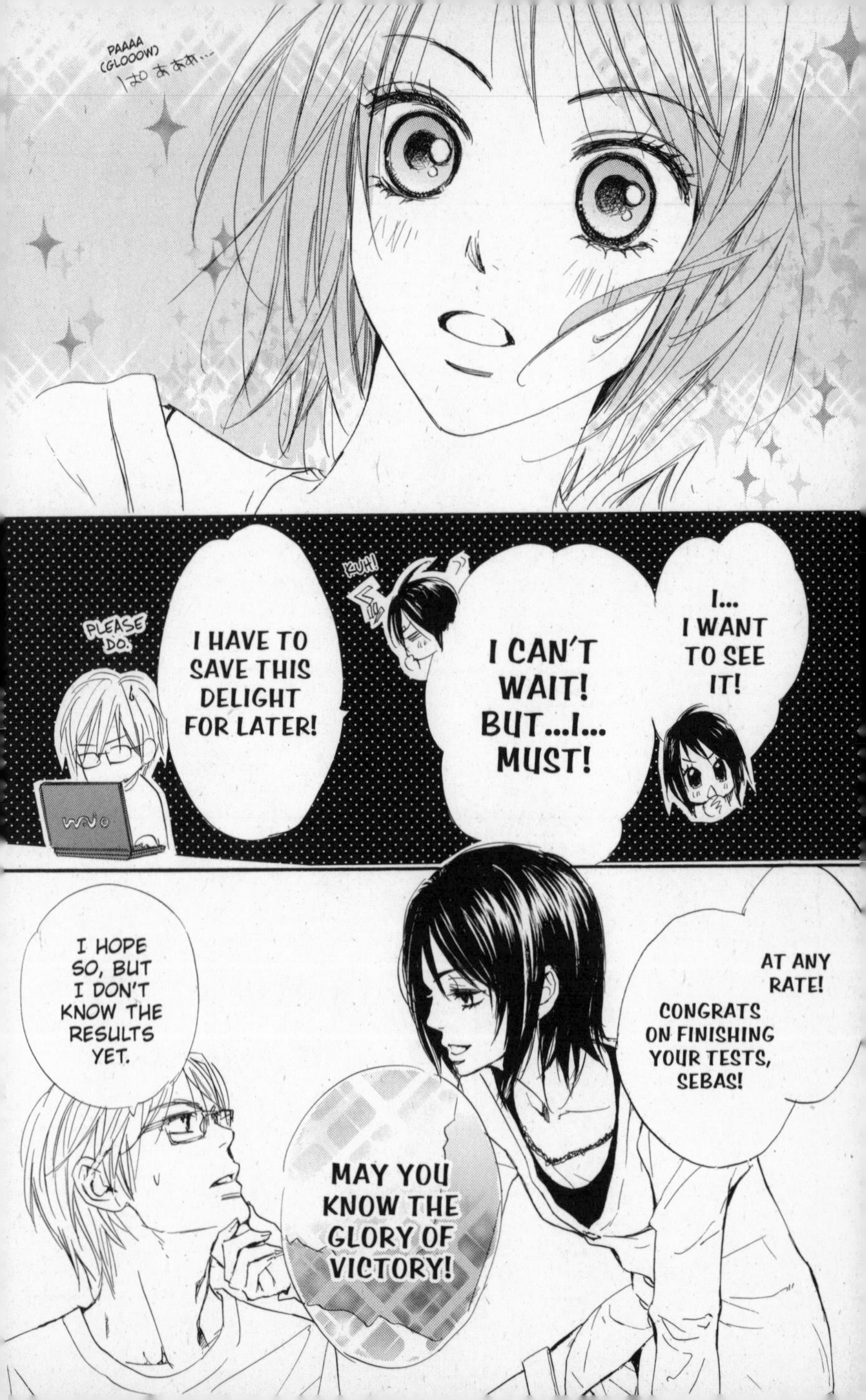
ぱあああ…
PAAAA (GLOOOW)
I... I WANT TO SEE IT!
KUH!
I CAN'T WAIT! BUT...I... MUST!
I HAVE TO SAVE THIS DELIGHT FOR LATER!
PLEASE DO.
AT ANY RATE!
CONGRATS ON FINISHING YOUR TESTS, SEBAS!
MAY YOU KNOW THE GLORY OF VICTORY!
I HOPE SO, BUT I DON'T KNOW THE RESULTS YET.

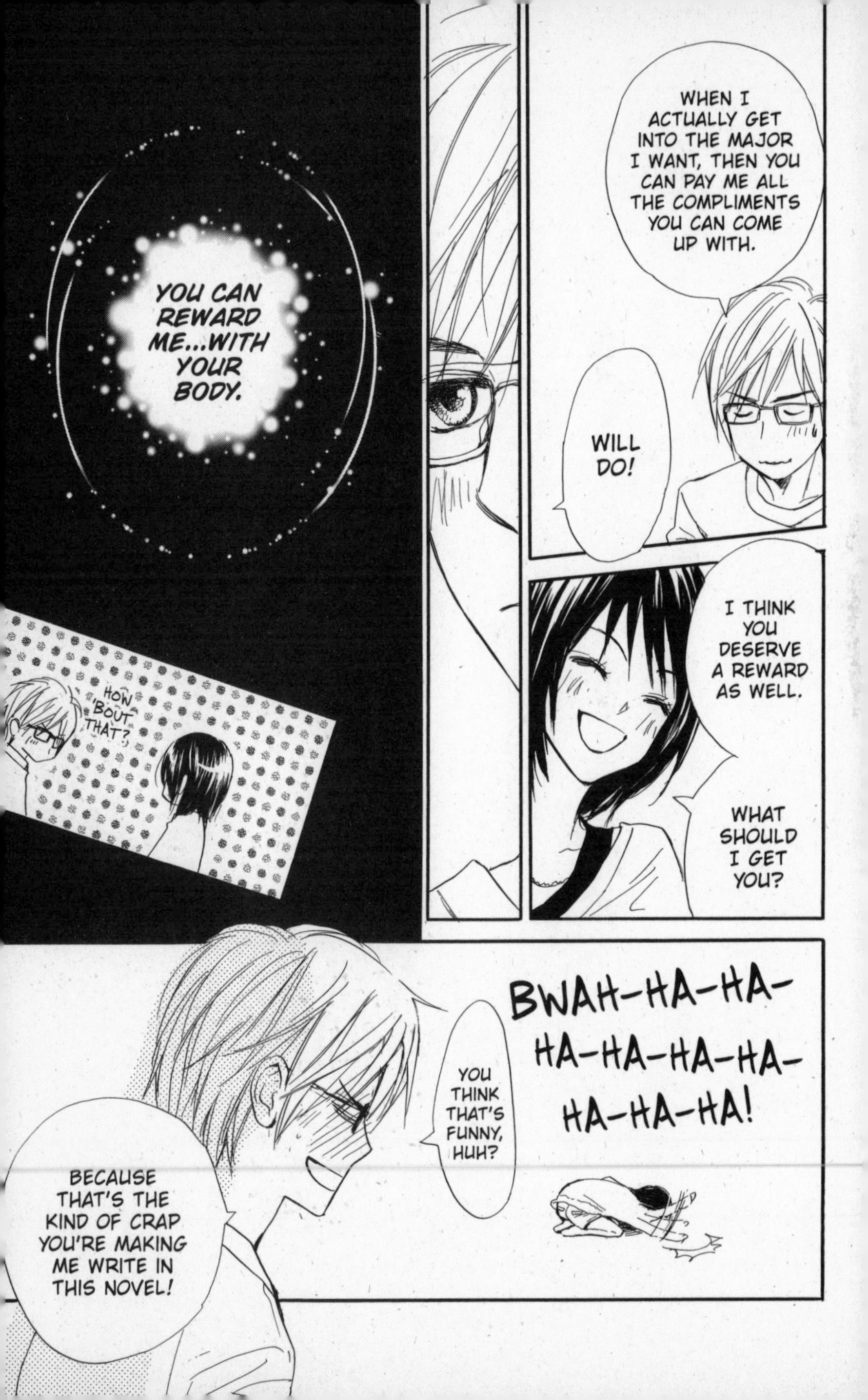
WHEN I ACTUALLY GET INTO THE MAJOR I WANT, THEN YOU CAN PAY ME ALL THE COMPLIMENTS YOU CAN COME UP WITH.
WILL DO!
I THINK YOU DESERVE A REWARD AS WELL.
WHAT SHOULD I GET YOU?
YOU CAN REWARD ME...WITH YOUR BODY.
HOW 'BOUT THAT?
BWAH-HA-HA-HA-HA-HA-HA-HA-HA-HA-HA!
YOU THINK THAT'S FUNNY, HUH?
BECAUSE THAT'S THE KIND OF CRAP YOU'RE MAKING ME WRITE IN THIS NOVEL!

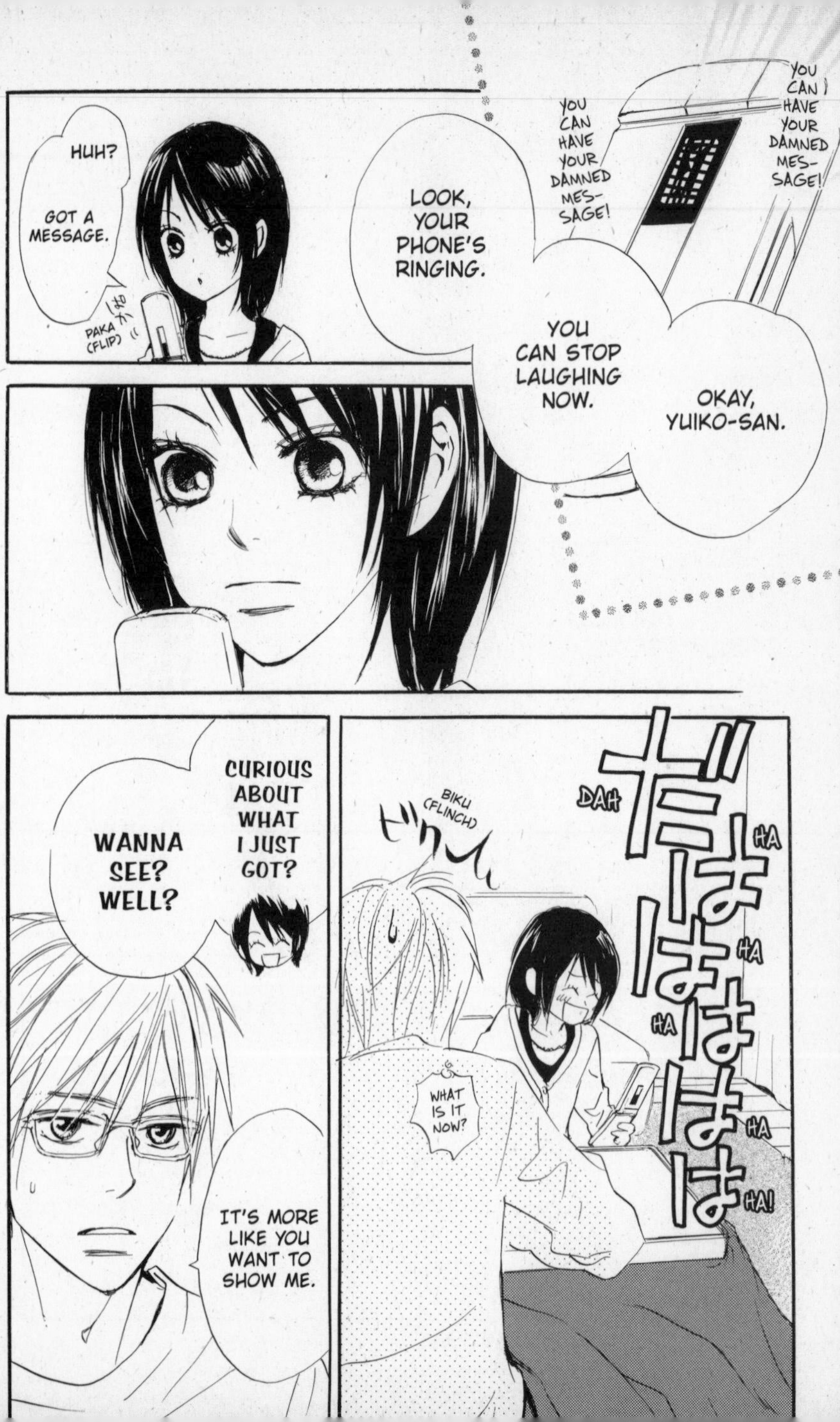
YOU CAN HAVE YOUR DAMNED MES-SAGE!
YOU CAN HAVE YOUR DAMNED MES-SAGE!
LOOK, YOUR PHONE'S RINGING.
OKAY, YUIKO-SAN.
YOU CAN STOP LAUGHING NOW.
HUH?
GOT A MESSAGE.
ぱか
PAKA (FLIP)
だははははは
DAH HA HA HA HA HA!
ビクッ
BIKU (FLINCH)
WHAT IS IT NOW?
CURIOUS ABOUT WHAT I JUST GOT?
WANNA SEE? WELL?
IT'S MORE LIKE YOU WANT TO SHOW ME.

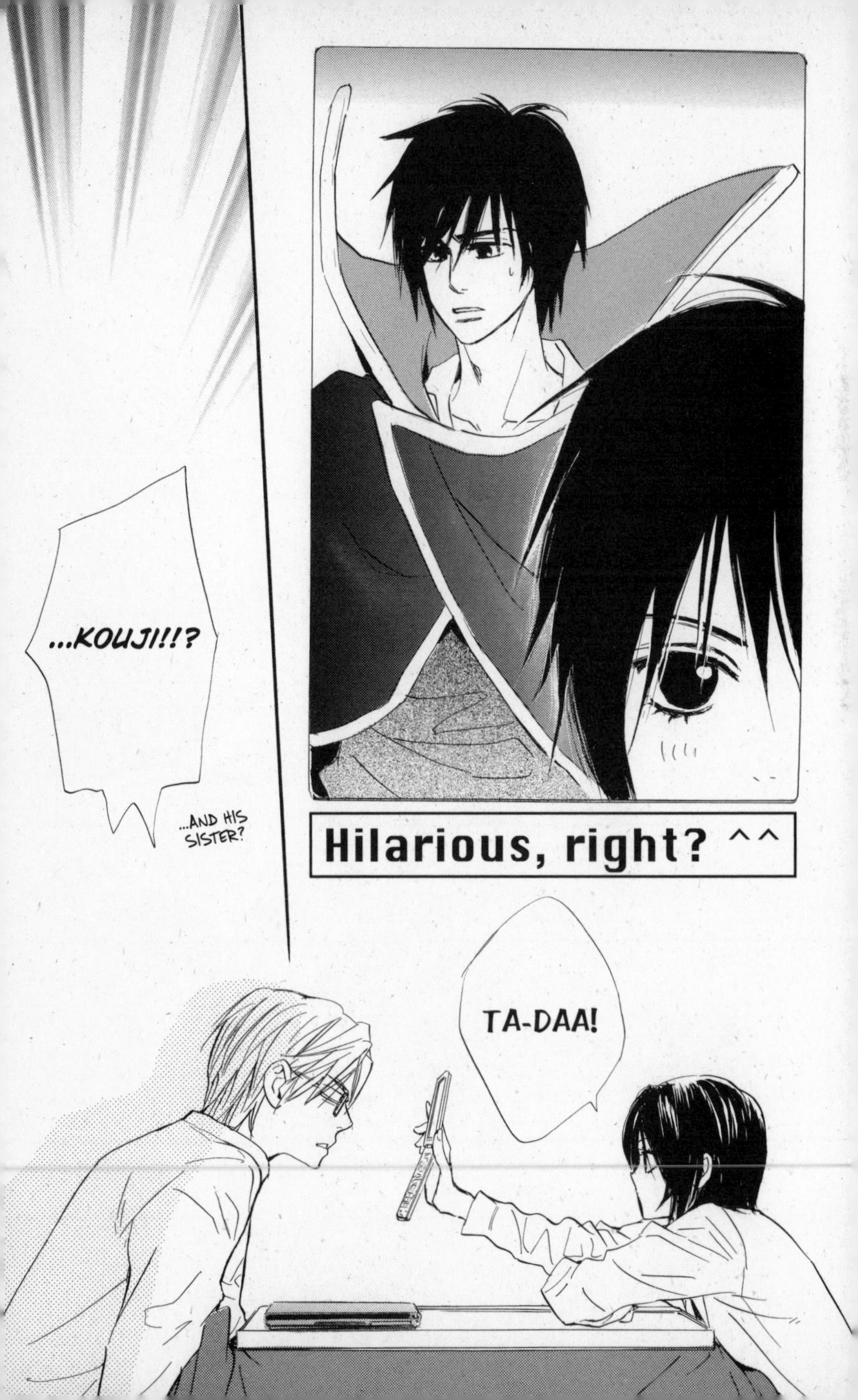
Hilarious, right? ^^
...KOUJI!!?
...AND HIS SISTER?
TA-DAA!

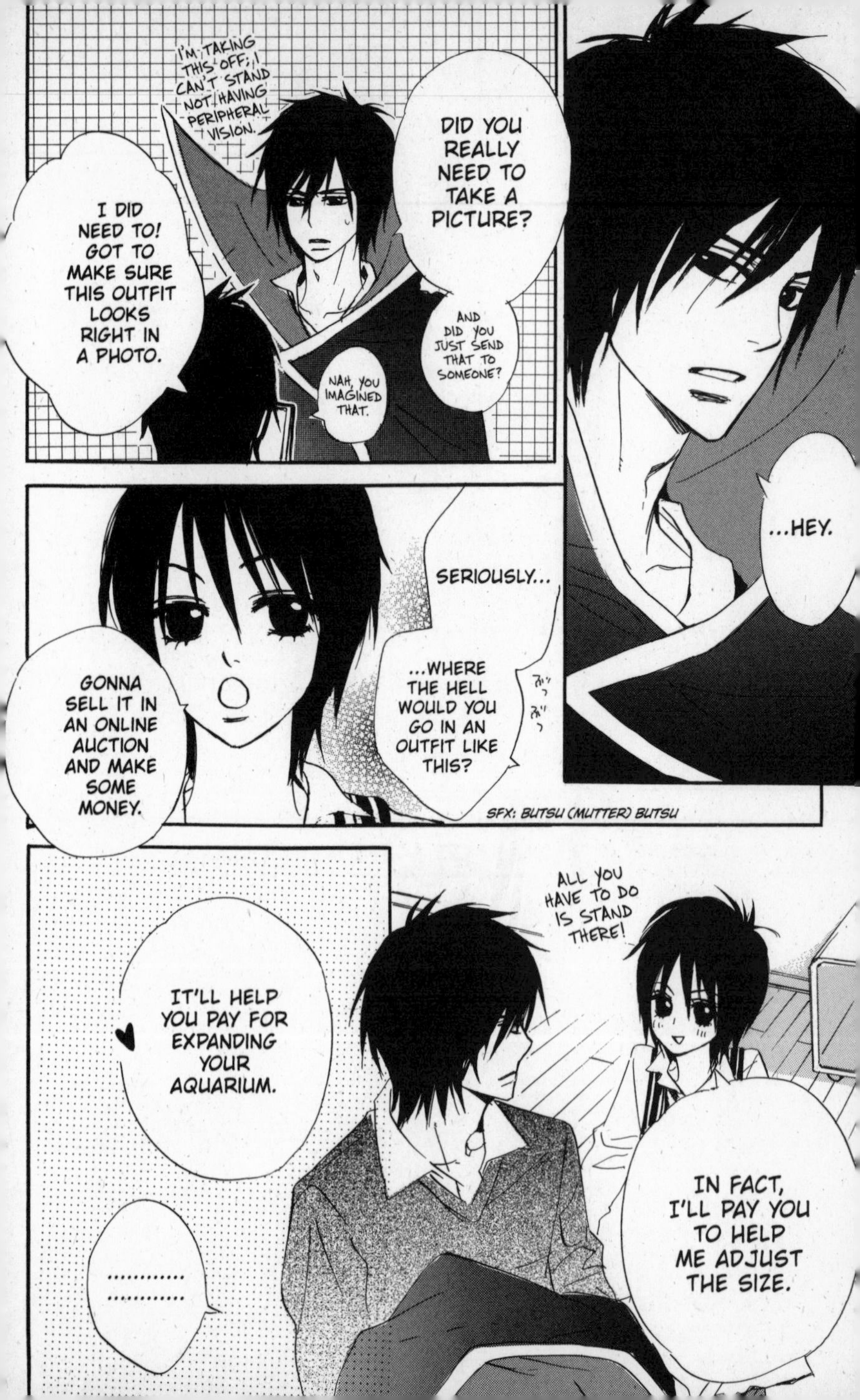
...HEY.
I'M TAKING THIS OFF; I CAN'T STAND NOT HAVING PERIPHERAL VISION.
DID YOU REALLY NEED TO TAKE A PICTURE?
I DID NEED TO! GOT TO MAKE SURE THIS OUTFIT LOOKS RIGHT IN A PHOTO.
AND DID YOU JUST SEND THAT TO SOMEONE?
NAH, YOU IMAGINED THAT.
SERIOUSLY...
...WHERE THE HELL WOULD YOU GO IN AN OUTFIT LIKE THIS?
GONNA SELL IT IN AN ONLINE AUCTION AND MAKE SOME MONEY.
SFX: BUTSU (MUTTER) BUTSU
ALL YOU HAVE TO DO IS STAND THERE!
IN FACT, I'LL PAY YOU TO HELP ME ADJUST THE SIZE.
IT'LL HELP YOU PAY FOR EXPANDING YOUR AQUARIUM.
....
....

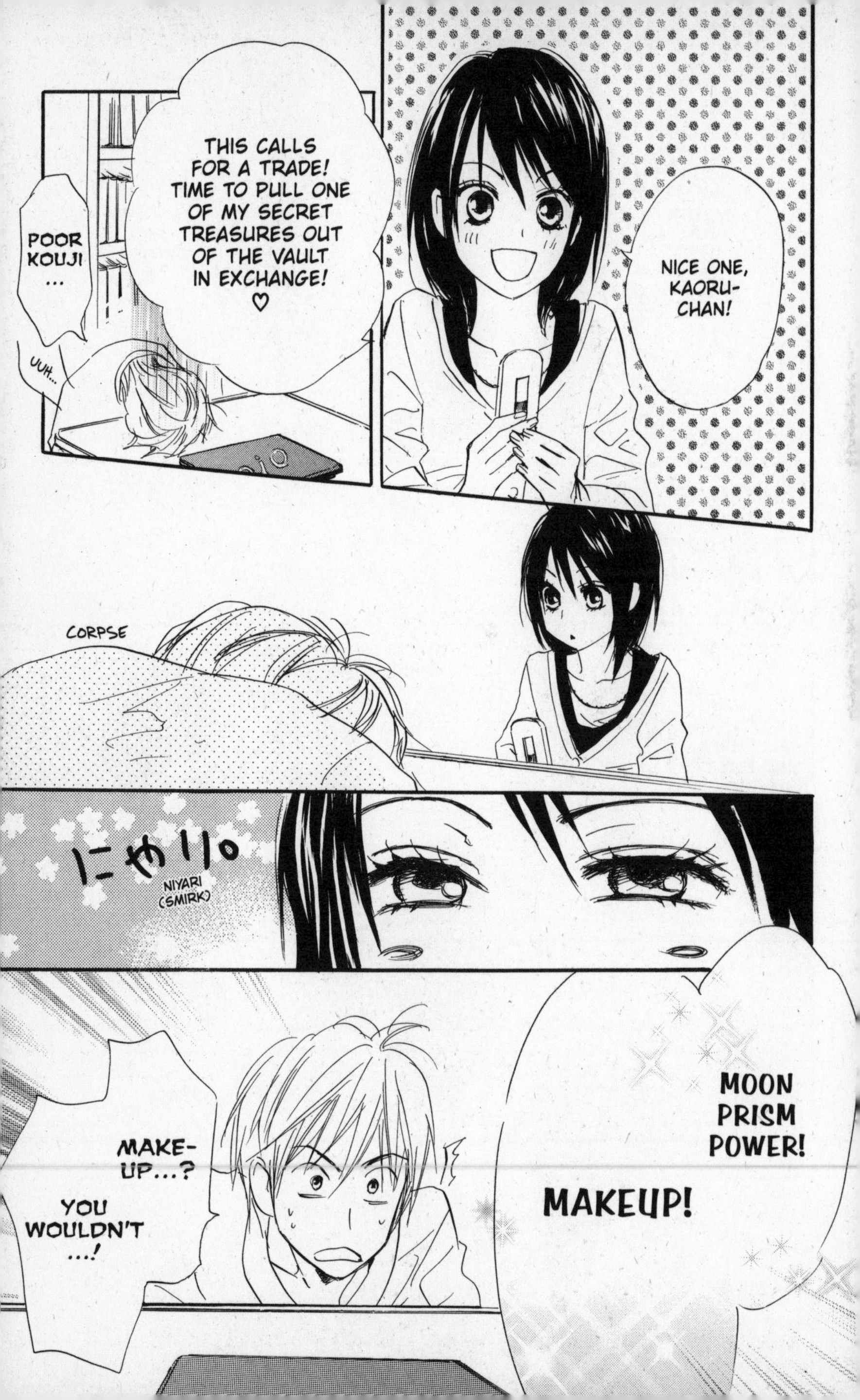
NICE ONE, KAORU-CHAN!
THIS CALLS FOR A TRADE! TIME TO PULL ONE OF MY SECRET TREASURES OUT OF THE VAULT IN EXCHANGE! ♡
POOR KOUJI ...
UUH...
CORPSE
にやり。
NIYARI (SMIRK)
MOON PRISM POWER!
MAKEUP!
MAKE-UP...?
YOU WOULDN'T ...!

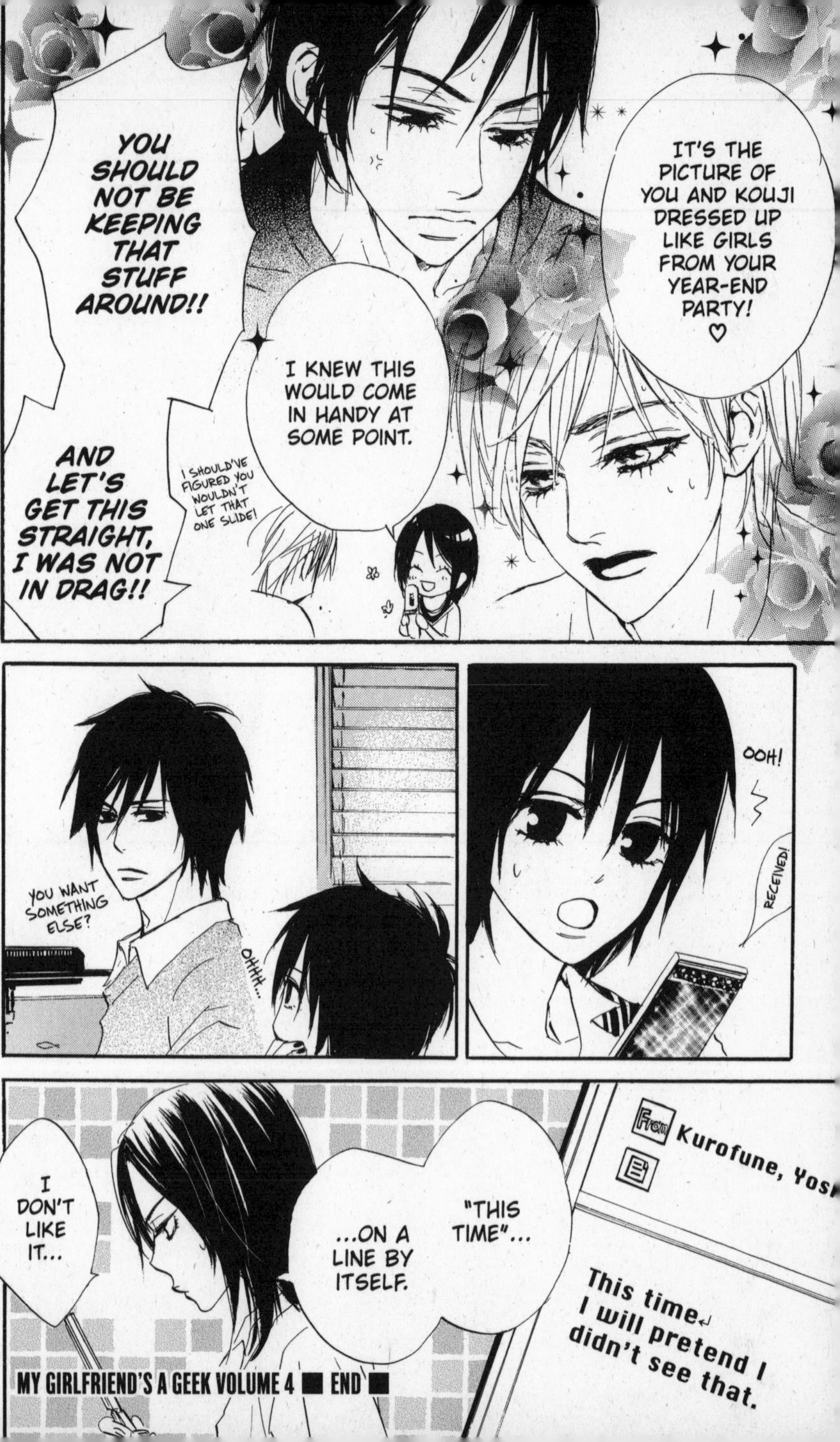
IT'S THE PICTURE OF YOU AND KOUJI DRESSED UP LIKE GIRLS FROM YOUR YEAR-END PARTY! ♡
I KNEW THIS WOULD COME IN HANDY AT SOME POINT.
YOU SHOULD NOT BE KEEPING THAT STUFF AROUND!!
I SHOULD'VE FIGURED YOU WOULDN'T LET THAT ONE SLIDE!
AND LET'S GET THIS STRAIGHT, I WAS NOT IN DRAG!!
OOH!
RECEIVED!
YOU WANT SOMETHING ELSE?
OHHH...
From Kurofune, Yos
This time↵ I will pretend I didn't see that.
"THIS TIME"...
...ON A LINE BY ITSELF.
I DON'T LIKE IT...
MY GIRLFRIEND'S A GEEK VOLUME 4 ■ END ■

FUJOSHI NEWS vol.13

YUIKO-SAN GLOSSARY

P.36
PERSONIFICATION - TO CREATE A HUMAN CHARACTER THAT REPRESENTS AN ANIMAL, PLANT, OR INANIMATE OBJECT. ANYTHING CAN BE A TARGET: COUNTRIES OF THE WORLD, STATES AND PREFECTURES, TRAIN LINES, LAWS, ETC.

P.61
TALK SHOW - AN EVENT WHERE YOU CAN GO SEE VOICE ACTORS BANTER ON STAGE. WHEN THE FRIENDSHIP BETWEEN ACTORS MIRRORS THAT OF THE CHARACTERS THEY PLAY, IT'S EVEN MORE EXCITING!

P.73
WEB RADIO - A RADIO SHOW THAT IS BROADCAST OVER THE INTERNET. THE ONE YUIKO-SAN LISTENS TO IS A LATE-NIGHT ANIME SHOW. THERE'S A FRANK, NO-HOLDS-BARRED ATMOSPHERE BETWEEN THE TWO MEN WHO RUN IT THAT SUITS THE TIME SLOT.

P.117
FLAG - AN EVENT OR LINE OF DIALOGUE IN A STORY THAT BRINGS ABOUT A FUTURE DEVELOPMENT. EXAMPLE: DEATH FLAG. IF A CHARACTER SAYS, "WHEN THIS WAR IS OVER, I'M GONNA GET MARRIED," HE IS LIKELY GOING TO DIE IN BATTLE.

P.118
FUDANSHI - A MAN WHO ENJOYS B.L. IN RECENT YEARS, THEY ARE ALSO CALLED "BUSHI," WHICH SOUNDS LIKE "WARRIOR" AND IS MORE MANLY.

P.131
MAIL-IN UPC - A CUT-OUT SLIP ON A BOOK'S DUST JACKET THAT CAN BE REDEEMED THROUGH THE MAIL FOR A PRIZE. MASA-NEE WANTED TO SEND IT IN FOR A BOOKSTORE GIFT CARD WITH AN ILLUSTRATION BY A GODLY ARTIST. THERE'S TOO MUCH SKIN SHOWING TO USE IT AT THE STORE WITHOUT EMBARRASSMENT, BUT SHE WAS PLANNING TO KEEP IT FOR HER COLLECTION ANYWAY.

P.132
GODLY ARTIST - AN ILLUSTRATOR WHOSE CONTRIBUTIONS TO A BOOK ARE SO GORGEOUS, THEY APPEAR TO HAVE COME DIRECTLY FROM THE HAND OF GOD.

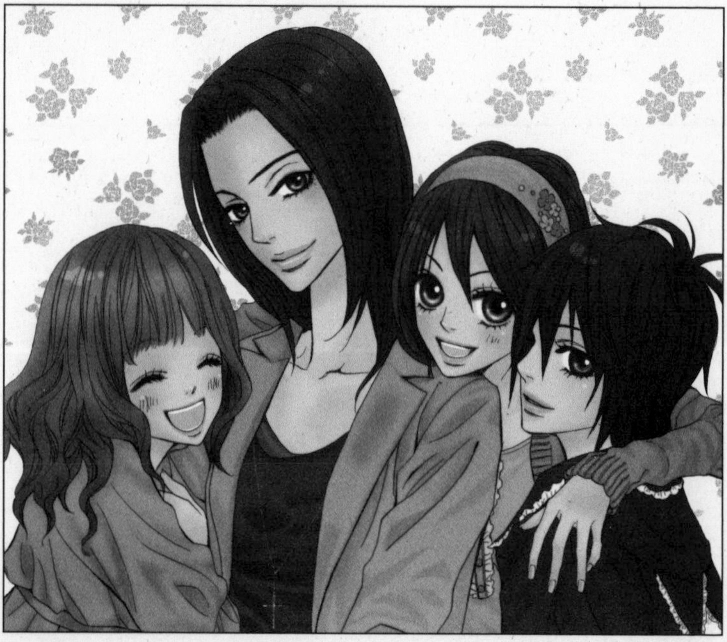

Afterword Essay

Pentabu

WELCOME TO THE ROTTEN WORLD OF FU-JOSHI!

MY GIRLFRIEND IS TWO YEARS OLDER THAN ME.

2009/03/03 23:31

My girlfriend is two years older than me...
.........and she's a *fujoshi*.

When I started my blog, a chronicle of life with my girlfriend, with these simple sentences, I never could have guessed it would someday be a book — and certainly never a manga drawn by a smash-hit artist like Shinba-sensei.

The happiness I experience every day with my girlfriend is being turned into a spectacular tale.
It is only through the help of Shinba-sensei and the people at the publisher, and the incredible support of the fans, that I've been blessed with this wonderful feeling.

As the creator and as simply a fan of the *My Girlfriend's a Geek* manga, I can only express myself in one simple statement: Thank you.

No other combination of words could possibly contain the sentiment that simple message holds, so let me try it one more time.
Thank you so much.

Now, then.
Even I, the guy who writes this stuff, can only half-believe what's happening.
In fact it's more like **30% believe**,
or possibly even **20% believe**. At any rate, it's hard to fathom.

After the book, after the manga...

The story of *My Girlfriend's a Geek*—
is being made into a movie.

Y-KO: I feel like we had this conversation when the whole manga thing came about, but...are you sure this isn't a dream? Let me have your cheek.

ME: Why do you need mine!? Pinch your own cheeks if you need to!

Y-KO: Huh? Why?

ME: Why would you say "why"!?

Y-KO: Because I don't like being in pain. But even worse than that would be painlessly finding out that it was all a dream.

ME: I don't want that either!

Y-KO: Well, you don't have to worry about it.
You're uke.

ME: That sentence makes no sense!

Y-KO: Well, **you're not seme**, are you?

ME: No, the proper way to frame your sentence was, "you're a masochist."

Y-KO: **...Huh? But...huh?** You're uke, right?

ME: Please don't pretend that you are honestly baffled by this conversation...

And no fair scratching your head like that!
It's too cute!

Y-KO: Oh, hey, if it's going to be a movie now, shouldn't we think up a new tagline?

ME: ...Pardon? A new tagline?

Y-KO: Yeah. You know how the blog's tagline was "My girlfriend is two years older than me...and she's a fujoshi"? I think it's about time we came up with a new one!

—Hmm.
A new tagline... She might have a point.
And more importantly, maybe it will get her mind off of this uke nonsense.

ME: Good idea. Let's put our heads together.

Y-KO: Actually, I've got an idea already.

ME: Oh? What's that?

Y-KO: # I am "uke."

......

I guess we weren't done with the uke stuff after all.

Y-KO: **"I do not yet have a name."**

ME: Uh, yes, I do! A very nice name given to me directly by my parents!

Y-KO: Yes, but this one's nice, isn't it? It has a real literary air to it.

ME: Right...if you say so!

Y-KO: Fine, then. Next idea!

"I am uke. Therefore I am."

ME: That's not the kind of affirmation of existence that I want associated with me! Rejected!

Y-KO: What? How about this? "In my dictionary, the only definition for 'uke' is **as it pertains to B.L.**"

ME: What kind of dictionary is that? Rejected!

Y-KO: "In fact, the **only** definition in my dictionary is 'uke.'"

ME: Rejected! Ultra-rejected!

Y-KO: Oh, nothing's ever good enough for you! What should it be, then?

ME: You can start by moving away from the uke thing!

Y-KO: Then... **"I'm going to be a moe seme."**

ME: Okay, so you did steer it away from uke like I asked, but still... Rejected!

Y-KO: **"Moe seme, grand opening."**

ME: Like a Chinese restaurant!?

Y-KO: —You see? **You can't be a seme!**

ME: Wait...are we discussing me now? What happened to the tagline!?

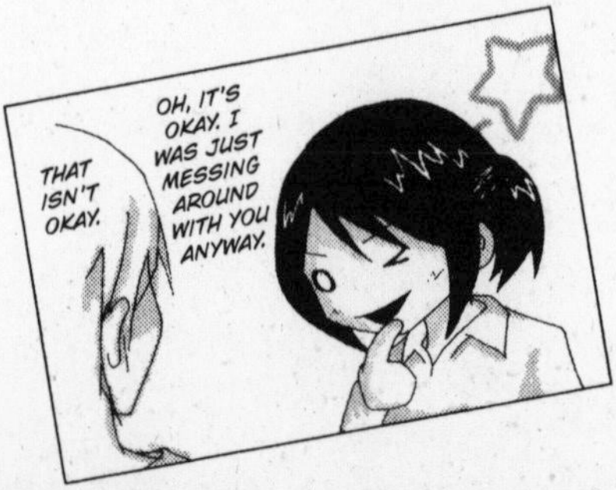
OH, IT'S OKAY. I WAS JUST MESSING AROUND WITH YOU ANYWAY.
THAT ISN'T OKAY.

—And there you have it.

Y-ko and I are living our lives to the fullest, just as Taiga and Yuiko are.

Not only do our lives go on, so do Taiga and Yuiko's, and now there will be even more of us to go around in the upcoming movie adaptation. I hope you enjoy it.

Spring 2009
Pentabu
Y-ko

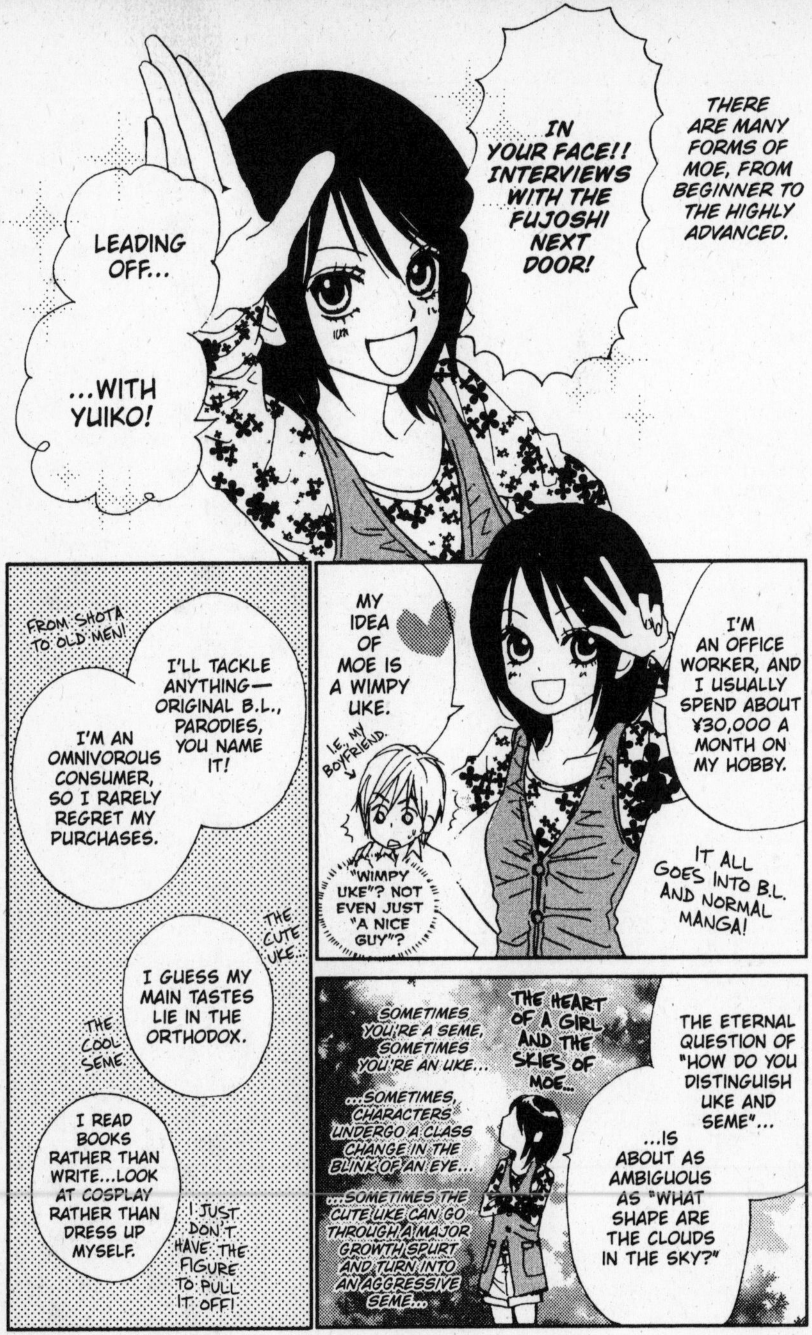
THERE ARE MANY FORMS OF MOE, FROM BEGINNER TO THE HIGHLY ADVANCED.
IN YOUR FACE!! INTERVIEWS WITH THE FUJOSHI NEXT DOOR!
LEADING OFF...
...WITH YUIKO!
I'M AN OFFICE WORKER, AND I USUALLY SPEND ABOUT ¥30,000 A MONTH ON MY HOBBY.
IT ALL GOES INTO B.L. AND NORMAL MANGA!
MY IDEA OF MOE IS A WIMPY UKE.
I.E., MY BOYFRIEND.
"WIMPY UKE"? NOT EVEN JUST "A NICE GUY"?
THE ETERNAL QUESTION OF "HOW DO YOU DISTINGUISH UKE AND SEME"...
...IS ABOUT AS AMBIGUOUS AS "WHAT SHAPE ARE THE CLOUDS IN THE SKY?"
THE HEART OF A GIRL AND THE SKIES OF MOE...
SOMETIMES YOU'RE A SEME, SOMETIMES YOU'RE AN UKE...
...SOMETIMES, CHARACTERS UNDERGO A CLASS CHANGE IN THE BLINK OF AN EYE...
...SOMETIMES THE CUTE UKE CAN GO THROUGH A MAJOR GROWTH SPURT AND TURN INTO AN AGGRESSIVE SEME...
FROM SHOTA TO OLD MEN!
I'LL TACKLE ANYTHING—ORIGINAL B.L., PARODIES, YOU NAME IT!
I'M AN OMNIVOROUS CONSUMER, SO I RARELY REGRET MY PURCHASES.
THE CUTE UKE...
I GUESS MY MAIN TASTES LIE IN THE ORTHODOX.
THE COOL SEME.
I READ BOOKS RATHER THAN WRITE...LOOK AT COSPLAY RATHER THAN DRESS UP MYSELF.
I JUST DON'T HAVE THE FIGURE TO PULL IT OFF!

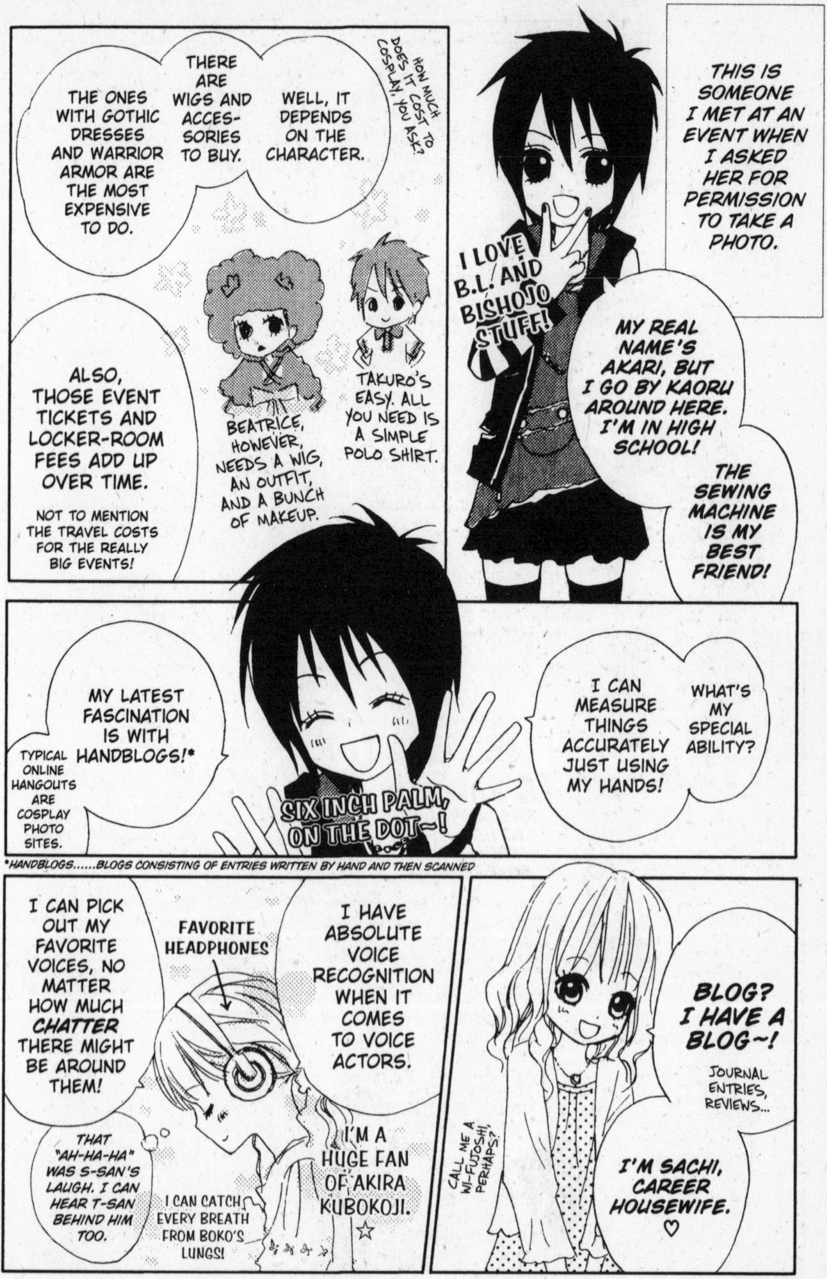

THIS IS SOMEONE I MET AT AN EVENT WHEN I ASKED HER FOR PERMISSION TO TAKE A PHOTO.
I LOVE B.L. AND BISHOJO STUFF!
MY REAL NAME'S AKARI, BUT I GO BY KAORU AROUND HERE. I'M IN HIGH SCHOOL!
THE SEWING MACHINE IS MY BEST FRIEND!
HOW MUCH DOES IT COST TO COSPLAY, YOU ASK?
WELL, IT DEPENDS ON THE CHARACTER.
THERE ARE WIGS AND ACCES-SORIES TO BUY.
THE ONES WITH GOTHIC DRESSES AND WARRIOR ARMOR ARE THE MOST EXPENSIVE TO DO.
TAKURO'S EASY. ALL YOU NEED IS A SIMPLE POLO SHIRT.
BEATRICE, HOWEVER, NEEDS A WIG, AN OUTFIT, AND A BUNCH OF MAKEUP.
ALSO, THOSE EVENT TICKETS AND LOCKER-ROOM FEES ADD UP OVER TIME.
NOT TO MENTION THE TRAVEL COSTS FOR THE REALLY BIG EVENTS!
WHAT'S MY SPECIAL ABILITY?
I CAN MEASURE THINGS ACCURATELY JUST USING MY HANDS!
SIX INCH PALM, ON THE DOT~!
MY LATEST FASCINATION IS WITH HANDBLOGS!*
TYPICAL ONLINE HANGOUTS ARE COSPLAY PHOTO SITES.
*HANDBLOGS......BLOGS CONSISTING OF ENTRIES WRITTEN BY HAND AND THEN SCANNED
BLOG? I HAVE A BLOG~!
JOURNAL ENTRIES, REVIEWS...
I'M SACHI, CAREER HOUSEWIFE. ♡
CALL ME A WI-FUJOSHI, PERHAPS?
I HAVE ABSOLUTE VOICE RECOGNITION WHEN IT COMES TO VOICE ACTORS.
FAVORITE HEADPHONES
I CAN PICK OUT MY FAVORITE VOICES, NO MATTER HOW MUCH CHATTER THERE MIGHT BE AROUND THEM!
I'M A HUGE FAN OF AKIRA KUBOKOJI. ☆
I CAN CATCH EVERY BREATH FROM BOKO'S LUNGS!
THAT "AH-HA-HA" WAS S-SAN'S LAUGH. I CAN HEAR T-SAN BEHIND HIM TOO.

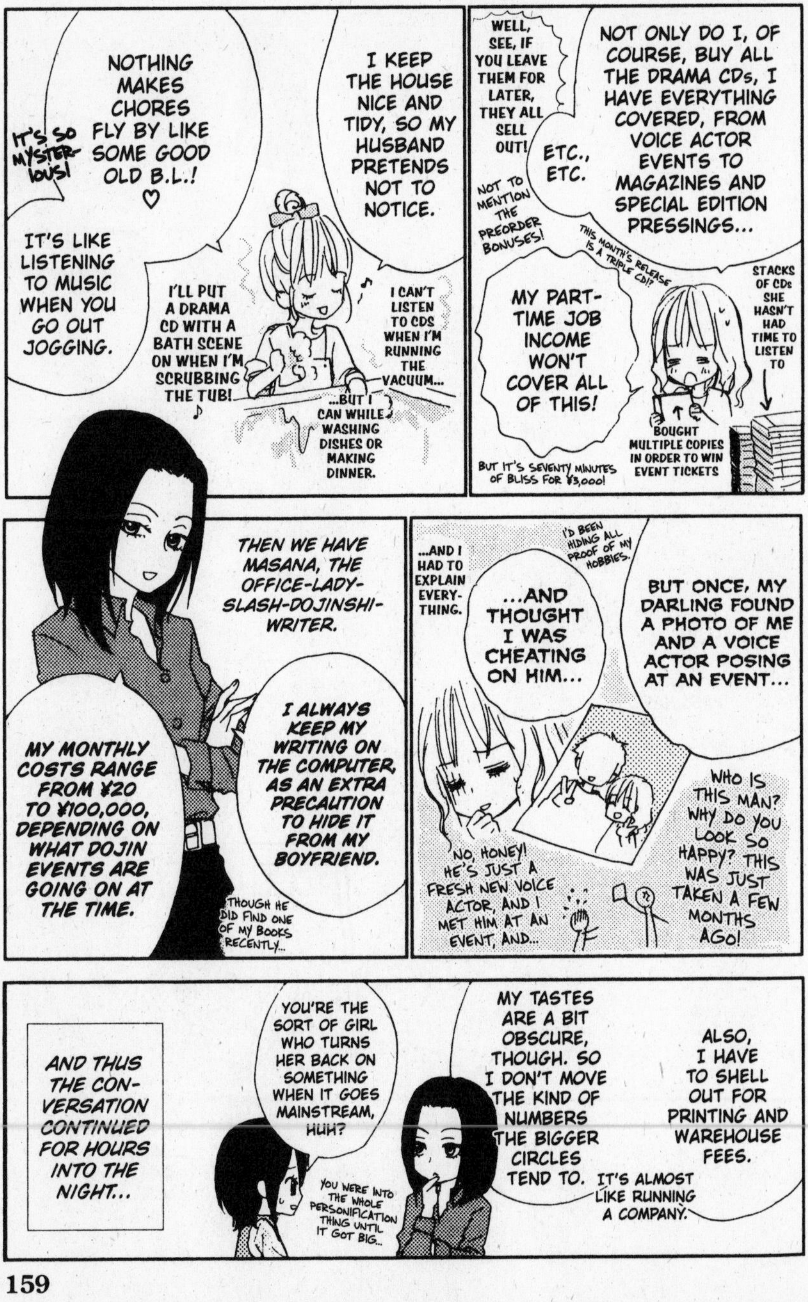
NOT ONLY DO I, OF COURSE, BUY ALL THE DRAMA CDs, I HAVE EVERYTHING COVERED, FROM VOICE ACTOR EVENTS TO MAGAZINES AND SPECIAL EDITION PRESSINGS...
WELL, SEE, IF YOU LEAVE THEM FOR LATER, THEY ALL SELL OUT!
ETC., ETC.
NOT TO MENTION THE PREORDER BONUSES!
THIS MONTH'S RELEASE IS A TRIPLE CD!?
STACKS OF CDs SHE HASN'T HAD TIME TO LISTEN TO
MY PART-TIME JOB INCOME WON'T COVER ALL OF THIS!
BOUGHT MULTIPLE COPIES IN ORDER TO WIN EVENT TICKETS
BUT IT'S SEVENTY MINUTES OF BLISS FOR ¥3,000!
I KEEP THE HOUSE NICE AND TIDY, SO MY HUSBAND PRETENDS NOT TO NOTICE.
NOTHING MAKES CHORES FLY BY LIKE SOME GOOD OLD B.L.! ♡
IT'S SO MYSTERIOUS!
I CAN'T LISTEN TO CDS WHEN I'M RUNNING THE VACUUM...
...BUT I CAN WHILE WASHING DISHES OR MAKING DINNER.
I'LL PUT A DRAMA CD WITH A BATH SCENE ON WHEN I'M SCRUBBING THE TUB! ♪
IT'S LIKE LISTENING TO MUSIC WHEN YOU GO OUT JOGGING.
BUT ONCE, MY DARLING FOUND A PHOTO OF ME AND A VOICE ACTOR POSING AT AN EVENT...
I'D BEEN HIDING ALL PROOF OF MY HOBBIES.
...AND THOUGHT I WAS CHEATING ON HIM...
...AND I HAD TO EXPLAIN EVERYTHING.
WHO IS THIS MAN? WHY DO YOU LOOK SO HAPPY? THIS WAS JUST TAKEN A FEW MONTHS AGO!
NO, HONEY! HE'S JUST A FRESH NEW VOICE ACTOR, AND I MET HIM AT AN EVENT, AND...
THEN WE HAVE MASANA, THE OFFICE-LADY-SLASH-DOJINSHI-WRITER.
I ALWAYS KEEP MY WRITING ON THE COMPUTER, AS AN EXTRA PRECAUTION TO HIDE IT FROM MY BOYFRIEND.
THOUGH HE DID FIND ONE OF MY BOOKS RECENTLY...
MY MONTHLY COSTS RANGE FROM ¥20 TO ¥100,000, DEPENDING ON WHAT DOJIN EVENTS ARE GOING ON AT THE TIME.
ALSO, I HAVE TO SHELL OUT FOR PRINTING AND WAREHOUSE FEES.
MY TASTES ARE A BIT OBSCURE, THOUGH. SO I DON'T MOVE THE KIND OF NUMBERS THE BIGGER CIRCLES TEND TO.
IT'S ALMOST LIKE RUNNING A COMPANY.
YOU'RE THE SORT OF GIRL WHO TURNS HER BACK ON SOMETHING WHEN IT GOES MAINSTREAM, HUH?
YOU WERE INTO THE WHOLE PERSONIFICATION THING UNTIL IT GOT BIG...
AND THUS THE CONVERSATION CONTINUED FOR HOURS INTO THE NIGHT...

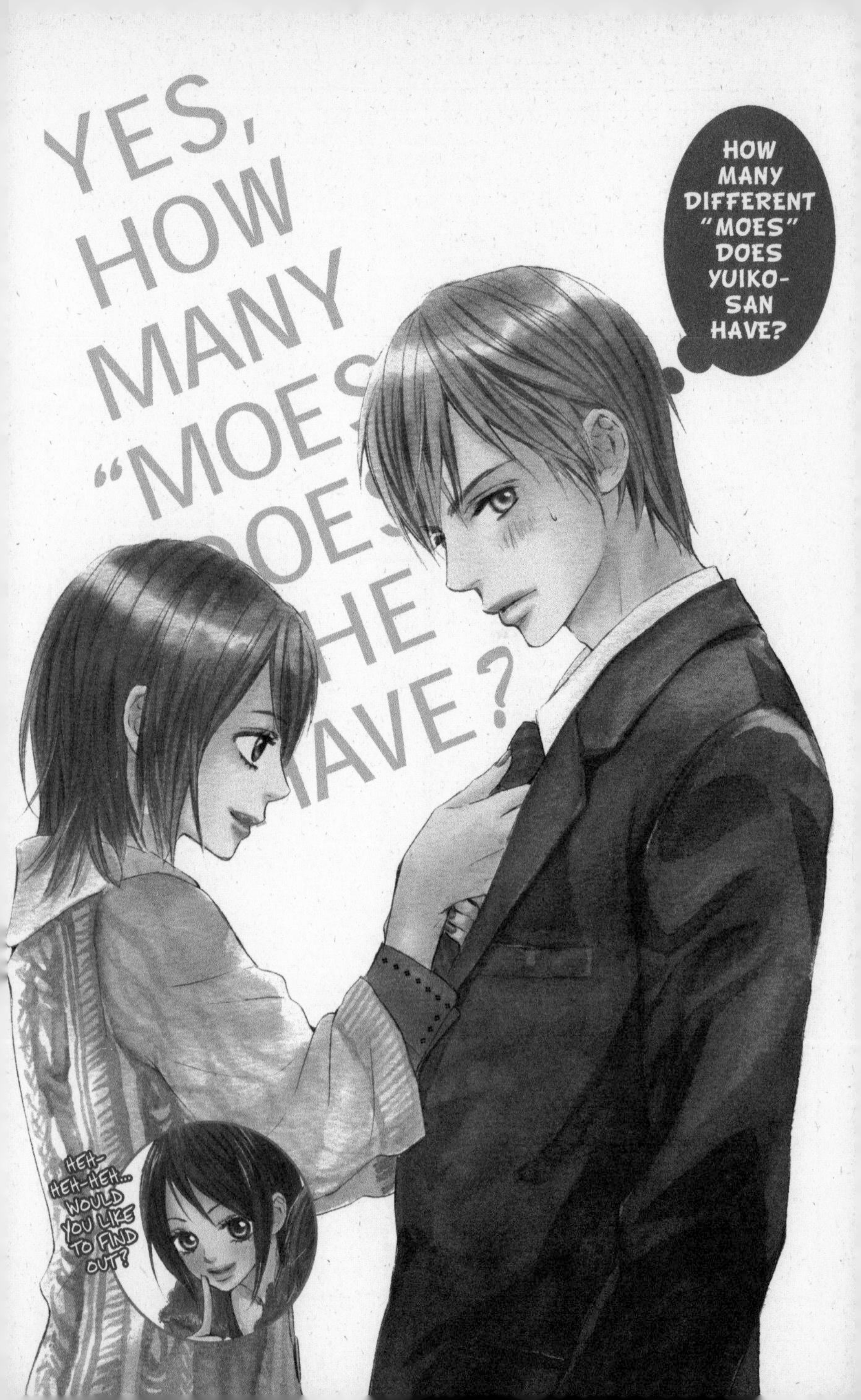
HOW MANY DIFFERENT "MOES" DOES YUIKO-SAN HAVE?
YES, HOW MANY "MOES" DOES SHE HAVE?
HEH-HEH-HEH... WOULD YOU LIKE TO FIND OUT?

MY GIRLFRIEND'S A GEEK ❹

RIZE SHINBA
PENTABU

Translation: Stephen Paul
Lettering: Alexis Eckerman

FUJYOSHI KANOJO Vol. 4 ©2009 Rize Shinba ©PENTABU 2006, 2007 All Rights
Reserved. First published in Japan in 2009 by ENTERBRAIN, INC., Tokyo. English
translation rights arranged with ENTERBRAIN, INC. through Tuttle-Mori Agency,
Inc., Tokyo.

Translation © 2011 by Hachette Book Group, Inc.

Yen Press
Hachette Book Group
237 Park Avenue, New York, NY 10017

BVG

Printed in the United States of America